QuickBooks® Pro 2014:
Level 1

TRISHA CONLON

LABYRINTH
LEARNING™

Berkeley, CA

QuickBooks Pro 2014: Level 1
by Trisha Conlon

Copyright © 2014 by Labyrinth Learning

Labyrinth Learning
2560 9th Street, Suite 320
Berkeley, California 94710
800.522.9746
On the web at lablearning.com

President:
Brian Favro

Product Manager:
Jason Favro

Development Manager:
Laura Popelka

Senior Editor:
Susan Scharf

Production Manager:
Rad Proctor

Editorial Assistant:
Alexandria Henderson

Production Assistant:
Andrew Kenower

eLearning Production Manager:
Arl S. Nadel

Indexing:
Joanne Sprott

Cover Design:
Mick Koller, SuperLab Design

Interior Design:
Mark Ong, Side-by-Side Studio

ITEM: 1-59136-687-9
ISBN-13: 978-1-59136-687-4

Manufactured in the United States of America.

10 9 8 7 6 5 4 3 2 1

Table of Contents

Quick Reference Tables

Preface

QuickBooks® Pro 2014: Level 1 provides essential coverage of QuickBooks 2014 software. Topics covered include basic accounting principles, backing up files, creating companies, working with vendors, working with customers, and banking with QuickBooks.

For almost two decades, Labyrinth Learning has been publishing easy-to-use textbooks that empower educators to teach complex subjects quickly and effectively, while enabling students to gain confidence, develop practical skills, and compete in a demanding job market. We add comprehensive support materials, assessment and learning management tools, and eLearning components to create true learning solutions for a wide variety of instructor-led, self-paced, and online courses.

Our textbooks follow the *Labyrinth Instruction Design*, our unique and proven approach that makes learning easy and effective for every learner. Our books begin with fundamental concepts and build through a systematic progression of exercises. Quick Reference Tables, precise callouts on screen captures, carefully selected illustrations, and minimal distraction combine to create a learning solution that is highly efficient and effective for both students and instructors.

This course is supported with *comprehensive instructor support* materials that include printable solution guides for side-by-side comparisons, test banks, customizable assessments, customizable PowerPoint presentations, detailed lesson plans, preformatted files for integration to leading learning management system, and more.

The full glossary associated with *QuickBooks Pro 2014: Comprehensive* is included here to offer more clarity and explanation. Some terms not included in this text may appear in the glossary.

Visual Conventions

This book uses many visual and typographic cues to guide students through the chapters. This page provides examples and describes the function of each cue.

`Type this text`   Anything you should type at the keyboard is printed in this typeface.

        Tips, Notes, and Warnings are used to draw attention to certain topics.

Command→   This convention indicates a Ribbon path. The commands are written: Ribbon
Command→   Tab→Command Group→Command→Subcommand.
Command, etc.

FROM THE KEYBOARD
Ctrl + S to save

These margin notes indicate shortcut keys for executing a task described in the text.

Features new to this edition of the software are indicated with this icon.

Visualize!

If there is an Intuit video related to the QuickBooks topic being discussed, this convention will point you to it.

Exercise Progression

The exercises in this book build in complexity as students work through a chapter toward mastery of the skills taught.

- **Develop Your Skills** exercises are introduced immediately after concept discussions. They provide detailed, step-by-step tutorials.
- **Reinforce Your Skills** exercises provide additional hands-on practice with moderate assistance.
- **Apply Your Skills** exercises test students' skills by describing the correct results without providing specific instructions on how to achieve them.
- **Extend Your Skills** exercises are the most challenging. They provide generic instructions, allowing students to use their skills and creativity to achieve the results they envision.

Acknowledgements

We are grateful to the instructors who have used Labyrinth titles and suggested improvements to us over the many years we have been writing and publishing books. This book has benefited greatly from the reviews and suggestions of the following instructors.

Jennifer Adkins, *North Central State College*

Marcia Bagnall, *Chemeketa Community College*

Elaine Barnwell, *Bevill State Community College*

Errol Belt, *San Juan Unified School District*

Ed Bonner, *National Career Skills Institute*

Kevin Bradford, *Somerset Community College*

David Campbell, *Northern Virginia Community College*

Margo Chaney Adkins, *Carroll Community College*

Valerie Chau, *Palomar College*

Marilyn Ciolino, *Delgado Community College*

Catherine Combs, *College of Applied Technology at Morristown*

Martha Cranford, *Rowan Cabarrus Community College*

Julie Dailey, *Central Virginia Community College*

Kerry Dolan, *Great Falls College MSU*

Dr. Vicky Dominguez, *College of Southern Nevada*

Gregory Drakulich, *Miami Jacobs Career College*

Sandra Dragoo, *Ivy Tech Community College Lafayette*

Susan Draper, *Williston State College*

Patricia Dukeman, *College of Central Florida*

Toiya Evans, *South Piedmont Community College*

Michael Fagan, *Raritan Valley Community College*

Connie Galvin, *Delta Montrose Technical College*

Evangelina Garner, *McAllen STVT*

Janet Garver, *Mid-Michigan Community College*

Mahnaz Ghaffarian, *Southwest Tennessee Community College*

Sharron Glover, *Black Chamber of Commerce, Metro OKC*

Yvette Gonzalez-Smith, *Savannah Technical College*

Nancy Gromen, *Eastern Oregon University*

Diane Hageman, *San Mateo Adult School*

Helen Hall, *College of Southern Maryland*

Diann Hammon, *JF Drake Community and Technical College*

Michele Hand, *Dickinson Lifelong Learning Center*

Sherry Harris, *University of Arkansas at Monticello*

Patricia Hartley, *Chaffey College*

Nancy Heinlein, *Nashua Adult Learning Center*

Lyle Hicks, *Danville Area CC*

Maggie Hilgart, *Mid-State Technical College*

Pam Hillman, *Gateway Technical College*

Rebecca Holden, *Southeastern Community College*

Peter Holland, *Napa Valley College*

Meredith Jackson, *Snead State Community College*

Stacie Jacobsen, *Pikes Peak Community College*

Carol Jensen, *City College of San Francisco*

Dr. Melanie S. Jones, *Mohave Community College*

Shawn Kendall, *Knox County Career Center*

Linda Kohnen, *North Central Technical College*

Dawn Krause, *Macomb Community College*

Denise Lawson, *Southern Westchester Board of Cooperative Educational Services*

Sue Lobner, *Nicolet Area Technical College*

Leonard Long, *Quincy College*

Diana Marquez, *Atlantic Technical Center*

Leslie Martin, *Gaston College*

Debbie McClanahan, *Balanced Books*

Autumn Matzat, *Alhambra Unified School District*

Vanessa May, *South Louisiana Community College*

Nancy Nibley, *Simi Valley Adult School and Career Institute*

Micki Nickla, *Ivy Tech Community College*

Susan Noble, *MiraCosta College*

Terry Mullin, *Cabrillo College*

John Oppenheim, *Dig-in Enterprises*

Arleen Orland, *Santa Clarita Technology & Career Development Center*

Carleen Powell, *Tri-County Adult Career Center*

Kathryn Quisenberry-Boyd, *Vista Adult School*

Kristina Rabius, *Pima Community College*

Traven Reed, *Canadore College*

Crystal Rhoades, *Wake Tech Community College*

Patrick Rogan, *Cosumnes River College*

William Simmons, *Austin Community College*

Sheila Smith, *Northwest Arkansas Community College*

Zachary Smulski, *South Seattle Community College*

Eric Stadnik, *Santa Rosa Junior College*

Traci Edmiston Thacker, *Texas State Technical College*

Mark Triller, *Blackhawk Technical College*

Laura Way, *Fortis College in Ravenna*

Sheree White, *Jupiter High School*

Diane Williams, *Colby Community College*

Alfred Worthy, *Rust College*

Peter F. Young, *San Jose State University*

Dora Zandarski, *Trumbull Career and Technical Center, Adult Training*

QuickBooks® Pro 2014:
Level 1

1

Introducing QuickBooks Pro

CHAPTER OUTLINE

CHAPTER OBJECTIVES

After studying this chapter, you will be able to:

- Discuss basic accounting concepts
- Determine if QuickBooks is right for your business
- Navigate the QuickBooks window
- Manage basic QuickBooks files
- Open a portable company file
- Back up a company file

QuickBooks has become the software of choice for many owners of small and medium-sized businesses. No doubt, this is due to the many functions and features that the software offers the smaller company. In this chapter, you will explore the various editions of QuickBooks and determine which is right for you. You will also examine what goes on behind the scenes and why it is so important for you to have a basic understanding of accounting. Finally, you will be introduced to some QuickBooks basics that are vital to your success as a QuickBooks user, and you will learn how to access valuable supplemental training tools right in your QuickBooks software.

Discovering What's New in QuickBooks 2014

Each year, Intuit introduces a new version of QuickBooks with new-and-improved features. As you work through this book, you will see these new aspects of the software called to your attention with a special icon.

 This is how you will be able to identify new or improved QuickBooks features.

The following list outlines some of the new QuickBooks 2014 features as well as the chapter in which each is introduced:

- The main color of the interface has changed from gray to blue (seen throughout the book)
- Alert and reminder links are located at the far right of the menu bar (Chapter 1, Introducing QuickBooks Pro)
- Income Tracker allows you to easily access income transactions from the Customer Center (Chapter 3, Working with Customers)
- Handling of bounced checks is dealt with in (Chapter 5, Banking with QuickBooks)
- Custom fields and Add Sales Rep can be added to purchase forms (Chapter 5, Banking with QuickBooks)
- Bank Feeds Center improves the online experience (Chapter 5, Banking with QuickBooks)
- Multiple attachments can be sent in a single email from transaction windows (*QuickBooks Pro 2014: Level 2*)

 Later in this chapter you will learn about the video tutorials available through the QuickBooks Learning Center. Once you have learned how to access tutorials, you will have a chance to view the "What's New in 2014" tutorial.

Presenting QuickBooks Pro

QuickBooks is a software program that allows companies to:

- Keep track of customers, vendors, employees, and other important entities
- Process sales transactions and cash receipts
- Process purchase transactions and payments to vendors
- Run payroll
- Track and sell inventory
- Run end-of-period financial reports
- Track assets (what you own) and liabilities (what you owe)
- Keep track of bank accounts
- Collaborate with accountants easily and efficiently

Types of Companies That Use QuickBooks Pro

QuickBooks Pro works well for different types of companies in a variety of industries. Ideally, your company should not have more than twenty employees and $1 million in annual revenue if you plan to use QuickBooks Pro (these are not strict rules, but guidelines). If your company is larger, you may want to consider using QuickBooks Enterprise Solutions. One type of business that QuickBooks Pro is not suited for is manufacturing, but Intuit has produced both Premier and Enterprise editions of QuickBooks especially for the manufacturing industry.

Aside from these issues, QuickBooks Pro can be customized and works well for many businesses, including not-for-profit organizations.

Editions of QuickBooks

Before you purchase your copy of QuickBooks, you should evaluate what you need QuickBooks to do for you. There are several editions of QuickBooks, all of which perform the basic tasks required for small-business bookkeeping. This book requires at the minimum the use of QuickBooks Pro, but it can be used with the Premier edition as well. If you are using a different edition, your screen may look a little bit different from what is displayed throughout this book.

Intuit also creates a QuickBooks edition for Mac users, which is similar to the Windows-based version in functions yet looks different because of the differences in the two platforms. The downloadable files associated with this book are *not* compatible with the Mac or International versions of QuickBooks.

Versions, as Compared to Editions

Now, don't let yourself become confused by the difference between editions and versions of QuickBooks. Intuit creates a new version of QuickBooks each year (such as QuickBooks 2012, 2013, or 2014). Each new version provides additional features that are new for that year. This book is designed for QuickBooks 2014, but once you learn how to use the features QuickBooks offers, it will be easy to switch between versions.

With each version, Intuit creates many editions from which a company may choose (such as QuickBooks Simple Start, QuickBooks Pro, QuickBooks Premier, and QuickBooks Enterprise Solutions). There are also online editions of QuickBooks available that, for a monthly fee, allow you to access your company's QuickBooks file via the Internet. Take a look at the Student Resource Center for this book to determine which edition will work best for your company.

Other Tools from Intuit

Intuit creates other tools that are a part of the "Quicken family" and are used by small businesses. You may find that software such as Quicken Home & Business or Quicken Rental Property Manager might be a better tool to track your small business' finances. To learn more about these other options produced by Intuit, browse the company's website at http://www.intuit.com.

The Online Editions of QuickBooks

Many companies are now using the online editions (Simple Start, Essentials, and Plus) of QuickBooks. The online versions look very similar to the traditional desktop editions but have some unique features, such as:

- The ability to access QuickBooks from any computer with Internet access, as well as from many popular smart phones
- A way for users in multiple or remote locations to easily utilize a single file
- Automatic online backups as all of your data is stored "in the cloud"

In addition, there is no need to worry about technological problems associated with desktop product installation and support when using QuickBooks online.

All of the users of a company file can access it through the web with a username and password, and all users work with the same up-to-date company file. It is recommended that you have a high-speed Internet connection to utilize these editions. The online editions, as with the desktop editions, allow you to set up users and determine the access level for each one.

The online interface is very similar to that of QuickBooks Pro, so once you learn the basics of the program from studying this book, you will be able to transfer your knowledge to the online editions. It is similar to learning to drive a Ford and then driving a Toyota—you will just need to familiarize yourself with the differences before you take off! You also have the ability to import your company data from a desktop edition of QuickBooks into your online account. You do not purchase software for an online edition but, instead, pay a monthly fee. Not all features are available in the online editions, though, so it is best to compare the different editions on the Intuit website in order to determine which is best-suited for your company's needs. You can find a link to the online edition comparison as well as current pricing in the Student Resource Center for this book.

QuickBooks App Center

The QuickBooks App Center is a web-based resource with tools to help you manage your business more effectively.

This link leads to the web page for the full App Center.

This is the window that appears when you click the Web and Mobile Apps task icon in the Company area of the Home page.

Types of Tasks

There are many types of tasks you can perform with QuickBooks. The tasks can be broken down into two main categories: those that affect the accounting behind the scenes (activities and company setup) and those that do not (lists and reporting). The following table lists the four basic types of tasks covered in this book.

QUICKBOOKS TASKS AND THEIR FUNCTIONS	
Task	**Function**
list (database)	Lists allow you to store information about customers, vendors, employees, and other data important to your business.
Activities	Activities affect what happens behind the scenes. They can be entered easily on forms such as invoices or bills.
Company Setup	This feature takes you through the steps necessary to set up a new company in QuickBooks.
Reports	QuickBooks provides many preset reports and graphs that are easily customizable to meet your needs.

Understanding Basic Accounting

Many business owners use QuickBooks to keep their own books and attempt to just learn the software. QuickBooks is quite intuitive, but you will find yourself running into problems if you don't understand the accounting basics on which QuickBooks is based. If you want to make sure you have a more solid understanding of accounting, you may wish to consider the book, *Accounting Basics: An Introduction for Non-Accounting Majors*, also published by Labyrinth Learning.

An Accountant's Worst Nightmare (or Greatest Dream?)

Picture yourself as an accountant who has just received a QuickBooks file from a client. The client has no idea how accounting works and, to him, debit and credit are just types of plastic cards he carries in his wallet. In his file you find duplicate accounts in the Chart of Accounts, accounts created as the wrong type, items posted to incorrect accounts, accounts payable inaccuracies, and payroll inaccuracies (to name just a few problems).

Now, as an accountant, you can consider this a nightmare because you will have to run numerous diagnostics to find all the mistakes (which could have been easily avoided if your client learned how to use QuickBooks properly in the first place) or a dream because your billable hours will increase at a rapid rate.

This scenario is exactly the reason why you, as the client, need to learn what happens behind the scenes in QuickBooks, as well as how to use the day-to-day functions of the software. By having a better understanding of the accounting and how to do things properly in the program, you will reduce the number of hours your accountant will have to spend and, thereby, save yourself the accountant fees in the end!

What's Up with GAAP?

GAAP stands for Generally Accepted Accounting Principles (GAAP). These are accounting rules used in the United States to prepare, present, and report financial statements for a wide variety of entities. The organization that creates the rules is called the FASB (Financial Accounting Standards Board). Publicly owned companies need to follow these rules unless they can show that doing so would produce information that is misleading. It is wise for the small-business owner to adhere to GAAP. These rules work to make taxation fair as it affects small-business owners.

As GAAP attempt to achieve basic objectives, they have several basic assumptions, principles, and constraints (described below). Throughout the book you will see reminders of how GAAP apply to tasks that you are completing in QuickBooks via the "Flashback to the GAAP" feature.

GENERALLY ACCEPTED ACCOUNTING PRINCIPLES (GAAP)	
Principle	Description
Business entity principle	The business is separate from the owners and from other businesses. Revenues and expenses of the business should be kept separate from the personal expenses of the business owner.
The assumption of the going concern	The business will be in operation indefinitely.

Principle	Description
Monetary unit principle	A stable currency is going to be the unit of record.
Time-period principle	The activities of the business can be divided into time periods.
Cost principle	When a company purchases assets, it should record them at cost, not fair market value. For example, an item worth $750 bought for $100 is recorded at $100.
Revenue principle	Publicly traded companies (not always sole proprietorships) record when the revenue is realized and earned, not when cash is received (accrual basis of accounting).
Matching principle	Expenses need to be matched with revenues. If a contractor buys a specific sink for a specific bathroom, it is matched to the cost of remodeling the bathroom. Otherwise, the cost may be charged as project expense. This principle allows a better evaluation of the profitability and performance (how much did you spend to earn the revenue?).
Objectivity principle	The statements of a company should be based on objectivity.
Materiality principle	When an item is reported, its significance should be considered. An item is considered significant when it would affect the decision made regarding its use.
Consistency principle	The company uses the same accounting principles and methods from year to year.
Prudence principle	When choosing between two solutions, the one that will be least likely to overstate assets and income should be selected.

INTRODUCING "BEHIND THE SCENES"

Throughout this book you will see a special section called "Behind the Scenes" whenever you are learning about an activity performed within QuickBooks. This section will go over the accounting that QuickBooks performs for you when you record a transaction. Please note that the account names used in this feature use QuickBooks, rather than traditional accounting, nomenclature.

Accrual vs. Cash Basis Accounting

There are two ways that companies can choose to keep the books. The method you choose to implement depends on the nature of your business. QuickBooks makes it easy for you to produce reports utilizing either method, and your data entry will be the same regardless of which method you choose. Talk to your accountant or tax advisor to determine which method you have been using (for an existing business) or should use (for a new business).

Accrual Basis

In the accrual basis of accounting, income is recorded when the sale is made and expenses recorded when accrued. This method is often used by firms and businesses with large inventories. As you just learned from the GAAP table, this is the basis you need to use for publicly traded corporations.

Cash Basis

In the cash basis of accounting, income is recorded when cash is received and expenses recorded when cash is paid. This method is commonly used by small businesses and professionals involved in occupations that are not publicly traded.

Where to Find More Help

You can learn more about accounting fundamentals in Appendix A, Need to Know Accounting, at the back of this book. It provides some basic definitions, theories, and a link to a web page with online resources. More in-depth coverage of accounting concepts can be found in the Labyrinth Learning book, *Accounting Basics: An Introduction for Non-Accounting Majors*.

In Appendix A, Need to Know Accounting, you will find information on:

■ The accounting equation

■ Debits and credits

■ Types of accounts and normal balances

Introducing the Integrative Case Studies

For the Develop Your Skills exercises, you will explore the operations of a company called Average Guy Designs. This company was started by Guy Marshall, a graphic arts and QuickBooks student from a community college, and provides production and design services to clients. In the second unit of the book, Guy will begin to sell his work and the work of other artists at his store.

You will further hone your QuickBooks skills with Reinforce Your Skills exercises that deal with Quality-Built Construction, a contractor specializing in home remodel and construction, and with Apply Your Skills exercises that deal with Wet Noses Veterinary Clinic. The Develop Your Skills exercises focus on using the Home page to perform tasks, while the Reinforce Your Skills exercises primarily use the menu bar since that is a preference for some QuickBooks users. Once you are on your own with QuickBooks, you should use whichever method(s) you prefer.

The exercises that you will complete for Average Guy Designs and Quality-Built Construction are set in the time frame of December 2014 through March 2015, and Wet Noses is set in the time frame of May through August 2014. Each exercise step that includes a date will have you set the correct date within these time frames. Tackle the Tasks exercises allow you to solidify your skills using the Develop Your Skills company file.

At the end of each chapter there are also Extend Your Skills exercises that will challenge you further. Sort Through the Stack exercises sit you down in the office of a not-for-profit organization. You will "look through" all of the papers at her desk and make the necessary entries into QuickBooks. Be Your Own Boss will allow you to create a company file for a business of your choice and then work with it throughout the entire book, and the culminating WebQuests send you to the Internet to learn more about QuickBooks and accounting.

How to Use This Book and the Student Files

You may be curious about the large number of student exercise files that come with this book and how using this book as a learning tool compares to working with your own company file. The following questions and answers should help to set you in the right direction!

Why is there a different company file for each exercise?

When you are learning QuickBooks, it is much easier to follow the instructions if your screen matches the illustrations in the book (or your instructor's screen). Having a fresh file at the beginning of each chapter helps to ensure that mistakes naturally made by students learning new material do not compound and cause a disconnect between student files and the example illustrations.

A fresh company file for each chapter also means that the chapters in this book can be completed in any order.

What if I want to use one file that continues from chapter to chapter?

You also have the option to use a file that continues from chapter to chapter. You can use each of the exercise files this way from Chapter 3 onward. This means that once you complete the Develop Your Skills exercise in Chapter 3, you can then use the file for Chapter 4 and Chapter 5 in order. The same is true for the Reinforce Your Skills and Apply Your Skills exercises. Note that, to use the same company file for the Develop Your Skill exercises from Chapter 3 onward, you must also complete the "Tackle the Tasks" exercise before continuing to the next chapter.

Is this how I will work in QuickBooks in "real life?"

No, using a separate file for each type of task (e.g., working with vendors, customers, inventory, etc.) is *not* how you will operate in "real life." In the real world, you will have *one* company file only. The multiple company files are for training purposes only.

Do I have to complete the chapters in the order presented in the book?

No, this book is entirely modular, and you can approach the chapters in any order you choose. Chapters may be worked through in any order. Fresh company files provided for each chapter make this possible.

Why do portable company files take so long to restore? What can I do while waiting for a file to restore?

Portable company files are compressed files that QuickBooks must "inflate" before you can use them. Think of the "space bags" you may have seen on an infomercial. Using a vacuum to remove all of the air from a space bag, you can fit some thirty sweaters into a shoebox. (Okay, this is a stretch, but hopefully you get the idea!) This is akin to QuickBooks creating a portable company file. Opening the seal and letting the air back in is like what happens when you restore a portable company file. It takes time for QuickBooks to prepare the portable company files just as it takes time for air to seep back into a space bag so the sweaters can return to their normal volume. If you are using an old computer system or a USB drive, the process will take longer than it will if you have a newer system.

Many users are not happy about waiting for the restore process to occur, but it is a necessity if you have chosen this file option. You may want to begin a chapter by restoring the portable company file first so you can read the concepts discussions while it restores.

What if I want to work with "real" company files rather than portable company files?

You can download either company files or portable company files for this course. Remember that company files will take longer to download and will use more space on your storage drive. On the plus side, you need not restore them in order to use them. For every portable company file there is also a regular company file—except for the Develop Your Skills exercise in Chapter 1, as the first task teaches you how to restore a portable company file.

Follow the exercise directions based on the file type you are using.

How do I save as a PDF?

Many instructors request students to save reports as PDF files. This makes it easier to submit your work and saves paper. To save a report as a PDF, first create and display the report. Next, click the Print button on the report toolbar and choose to Save As PDF.

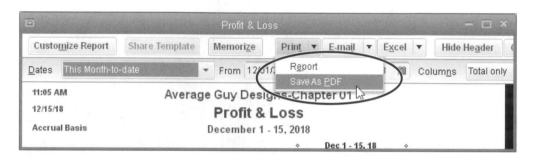

Managing Basic QuickBooks Files

Before you can begin working with a QuickBooks file, you need to understand some basic file-management operations. This section will cover how to launch the program, store files, and restore QuickBooks portable company files.

Launching the Program

There is more than one way to do just about everything on a computer, and launching QuickBooks is no exception. Each computer is set up a little differently and may have different options for launching the program depending on shortcuts that have been created. Ask your instructor how he wishes for you to launch QuickBooks in your computer lab. Depending on the version of Windows you are running, QuickBooks will be found in the All Programs or Programs menu accessed via the Start button or on the Windows 8 Start screen. In addition, there may be a shortcut to QuickBooks on the Windows Desktop.

"There is more than one way to do just about everything on a computer" is not meant to confuse you! You will be introduced to various ways to perform tasks in QuickBooks. Choose whichever methods work best for you.

Types of QuickBooks Files

There are three different types of files in which you can store your QuickBooks data: company files, backup files, and portable company files. The type of file that you will utilize when working with your business is the company file. A backup file is used to store a copy of your data in case your main file becomes corrupted and needs to be restored. A portable company file is much smaller than both company and backup files and is a convenient way to send your company information by email.

There are two other QuickBooks file types that play important support roles for your company data. A network data file has a file extension of .nd, and it contains important configuration data. A transaction log has a file extension of .tlg, and it can help you to recover any data entered after the last backup operation you have performed.

Your company file can be stored anywhere on your computer. The QuickBooks default storage location is the QuickBooks folder for the current version you are using.

Backup and portable company files contain all data stored from the company file—just compressed. These files are substantially smaller than company files, and portable company files are great for sending by email. The other "auxiliary" files do not store company data, but they do have important support functions.

WARNING

Even though .nd and .tlg. files do not allow you to work with your company information, do *not* delete them. This can affect the integrity of your company data.

Opening and Restoring QuickBooks Files

In order to open a QuickBooks company file, or to restore either a backup or portable company file, you access the command via the File menu. QuickBooks doesn't save files as other applications like word-processing programs do. When you enter transactions, they are saved automatically to the QuickBooks file. To save a QuickBooks file for backup purposes, you create a compressed file—either a backup or portable company file. The act of decompressing a backup or portable company file for use is called restoring.

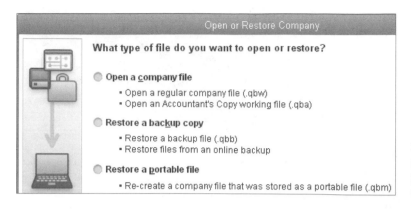

Open or Restore Company

What type of file do you want to open or restore?

○ Open a **c**ompany file
  - Open a regular company file (.qbw)
  - Open an Accountant's Copy working file (.qba)

○ Restore a bac**k**up copy
  - Restore a backup file (.qbb)
  - Restore files from an online backup

○ Restore a **p**ortable file
  - Re-create a company file that was stored as a portable file (.qbm)

When you open or restore a company file from the File menu, you must choose the file type you are accessing.

QUICK REFERENCE	OPENING AND RESTORING QUICKBOOKS DATA FILES
Task	**Procedure**
Open a QuickBooks company file	■ Choose File→Open or Restore Company. ■ Choose Open a company file; click Next. ■ Navigate to and select the desired file; click Open.
Restore a backup file	■ Choose File→Open or Restore Company. ■ Choose Restore a backup copy; click Next. ■ Navigate to the desired backup copy, either locally or online; click Next. ■ Locate the backup copy you wish to restore; click Open. ■ Click Next, choose the save-to location, and then click Save.
Restore a portable company file	■ Choose File→Open or Restore Company. ■ Choose Restore a portable file; click Next. ■ Navigate to the portable file you wish to restore; click Open. ■ Click Next, choose the save-to location, and then click Save. ■ Be patient as the file restores! Click OK to acknowledge the successful restoration.

Restore a Portable Company File

In this exercise, you will restore a QuickBooks portable company file.

Before You Begin: Navigate to the Student Resource Center to download the student exercise files for this book. Two versions of the files are available from which you must choose—portable company files and company files.

Even if you choose to download the company files, you will use a portable company file for this exercise.

1. If necessary, start your computer.

2. Follow the steps for your version of Windows:

You may see one of two editions of QuickBooks installed on your computer: Pro or Premier. This book works with both of these editions, so choose whichever edition is installed. Make sure to correct the operating system you are using.

Windows 7

■ Click the **Start** 🔵 button at the left edge of the taskbar and choose **All Programs**.

■ Choose **QuickBooks,** and then choose **QuickBooks 2014** from the menu.

Windows 8

■ Locate the **QuickBooks 2014** tile.

■ Click the tile to start **QuickBooks**.

A "splash screen" displays the version of QuickBooks you are launching and opens the program window. If this is the first time you have used the QuickBooks installation on this computer, you will see a QuickBooks Setup window.

Intuit provides maintenance releases throughout the lifetime of the product. These updates may require you to update your student exercise files before you begin working with them. Please follow the prompts on the screen if you are asked to update your company file to the latest QuickBooks release.

3. Choose **File**, and then choose the **Open or Restore Company** command.

In the future, a menu bar command like this will be written as Choose File→Open or Restore Company.

QuickBooks displays the Open or Restore Company window.

4. Click in the circle to the left of **Restore a portable file**.

5. Click **Next**.

6. Follow these steps to restore your file:

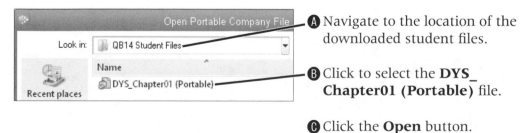

Ⓐ Navigate to the location of the downloaded student files.

Ⓑ Click to select the **DYS_ Chapter01 (Portable)** file.

Ⓒ Click the **Open** button.

7. Click **Next**, and then follow these steps to determine where the resulting company file will be located:

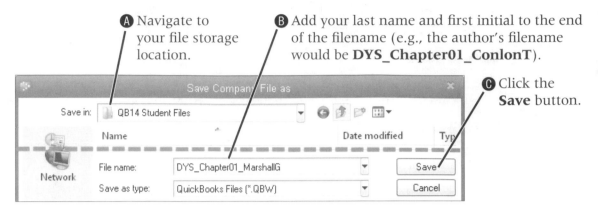

Ⓐ Navigate to your file storage location.

Ⓑ Add your last name and first initial to the end of the filename (e.g., the author's filename would be **DYS_Chapter01_ConlonT**).

Ⓒ Click the **Save** button.

It may take a few moments for the portable company file to open. The QuickBooks window opens with the Average Guy Designs company file ready to go. Leave this window open for the next exercise.

8. Click **OK** to close the QuickBooks Information window.

9. Click **No** in the Set Up External Accountant User window, if necessary.

10. Close the **Accountant Center** window, if necessary.

For the rest of the Develop Your Skills exercises in this book, you can restore a portable company file or open a company file. This exercise showed you how to restore a portable company file. Use this process as applicable moving forward.

Working with the QuickBooks Window

There are many screen elements with which you are probably familiar if you have ever worked with a Windows-based PC. Many of the elements remain similar regardless of the program in which you are operating. The elements in common are the title bar and quick-sizing buttons. In addition, many programs utilize menu, toolbar, and Icon bars as well as a Ribbon and tabs that you will see in QuickBooks.

Viewing the QuickBooks Window

The QuickBooks window features many components designed to help you complete all of the tasks necessary to manage your business effectively.

Click a button on the menu bar to see a drop-down menu of options specific to that button.

The title bar shows the company name and the QuickBooks version/edition you are using.

Alerts and reminders can be easily accessed from the far right of the menu bar.

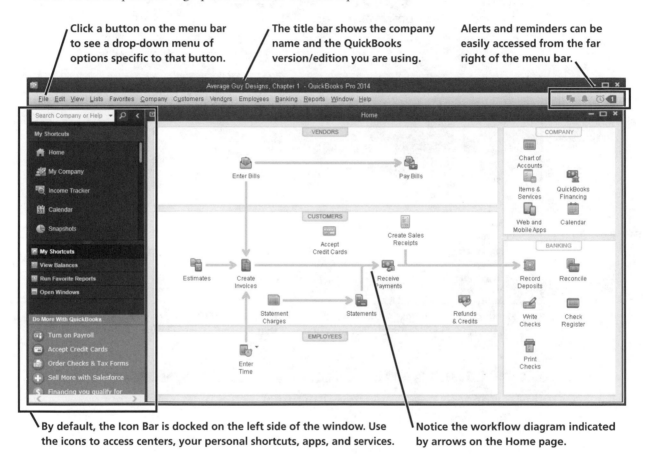

By default, the Icon Bar is docked on the left side of the window. Use the icons to access centers, your personal shortcuts, apps, and services.

Notice the workflow diagram indicated by arrows on the Home page.

Flowing Through the Home Page

The workflow diagram on the Home page is indicated by arrows going from one task icon to another. It is important to follow the diagram so as not to run into trouble. Some instances of trouble that you may encounter are listed below:

- If you write a check rather than pay a bill (for which a bill has been entered), you will overstate expenses.
- If you make a deposit rather than receive a payment for an invoiced amount, you will overstate income.

Sales tax errors can also occur by not following the proper flow outlined on the Home page.

The QuickBooks Icon Bar

The Icon Bar provides a quick way to access QuickBooks centers, snapshots, shortcuts, apps, and services. It is docked on the left side of the QuickBooks window by default, but you can move it to the top of the window or hide it altogether.

All commands accessible on the Icon Bar and Home page can be found through the menu bar, but the opposite is not also true. (They would be a bit too crowded!)

QuickBooks Calendar

The QuickBooks Calendar allows you to keep up with deadlines. This feature also integrates a to-do list so you can keep track of your calendar and tasks in one handy place. The calendar can be accessed via the Company area of the Home page or via the Icon Bar.

The to-do list is displayed to the right of the calendar.

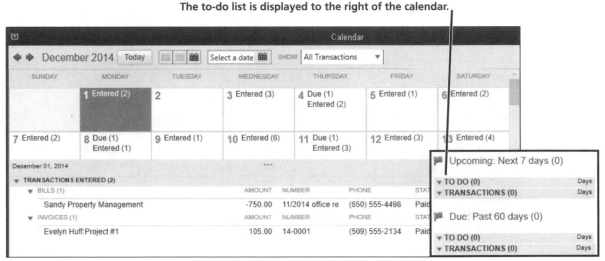

The calendar shows you how many transactions have been entered and are due on a specific day. When a date is selected, you can view details of what took place on that day in the panel at the bottom of the window.

Controlling the QuickBooks Display

If you cannot see the Icon Bar, you can turn it on through the View menu. To show or hide the Icon Bar, choose View from the menu bar.

The Icon Bar is docked to the left side of the screen.

Note where you can go to customize the Icon Bar.

To single-click or double-click—that is the question. Always single-click first; double-click only if the single-click doesn't work. Most students are "happy double-clickers," and this can get you into trouble (especially if you double-click a toggle button, which is like flipping a light switch up and down and then wondering why the light doesn't stay on). Remember, always single-click a button and a hyperlink!

The Open Window List

You may wish to display the Open Window List at the top of the Icon Bar in order to keep track of all of the windows you have open. The active window will always appear at the top of the list.

Customizing the Home Page

QuickBooks allows users to customize the Home page based on their preferences and how they use the software. The task icons displayed on the Home page will change when a user makes changes to certain preferences. For instance, if a user decides to track inventory in QuickBooks and so turns on the "Inventory and purchase orders are active" preference, additional task icons will be added to the Vendor area of the Home page to assist with the inventory-related tasks. You will learn how to change this preference in *QuickBooks Pro 2014: Level 2*. Changes to other preferences that result in changes to the Home page will be dealt with throughout this book as well.

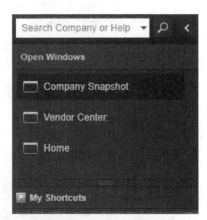

Pictured is the Icon Bar with the Open Window List displayed. Note that the Company Snapshot is the active window.

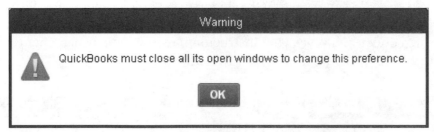

When you change a preference that will alter the content of the Home page, QuickBooks displays a warning message first.

In addition, you can choose to not display some of the task icons that you may not use as often. The commands will still be available through the menu, just not accessible via a task icon on the Home page.

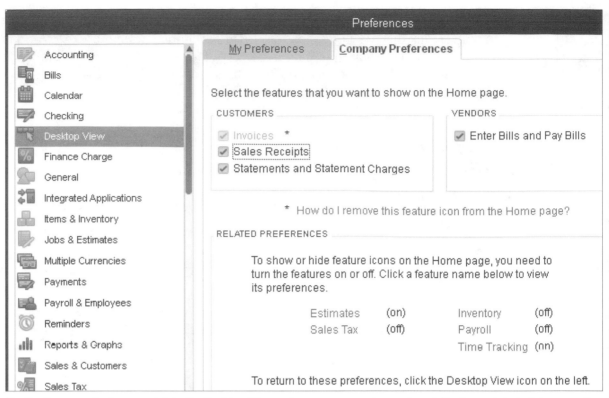

On the Company Preferences tab in the Desktop View category, you can choose to not display certain task icons on the Home page. Add them back at any time by returning to the Preferences window and reselecting the option.

Maximized vs. Restored Down Windows

Some QuickBooks users prefer to work with windows maximized and others with them restored down. This is based entirely on user preference! In this book, we will work with windows "restored down;" however, your instructor may choose to display them as maximized. It will only look different; all functions will be the same.

When you work with all windows maximized, the name of the active window will appear in the Title Bar of the QuickBooks window in square brackets and the quick-sizing buttons will be a part of the menu bar.

If you choose to work with windows restored down, you will see separate windows for each open window, and each will have its own Title Bar and quick-sizing buttons.

Exiting QuickBooks

When you are finished working with QuickBooks, you will need to close the company file and the program. This can be accomplished by clicking the Close button at the top-right corner of the QuickBooks window or by selecting File→Exit.

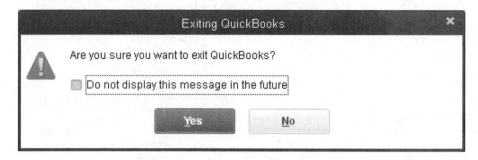

QuickBooks displays a warning message when you click the Close button at the top-right corner of the window. Notice that you can choose to not have this message appear again.

Close All Windows with One Command

If you have a lot of windows open and wish to close them all simultaneously, QuickBooks makes it easy with the Close All command. This command can be accessed by choosing Windows from the menu bar.

Task Icon ToolTips

There are many task icons on the Home page. As you customize your QuickBooks file, you may see more or fewer appear, depending on how you use the program. If you are not sure what a certain task item is used for, simply "mouse over" it (place your mouse pointer over the icon and hold it still, without clicking), and a ToolTip that explains what the task will accomplish for you will appear.

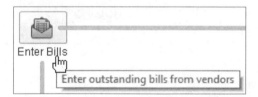

Notice that when you "mouse over" the Enter Bills task icon, a ToolTip appears to explain what task you can accomplish if you click the icon.

QuickBooks Learning Center Tutorials

Sure to be a valuable resource during your study is the QuickBooks Learning Center. It features a large number of instructional QuickBooks videos that are great learning tools for many students. You will find yourself directed to these tutorials through the "Visualize!" element in this book. Develop Your Skills 1-2 includes steps to show you how to access a video. In this book you will see a special icon and text whenever a QuickBooks Learning Center tutorial is available (see below).

Tab: Thank you for upgrading
Topic: What's New in 2014

In addition, QuickBooks provides help for some topics that are not in video format. When you choose one of these topics in the Learning Center, a web page with more information will open.

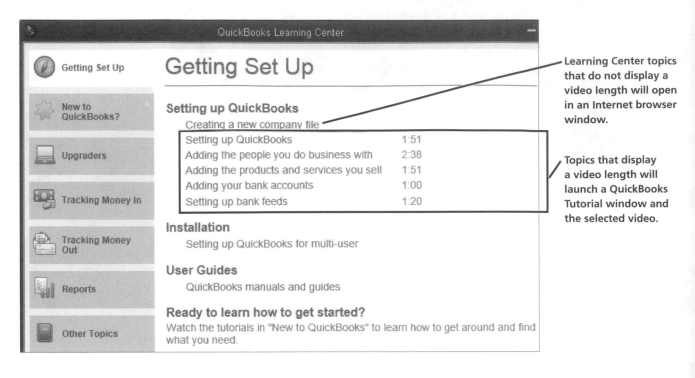

Learning Center topics that do not display a video length will open in an Internet browser window.

Topics that display a video length will launch a QuickBooks Tutorial window and the selected video.

Explore the QuickBooks Window

In this exercise, you will have a chance to explore the QuickBooks window.

1. Click the **Vendors** button on the Home page.

The Vendor Center will open, from where you can work with the vendors on your list, manage various vendor transactions, and create new vendors.

2. Choose **Lists→Chart of Accounts**.

The Chart of Accounts window opens. This is an example of a list in QuickBooks. It lists the various accounts this company utilizes.

3. Click the **Snapshots** icon on the Icon Bar, scrolling down if necessary.

The Company Snapshot window opens.

4. Choose **Window**.

Notice that all four of the open windows are listed.

5. Click the **Chart of Accounts** item.

The Chart of Accounts window appears on top of the other windows and is active. Look at the windows you have opened within QuickBooks and notice that each one is restored down and has its own set of quick-sizing buttons (Close, Restore/Maximize, Minimize), which you can use to control the display of each window within the QuickBooks program window.

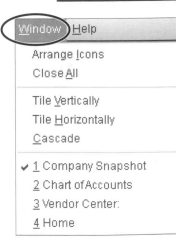

6. Click the **Close** [x] button for the Chart of Accounts window.

7. Choose **View→Open Window List**.

   QuickBooks will display the Open Window List at the top of the Icon Bar.

8. Choose **Window→Close All**.

   This command will close all open windows for you so you don't have to go chasing "Xs" around the screen! Notice that the Home page is closed since it is a window, but that the Open Window List/Icon Bar is still displayed since it is not.

9. Open the Home page by choosing **Company→Home page**.

10. Choose **View→Hide Icon Bar**.

    QuickBooks no longer displays the Icon Bar.

Exit and Reopen QuickBooks

11. Choose **File→Exit**.

12. Click **No** in the Automatic Backup window, if necessary.

    The QuickBooks window closes.

13. Open QuickBooks, based on the version of Windows you are using.

    Notice that QuickBooks opens the file that you were last working on and that the Icon Bar is not visible.

14. Click **No** in the Set Up an External Accountant User window, if necessary.

15. Close the **Accountant Center** window, if necessary.

16. Maximize the QuickBooks program window, if necessary.

17. Choose **View→Left Icon Bar**.

    The Icon Bar reappears.

Mouse Around the Home Page

18. Mouse over the task icon for the following tasks on the Home page, and then write the ToolTips in the spaces provided.

19. If you do not wish to write in the book, print the Mouse Around the Home Page worksheet from the Student Resource Center.

■ Chart of Accounts

_____

_____

■ Create Invoices

_____

_____

■ Pay Bills

_____

_____

■ Reconcile

_____

_____

20. Submit your responses to step 19 based on the guidelines provided by your instructor.

Explore the QuickBooks Learning Center

Throughout this book, the "Visualize!" feature will point you to QuickBooks video tutorials. These steps will show you how to access these tutorials.

21. Choose **Help→Learning Center Tutorials**.

22. Follow these steps to view a tutorial that will show you how to get around in QuickBooks:

Ⓐ Click **New to QuickBooks?**.

Ⓑ Click **Getting around in QuickBooks**. The QuickBooks Tutorial window will launch, and the video will begin.

Ⓒ Watch the tutorial and then click the **Close** button on the tutorial window.

23. Click the Go to QuickBooks button.

Leave QuickBooks open with the Home page displayed for the next exercise.

In the future, you will see text and an icon like the following to direct you to available videos.

Tab: New to QuickBooks?
Topic: Getting Around in QuickBooks

Backing Up and Updating Your Company File

You have already learned how to restore a portable company file. Now you will learn how to create a backup file. If you have ever lost a file or had your computer "crash" on you, you surely can understand the importance of backing up your data!

When working in QuickBooks, you cannot save your file as you may be used to doing in programs such as Microsoft® Word. Transactions are automatically saved to your company file as you enter them, so the backup operation will back up the entire file.

How often you back up your file is up to you, but you should not let too much time go between backups. If you lose your company file and are forced to restore the backup copy, you will have to enter all of the transactions since your last backup.

Backup Location

Do not back up your company file to your hard drive or where your main company file is stored. Choose an alternate backup location such as a network drive, USB drive, external hard drive, cloud storage, or the QuickBooks' online backup option. If you back up your file to a USB drive or some other removable media, make sure to store the backup copy someplace other than where the original file is physically located. For instance, do not set the backup media on the PC where the original file is, just in case something such as fire or water damage occurs at the physical location.

Protecting Your Data Online

To ensure the security of your QuickBooks data in the event of human error, natural disaster, or a computer crash, you may wish to use Intuit Data Protect. This online service allows you to recover your data in the event you lose your working company file. Data is encrypted and backed-up automatically each day to secure servers. You can also use the service to back up other important files, such as reports and contracts, or personal items, such as valuable photos. Learn more about Intuit Data Protect through the File menu bar command.

There is a fee associated with this service.

If your data is not backed up properly, Intuit Data Protect cannot help you. Make sure to back up your data properly!

When to Save a Backup Copy

In QuickBooks, you can choose when to back up your company file. QuickBooks allows you to choose among three options:

- Save it now
- Save it now and schedule future backups
- Only schedule future backups

The future backup options make it easy to back up your company file on a regular basis without having to remember to physically issue the command. If you choose scheduled backups, make sure the backup location is available to QuickBooks at the scheduled times. For instance, ensure that you have your USB flash drive available if that is your backup location.

Updating Your QuickBooks Company File

Earlier in this chapter you learned about the different editions of QuickBooks that are available for purchase each year. In addition, Intuit releases free updates for your QuickBooks software throughout the life of the version. (At some point, Intuit will announce that they will no longer support each version of QuickBooks based on the length of time since it was released.) These updates are available for download over the Internet and may include such things as a new service, a maintenance release, a new feature, or something else relevant to your company.

The easiest way to stay abreast of these updates is to have QuickBooks automatically check for and download them for you through the Automatic Update feature.

Verifying the QuickBooks Release Number

You can easily find out which release number you are working with for your current version of QuickBooks by tapping the F2 key. This will launch a Product Information window that displays not just the release number, but also a lot of other information about your QuickBooks file such as your license and product numbers. In addition, if you choose to open the Update QuickBooks window from the Help menu, you can also find your release number displayed at the top of that window.

FROM THE KEYBOARD

Tap F2 to display the QuickBooks Product Information window

QUICK REFERENCE	BACKING UP AND UPDATING A QUICKBOOKS FILE
Task	**Procedure**
Create a portable company file	<ul><li>Choose File→Create Copy.</li><li>Choose Portable company file; click Next.</li><li>Choose your file storage location; click Save.</li><li>Click OK to allow QuickBooks to close and reopen your file.</li><li>Click OK to acknowledge the portable company file creation.</li></ul>
Create a backup file	<ul><li>Choose File→Back Up Company→Create Backup.</li><li>Choose to create a local or online backup; click Next.</li><li>Choose your file storage location; click OK.</li><li>Choose when you wish to create the backup copy; click Next.</li><li>Ensure the location for the backup file is correct; click Save.</li><li>Click OK to acknowledge the backup file creation.</li></ul>

Task	Procedure
Start Intuit Data Protect	■ Choose File→Back Up Company→Setup/Activate Online Backup. ■ View the web page with information about Intuit Data Protect that opens.
Set up QuickBooks to update automatically	■ Choose Help→Update QuickBooks. ■ Click the Options tab; choose Yes to automatically update your QuickBooks file. ■ Click Close.
Update QuickBooks manually	■ Choose Help→Update QuickBooks. ■ Click the Update Now tab; click to select/deselect the updates you wish to receive. ■ Click Get Updates.
Determine the release number of QuickBooks	■ Choose Help→Update QuickBooks. ■ With the Overview tab displayed, look at the upper-right area of the Update QuickBooks window for the release number; tap F2 to view the full Production Information window.

DEVELOP YOUR SKILLS 1-3

Back Up Your QuickBooks Data File

In this exercise, you will create a backup copy of your company file. Ask your instructor where he wants you to back up your file. A cloud storage option in the form of Dropbox is used in this example.

1. Choose **File→Back Up Company→Create Local Backup**.

2. Verify that **Local Backup** is selected, and then click **Next**.

3. Click the **Browse** button.

4. Choose your file storage location in the **Browse for Folder** window. (The drive or folder name will probably be different from the one shown here.)

If you are not sure where to save your backup copy, ask your instructor.

5. Click the **OK** button two times.

   If you have chosen to save the file to the same drive on which the company file is stored, QuickBooks will display a warning window.

6. Read the information in the QuickBooks window, and then click the **Use this location** option, if necessary.

7. Ensure **Save it now**, and then click **Next** again.

   A Save Backup Copy window will appear and should display the file storage location you chose in step 4.

8. Ensure that the correct file storage location is displayed, and then click **Save**.

   QuickBooks will first verify that your file is not corrupted and will then create a backup copy in the location you specified.

9. Click **OK** to acknowledge the information window that tells you a backup file has been created.

10. Choose the appropriate option for your situation:
    - If you will continue working, leave QuickBooks open.
    - If you are finished working in QuickBooks for now, choose **File→Exit**.

Concepts Review

To check your knowledge of the key concepts introduced in this chapter, complete the Concepts Review quiz on the Student Resource Center.

Reinforce Your Skills

In all of the Reinforce Your Skills exercises, you will be working with a company called Quality-Built Construction. This business is an S corporation that builds and remodels homes. Angela Stevens is the proprietor of the business. You will assist Angela in a variety of QuickBooks tasks as you work your way through this book.

REINFORCE YOUR SKILLS 1-1
Find Your Way Around QuickBooks

In this exercise, you will take a look at Angela's QuickBooks company file. You will begin by opening a portable company file.

1. Start **QuickBooks**, if necessary.

2. Choose **File→Open or Restore Company**.

3. Choose to **Restore a portable file**, and then click **Next**.

4. Follow these steps to select the file to restore:

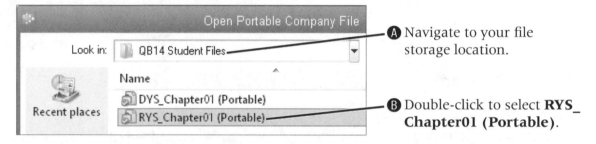

Double-clicking the filename works the same as if you had single-clicked the filename and then clicked the Open button.

5. Click **Next** to move to the next screen.

6. Follow these steps to choose where to locate your new company file:

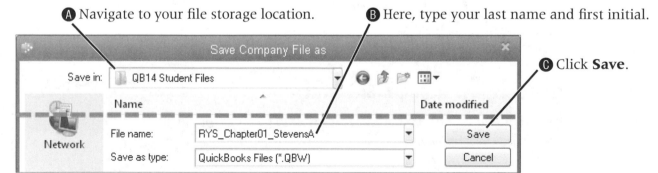

There is a long pause as QuickBooks opens the portable company file.

7. Click **OK** in the QuickBooks Information window, if necessary.

QuickBooks opens the company file and displays the Home page.

Navigate in the Company File

Now you will explore the QuickBooks window.

8. Click the **Items & Services** task icon in the Company area of the Home page.

   QuickBooks displays the Item List window.

9. Click the **Calendar** button on the Icon Bar.

10. Choose **Vendors→Enter Bills**.

    QuickBooks displays the Enter Bills window, ready for you to enter a bill from a vendor.

11. Choose **Company→Lead Center**.

12. Choose **Window→Item List**.

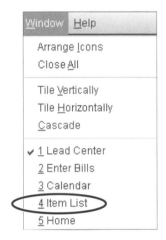

The Item List window appears on top of the other open windows. Notice that all open windows are listed at the bottom of the Window menu list. Clicking on one of them will make that window active.

13. Choose **Window→Close All**.

    The Close All command closes all open windows, including the Home page.

14. Click the **Home** icon on the Icon Bar.

    QuickBooks displays the Home page.

 Tab: New to QuickBooks?
Topic: Using the Home Page

Get to Know QuickBooks Better

15. Complete the **Get to Know QuickBooks Better** worksheet.

    Print or save the worksheet from the Student Resource Center.

16. Submit your worksheet based on the guidelines provided by your instructor.

17. Choose the appropriate option for your situation:

    ■ If you will continue working, leave QuickBooks open.

    ■ If you are finished working in QuickBooks for now, choose **File→Exit**.

Work with T-Accounts

In this exercise, you will use your accounting knowledge. Refer to Appendix A, Need to Know Accounting if you need assistance. You can either write directly in the book or download the Work with T-Accounts worksheet from the Student Resource Center.

1. Below or on your printed worksheet, write the following account names at the tops of the T-charts:
   - Bank Service Charges
   - Construction Income
   - Company Checking Account
   - Loans Payable
   - Machinery & Equipment
   - Common Stock

2. Next to each account, write the account type (asset, liability, equity, income, or expense).

3. Label the debit and credit side of each T.

4. Place an **NB** on the appropriate side of the T to indicate the normal balance of each account.

5. Submit your work based on the guidelines provided by your instructor.

Apply Your Skills

In all of the Apply Your Skills exercises, you will be working with a company called Wet Noses Veterinary Clinic run by Dr. Sadie James, DVM. She is a small-animal veterinarian specializing in dogs and cats.

APPLY YOUR SKILLS 1-1

Restore a Portable Company File and Explore QuickBooks

In this exercise, you will restore a portable company file and take a look at Dr. Sadie James' QuickBooks company file.

1. Start **QuickBooks**.

2. Restore the **AYS_Chapter01 (Portable)** backup company file. Name the restored company file `AYS_Chapter01_LastNameFirstInitial`.

3. Open the following windows using any of the methods described in this chapter:
   - Create Invoice
   - Item List
   - Customer Center
   - Chart of Accounts
   - Pay Bills
   - Company Snapshot

4. Display the **Item List** window above the other open windows.

   Next you will create a screen capture to submit to your instructor. Two options are presented. Use the option as directed by your instructor.

Option 1: Capture Your Work Using Microsoft Word

5. Tap `PrtScn`, and then launch **Microsoft Word**.

   Your screen capture is automatically copied to the Window's Clipboard, ready for pasting.

6. Display a blank document, and then press `Ctrl`+`v`.

   Your screen capture is pasted into the Word document.

7. Save your Word document as `AYS_Chapter01_Capture_LastnameFirstIntial` and submit it according to the guidelines provided by your instructor.

8. Choose the appropriate option for your situation:
   - If you will continue working, leave QuickBooks open.
   - If you are finished working in QuickBooks for now, choose **File→Exit**.

Option 2: Complete a Worksheet to Capture Your Work

9. Print or save the **Capture Your Work** worksheet from the Student Resource Center.

10. Complete and then submit the worksheet according to the guidelines provided by your instructor.

11. Choose the appropriate option for your situation:

- If you will continue working, leave QuickBooks open.
- If you are finished working in QuickBooks for now, choose **File→Exit**.

Get a Grasp on Accounting Principles

In this exercise, you will use your accounting knowledge to brainstorm the accounts that would be required for the business that you will be working with in the Apply Your Skills exercises throughout the rest of this book.

You can either write directly in the book or download the Get a Grasp on Accounting Principles worksheet from the Student Resource Center.

1. Think about a veterinary practice. On the printed worksheet or in the following space, list the accounts that you feel would be required on the business's Chart of Accounts.

2. In the second column, list the type of account for each.

3. In the third column, state whether the normal balance for the account would be a debit or a credit.

ACCOUNT NAME	ACCOUNT TYPE (ASSET, LIABILITY, EQUITY, INCOME, EXPENSE)	NORMAL BALANCE (DR/CR)

4. Submit your work based on the guidelines provided by your instructor.

Extend Your Skills

1-1 Sort Through the Stack

You have been hired by Arlaine Cervantes to help her with her organization's books. She is the founder of Niños del Lago, a nonprofit organization that provides impoverished Guatemalan children with an engaging educational camp experience. You will begin your work with Ninos del Lago in Chapter 2, Creating a Company.

1-2 Be Your Own Boss

In this exercise, and throughout the entire book, you will be working with a company file that you create from scratch. The company should either be based on your own company or a company you would like to own or manage someday. In this first chapter you will determine what edition of QuickBooks is best for your company as well as the name and type of business formation.

Download the EYS_Chapter01 Word file from the Student Resource Center to complete this exercise. Save the completed file as **EYS2_Chapter01_LastnameFirstInitial** and submit it to your instructor based on the instructions provided.

1-3 Use the Web as a Learning Tool

Throughout this book, you will be provided with an opportunity to use the Internet as a learning tool by completing WebQuests. According to the original creators of WebQuests, as described on their website (http://WebQuest.org), a WebQuest is "an inquiry-oriented activity in which most or all of the information used by learners is drawn from the web." To complete the WebQuest projects in this book, navigate to the Student Resource Center and choose the WebQuest for the chapter on which you are working. The subject of each WebQuest will be relevant to the material found in the chapter.

WebQuest Subject: Learn more about QuickBooks versions and determine which one is most appropriate for your business

2 Creating a Company

CHAPTER OBJECTIVES

After studying this chapter, you will be able to:

- Plan and create a company
- Edit your QuickBooks preferences and customize a company file
- Enter opening balances and historical transactions
- Run list reports and find help for QuickBooks
- Set up QuickBooks users
- Close the books "QuickBooks style"

Now that you have had a chance to explore the QuickBooks window and learn about how to work with QuickBooks files, it is time to create a company file. By taking the knowledge that you gain from this chapter and coupling it with what you will learn in the rest of the book, you will be ready at the end of your QuickBooks studies to create a file for your own company.

Average Guy Designs

Guy Marshall is a community college student who is completing his degree in visual communications. He began his own graphic design business a year ago and has chosen to start using QuickBooks as the tool to track his business finances. Guy just took a class that focused on the business of graphic arts, and he learned that there is some important information that he needs to gather before setting up his new QuickBooks company.

Average Guy Designs
Checklist for New QuickBooks Company

Company Name	Average Guy Designs	Need from accountant	Chart of accounts, what should I use for items?
Address	110 Sampson Way, Bayshore, CA 91547	Vendors	need names, addresses, account numbers, and payment terms for each
Office	(650) 555-5555	Customers	need names and contact information, payment terms, and account numbering system
Cell	(650) 555-4455		
Fax	(650) 555-5252		
Start date	11/30/2014	Accounting basis	Cash
Fiscal year	January	Email	averageguydesigns@outlook.com
EIN	94-4555555	Website	averageguydesigns.wordpress.com
Income Tax Form	1040 (Sole Proprietor)		

Guy has written out the information he needs to have handy to start his new company file.

Planning and Creating a Company

Before you begin to set up your QuickBooks company, it is important to do careful planning. You must think about the information you want to get from QuickBooks before you begin. As with many situations, garbage in will equal garbage out!

Choosing Your Start Date

Choosing the start date that is right for you is important. Very ambitious people may think they want to start their QuickBooks file the day they started their company. This is a nice idea, but not very practical for a busy or cost-conscious entrepreneur.

Keep in mind that you must enter all transactions for your company (invoices, checks, bills paid, etc.) from the start date forward. If you choose a date too far in the past, this process will take a long time to complete.

You should strive to start your QuickBooks company file at the beginning of a month, a quarter, or your fiscal year. You may want to discuss this matter with your accountant to help determine the best and most practical starting date for your business. The actual start date should be the last day of the prior period rather than the first day of the current period; for example, we will use 11/30/18 rather than 12/1/18.

The Five Ps

Sit down and think about what you want QuickBooks to do for you. It is difficult to go back and add a new field for every customer or change every transaction! A little planning at the beginning can save you a lot of time in the future. Think about the five Ps (Prior Planning Prevents Poor Performance) as you get ready to start your company and take into account the needs of all of the stakeholders involved. What type of information will each stakeholder need to be able to interact efficiently with your business? Potential stakeholders may include your accountant, customers, vendors, employees, stockholders, partners, etc.

How Many Companies Should You Create?

Generally, the best guideline is to set up a separate QuickBooks company file for each tax return you will file.

FLASHBACK TO GAAP: BUSINESS ENTITY

Remember that the business is separate from the owners and from other businesses. Revenues and expenses of the business should be kept separate from the personal expenses of the business owner. Also, revenues and expenses for separate companies must be kept separate from the other companies that may be operated by the same owner.

Creating a New QuickBooks File

There are several ways you can go about creating your new QuickBooks file. Look at the following list to determine which one will work best for your situation:

- Create a company from scratch
- Upgrade from a previous version of QuickBooks
- Convert from a different QuickBooks edition
- Convert a Quicken file
- Convert a file from other accounting software

Choosing a Setup Path

When creating a new company, QuickBooks makes it easy for you to select from a variety of options. Express Start is the easiest method; use the Detailed Start method if you wish to fine-tune your company file as you set it up.

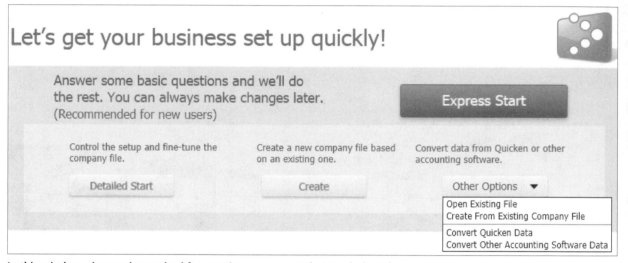

In this window, choose the method for creating a company that works best for you.

Express Start

The Express Start option for company setup allows you to provide a minimum amount of information and get started with QuickBooks right away. Once you have entered the Express Start information and your company file is created, QuickBooks helps you to set up the rest of the information needed to run your business. You will use this method in the Develop Your Skills exercises in this chapter.

Detailed Start (EasyStep Interview)

A click of the Detailed Start button takes you to the EasyStep Interview window. Here you provide more information when creating your company file. You will use this method in a Reinforce Your Skills exercise at the end of the chapter.

Using an Old QuickBooks File as a Template for a New File

If you wish to create your new company file based on an older one, QuickBooks will allow you to keep the lists and preferences from the old file while removing the old, unneeded transactions. Some QuickBooks users prefer to keep a separate company file for each fiscal year of the business, and being able to keep preferences and list data while removing transactions makes this easy.

To complete this task, you must clean up your company data from the old file using the Clean Up Company Wizard. Be sure you have a large window of time available before you start this process, as it can take some time to clean up a large file. QuickBooks will create a backup and archive copy of your file as a part of this process, as well as verify file integrity.

Converting Data to Start a New Company File

An additional option available to you when creating a new company file is to convert an existing file from Quicken or other accounting software data.

A Setup Checklist

There are some items that you should gather before you begin to set up your company. Review the checklist of items to collect in the Student Resource Center for this book.

A Quick Payroll Primer

You will be introduced to running payroll in QuickBooks in *QuickBooks Pro 2014: Level 2*. If you choose to create your new company using the Detailed Start method, you need to understand a bit about how QuickBooks deals with payroll first.

If you wish to include an addition or deduction on an employee's paycheck, you must first set it up as a payroll item. During the EasyStep interview you will have an opportunity to create payroll items. If you will be using QuickBooks for payroll and wish to set it up during the setup process (you can also set this up after the fact if you choose, and that process will be covered in *QuickBooks Pro 2014: Level 2*), you will need to have the following information ready:

- Information for each employee: name, address, social security number, and withholding information (from their W-4 forms)
- All "additions" that will be found on a paycheck, such as salaries, hourly wages, and bonuses
- All payroll taxes the employees are required to pay
- All payroll taxes you, as the employer, are required to pay
- Any additional deductions you will be withholding from paychecks, such as investment plan contributions or child support payments

Your Starter Chart of Accounts

During the setup process, QuickBooks will ask you to search for the business type that your company most closely resembles. QuickBooks will use your choice to create a Starter Chart of Accounts close to what you need. (It will take you less time to edit it to fit your unique business than to start from scratch.) QuickBooks will also create profile lists based on your selection. You will work with the customer and vendor profile lists in *QuickBooks Pro 2014: Level 2*. Choose carefully here, as you cannot go back and change the business type option.

In order to ensure your books are set up properly, you should talk to your accountant to make sure that your Chart of Accounts is set up correctly. A quick conversation and small bill now can prevent a large bill in the future.

QuickBooks has several predefined company Chart of Accounts for specific industries that will help users in those or similar industries to streamline their setup processes.

 Once you select a business type during the setup process, you cannot change it later. You can edit and delete accounts and list entries, though.

Account Beginning Balances

If you have an existing company for which you are setting up QuickBooks, you should enter the balances of all asset and liability accounts during the setup process (although you can also enter them in the registers later). These account beginning balances are termed "opening balances" in QuickBooks. You will learn more about entering and editing these balances later in the chapter.

After you create your first balance sheet account, QuickBooks will create an Opening Balance Equity account, in which the account beginning balances you enter will be placed. Asset beginning balances credit the account, while liability beginning balances debit it. This account is created so you can have a balance sheet that is accurate from the start even if you haven't entered all assets and liabilities for your company.

TYPES OF ACCOUNTS IN QUICKBOOKS

Account Type	Example	Normal Balance
Bank	Checking Account	Debit
Accounts Receivable	Accounts Receivable	Debit
Other Current Asset	Prepaid Rent	Debit
Fixed Asset	Machinery	Debit
Other Asset	Long Term Notes Receivable	Debit
Accounts Payable	Accounts Payable	Credit
Credit Card	Silver Falls Bank Visa	Credit
Other Current Liability	Short Term Loan	Credit
Long Term Liability	Auto Loan	Credit
Equity	Opening Balance Equity	Credit
Income	Sales	Credit
Cost of Goods Sold	Cost of Goods Sold	Debit
Expense	Telephone Expense	Debit
Other Income*	Interest Income	Credit
Other Expense*	Corporate Taxes	Debit

*Other Income and Other Expense accounts are used to track income and expenses that are not the result of normal day-to-day business operations.

QUICK REFERENCE	CREATING A NEW COMPANY FILE
Task	**Procedure**
Create a new company in QuickBooks	■ Review the checklist to make sure you have all necessary information. ■ Plan what you want QuickBooks to do for you. ■ Choose File→New Company. ■ Choose a method set up your company file.
Edit information for a new company	■ Choose Company→Company Information. ■ Edit the information in the Company Information window.
Create a new company file based on a prior one, keeping list data and preferences	■ Choose File→Utilities→Clean Up Company Data. ■ Choose to remove all transactions as of a specific date or all transactions in the file. ■ Continue through the wizard screens. ■ Click Begin Cleanup. ■ Click OK to close the "message;" click Create Back Up.

Create a New Company

In this exercise, you will use Express Start to set up the company for Average Guy Designs.

1. Launch **QuickBooks**.

2. Choose **File→New Company**.

3. Click the **Express Start** button.

Express Start

4. Follow these steps to enter the first set of company data:

Ⓐ Type **Average Guy Designs**. Ⓑ Tap Tab, and then type **design**.

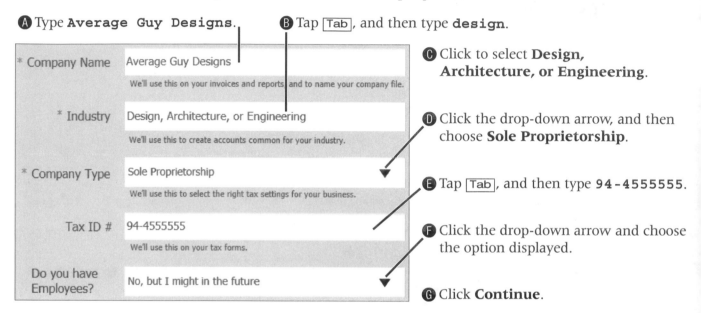

Ⓒ Click to select **Design, Architecture, or Engineering**.

Ⓓ Click the drop-down arrow, and then choose **Sole Proprietorship**.

Ⓔ Tap Tab, and then type **94-4555555**.

Ⓕ Click the drop-down arrow and choose the option displayed.

Ⓖ Click **Continue**.

5. Follow these steps to enter your business contact information:

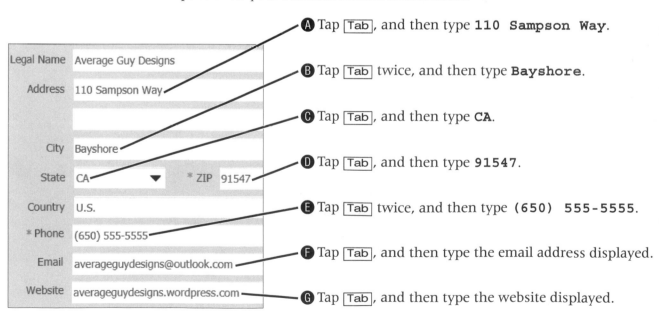

Ⓐ Tap Tab, and then type **110 Sampson Way**.

Ⓑ Tap Tab twice, and then type **Bayshore**.

Ⓒ Tap Tab, and then type **CA**.

Ⓓ Tap Tab, and then type **91547**.

Ⓔ Tap Tab twice, and then type **(650) 555-5555**.

Ⓕ Tap Tab, and then type the email address displayed.

Ⓖ Tap Tab, and then type the website displayed.

In this window, you will need to type the phone number and address just as you wish them to appear on forms—including punctuation such as parentheses, dashes, or periods. Take care to spell everything correctly when entering this company information. Imagine how embarrassing it would be to send out invoices, bills, and other correspondence with your own company name and information incorrect!

6. Click **Preview Your Settings**.

   QuickBooks will open the Preview Your Company Settings window, where you can choose where to save your file.

7. Click the **Company File Location** tab, and then click **Change Location**.

8. Choose your file storage location in the **Browse For Folder** window, and then click **OK**.

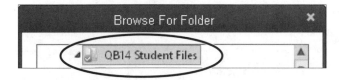

9. Click **OK** again, and then click **Create Company File**.

   QuickBooks creates your new company file, which will take a minute or so. Once the file is created, the QuickBooks Setup window will appear.

10. Click **Start Working**.

    We will be adding information in the next several chapters, but not right now.

    The Quick Start Center, which is designed to help you perform basic tasks, will appear. We will be working from the QuickBooks Home page as we progress through this book, so this window is not necessary.

11. Close the **Accountant Center** window, if necessary.

12. Click the **Close** button at the top-right corner of the Quick Start Center window.

    The QuickBooks Home page for your new company file will be displayed. Leave it open and continue to the next topic.

Editing Your QuickBooks Preferences

The way you interact with QuickBooks is controlled by the preferences you select. The Preferences window has twenty-three categories of preferences you can set or modify so QuickBooks can work more efficiently for your company.

Here are twenty-one of the twenty-three preference categories.

Use these tabs to switch between company and personal preferences with a click of the mouse.

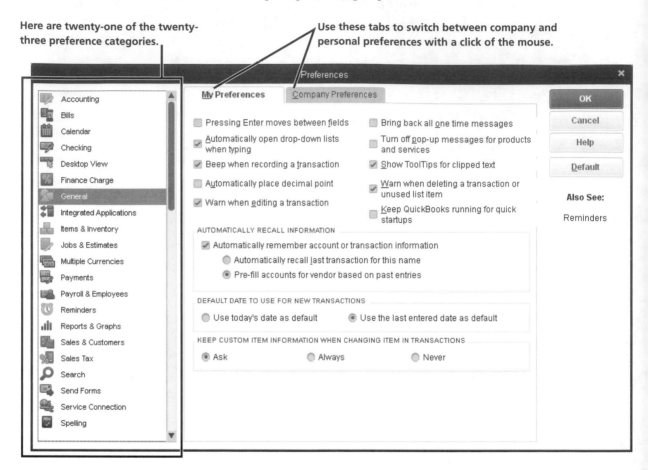

Tab: Getting Set Up
Topic: Setting up QuickBooks

Company vs. Personal Preferences

Each category has two tabs on which changes to preferences can be set: the Company Preferences tab and the My Preferences (personal) tab. Company preferences are controlled by the administrator. They determine how the entire company interacts with QuickBooks. Personal preferences are controlled by each individual user. They dictate interactions between QuickBooks and that one user only.

The following illustrations show an example of a company and a personal preference.

Changes made by an administrator affect all users. Here, an administrator turned on the preference to use account numbers. In the Chart of Accounts, there would then be an account number associated with each account.

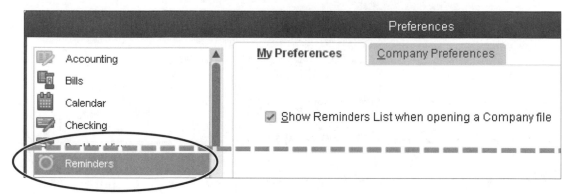

Here, a user can change the setting for the Reminder List to be shown on the My Preferences tab that will affect only her individual QuickBooks user login.

Setting a Company Preference: Account Numbers

Many businesses use account numbers for the accounts in their Chart of Accounts. You will be using account numbers as you work with the company file for Average Guy Designs. Account numbers are somewhat standard within the accounting world. "Somewhat" means that each account type begins with the same number, but the accounts listed within the account type are not universally numbered. Examine the following table to understand how account numbers work. Note that account numbers have a minimum of four characters, and you can use five or six. For instance, a Checking account (which is an asset) could be numbered 1000, 10000, or 100000.

ACCOUNT TYPES AND NUMBERS		
Account number starts with:	Type of account	Example
1	Asset	Checking Account
2	Liability	Accounts Payable
3	Equity	Retained Earnings
4	Income	Retail Product Sales
5	Cost of Goods Sold	Purchases – Resale Items
6	Expenses	Utilities Expense
7	Other Income	Interest Income
8	Other Expense	Sales Tax Penalty

Setting a Personal Preference: Show Reminders List

In many of the Preferences categories, an individual user can choose from a variety of options. In the following exercise, you will choose to show the Reminders List when starting your QuickBooks file.

QUICK REFERENCE	EDITING BASIC QUICKBOOKS PREFERENCES
Task	**Procedure**
Edit QuickBooks file preferences	■ Choose Edit→Preferences.
	■ Click the category (on the left side of the window) in which you wish to make a change.
	■ Choose the Company Preferences or My Preferences tab.
	■ Make any necessary changes.
	■ Click OK to save the new preferences.

Change Your Preferences

In this exercise, you will turn on the account number preference for the company and choose for the Reminders List to be displayed when opening QuickBooks.

Whether to turn on the use of account numbers is a company preference, is set by the company administrator, and cannot be changed by other users.

1. Choose **Edit→Preferences**.

2. Follow these steps to turn on the account numbers preference:

Ⓐ Click **Accounting**.

Ⓑ Click the **Company Preferences** tab.

Ⓒ Click in the box to the left of **Use account numbers**.

The Show lowest subaccount only preference will be introduced in QuickBooks Pro 2014: Level 2.

3. Click **OK** to accept the new preference.

Change a Desktop View Personal Preference

Now, you will turn on the Reminder List.

4. Choose **Edit→Preferences**.

5. Follow these steps to choose to have the Reminders List displayed when you open your company file:

Ⓐ Click **Reminders**.   Ⓑ Ensure that the **My Preferences** tab is displayed.

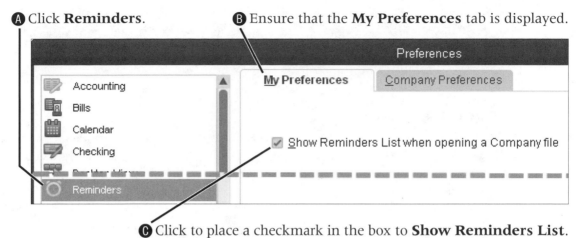

Ⓒ Click to place a checkmark in the box to **Show Reminders List**.

6. Click **OK** to accept the new preference.

Leave the QuickBooks window open and continue with the next topic.

Customizing a Company File

During the setup process, QuickBooks allows you to choose a business type similar to your own. It is up to you to take this generic file and customize it to fit your company.

Modifying the Lists in a New File

You will need to look at several lists after you set up your new QuickBooks company to ensure they are correct. If any of them are incorrect or incomplete, you will need to edit, delete, or add entries to them. These lists include the following:

- The Chart of Accounts
- The Customers & Jobs List
- The Vendor List
- The Item List
- Customer & Vendor Profile Lists

- The Fixed Asset Item List
- The Employees List
- The Payroll Items List
- The Price Level List

Entries in these lists can be created during the EasyStep interview. If you choose to skip the interview, you will need to populate these lists once the company has been created.

The Chart of Accounts

The Chart of Accounts is composed of all of the asset, liability, equity, income, and expense accounts your company utilizes. You use the Chart of Accounts list window to create new accounts, edit existing accounts, and delete unused accounts.

Customizing the Chart of Accounts

The first task you have with your new company file is to fine-tune your Chart of Accounts. If you are using QuickBooks for an existing business, you will want to talk to your accountant and get a copy of your current Chart of Accounts. If you are starting a new business, you may also want to contact your accountant for guidance on how best to set up your Chart of Accounts for your unique company.

Adding Accounts

When you add an account to the Chart of Accounts, make sure to select the correct account type, as this is one of the most prevalent errors accountants find in their clients' QuickBooks files. Keep in mind that your "behind the scenes" action will be incorrect if the wrong account type is selected.

To Edit or Delete—That Is the Question...

The generic Chart of Accounts that QuickBooks provides will have some accounts you probably won't need for your unique business. You can choose to either rename (edit) these accounts or delete them. Renaming an account is appropriate if you are working with the same account type. Deleting is appropriate if you no longer need additional accounts of the same type.

Moving and Sorting Accounts Within the List

You can change the order in which accounts appear within your Chart of Accounts. By default, QuickBooks alphabetizes accounts by type. The Chart of Accounts is structured so that assets are listed first, liabilities second, equity accounts third, income accounts fourth, cost of goods sold accounts fifth, and expense accounts last. This structure must remain intact; you can only move accounts around within their own type.

Moving list items works the same way in the various lists in QuickBooks—by clicking and dragging the diamond to the left of the list entry.

If you move your accounts and later decide you want them alphabetized by type once again, QuickBooks allows you to re-sort the list. Re-sorting the list restores the QuickBooks default.

Subaccounts

To keep precise records, you may wish to use QuickBooks subaccounts. For instance, to keep the number of expense accounts within reason, you are likely to utilize only one telephone expense account for all of your telephone lines. To track expenses more closely, though, you may want to have separate accounts for your office phone, office fax, and cellular phone. Subaccounts are a great way to track these separate expenses while keeping the number of expense accounts down.

When you run Profit & Loss reports and budgets, you have the option to expand the report (show subaccounts) to show detail or collapse the report (show only main accounts) for brevity.

Using Classes in QuickBooks

In *QuickBooks Pro 2014: Level 2*, you will go into depth in regard to using classes in QuickBooks. Classes allow you to track income and expenses for one specific aspect of your company, and they are not tied to any particular customer, job, vendor, or item. For right now, understand that if you choose to use classes for your own business, the best option is to set them up when you create your new company file.

QUICK REFERENCE	CUSTOMIZING THE CHART OF ACCOUNTS
Task	**Procedure**
Add an account	■ Click the Account menu button; choose New. ■ Choose the correct account type; click Continue. ■ Enter all necessary information. ■ Click Save & Close or Save & New.
Edit an account	■ Single-click the account you wish to edit. ■ Click the Account menu button; choose Edit. ■ Make any necessary changes; then click Save & Close.
Delete an account	■ Single-click the account you wish to delete. ■ Click the Account menu button and choose Delete; click OK.
Create a subaccount	■ Click the main account for which you wish to create a subaccount. ■ Click the Account menu button; choose New. ■ Choose the correct account type; click Continue. ■ Type the subaccount name; click in the box for Subaccount of. ■ Click the drop-down arrow, click the main account from the list, and then click OK.
Move an account	■ Click the account to move. ■ Place the mouse pointer over the diamond to the left of the account name so the four-way arrow appears. ■ Click and drag the account to the new location within the same account type.
Re-sort accounts	■ Click the Account menu button; choose Re-sort.

DEVELOP YOUR SKILLS 2-3

Make the File Fit Your Business

In this exercise, you will take the generic Chart of Accounts created for Average Guy Designs and make it fit the needs of the company. The first task is to add an account that Guy needs but that was not provided in the generic Chart of Accounts, Checking.

FROM THE KEYBOARD

Ctrl + a to open the Chart of Accounts

1. Click the **Chart of Accounts** task icon in the Company area of the Home page.

   QuickBooks opens the generic Chart of Accounts created for you. Notice the account numbers that you turned on in the previous exercise.

Chart of Accounts

2. Follow these steps to create the new account:

FROM THE KEYBOARD

Ctrl+n to create a new account

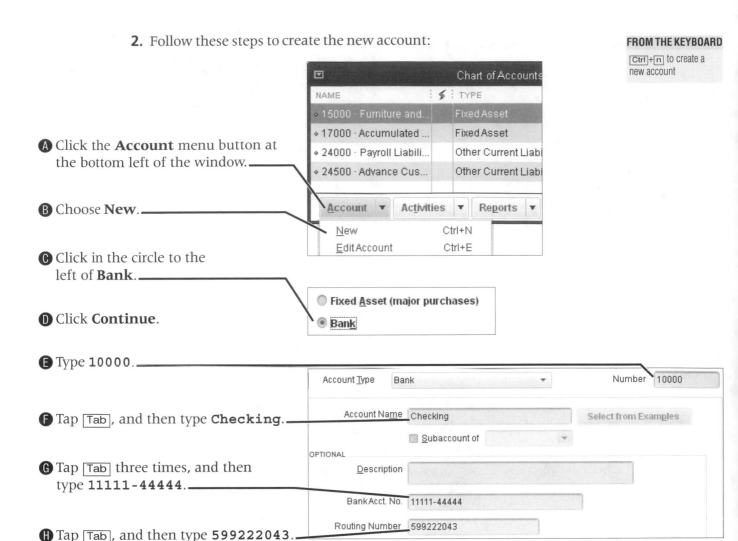

A Click the **Account** menu button at the bottom left of the window.

B Choose **New**.

C Click in the circle to the left of **Bank**.

D Click **Continue**.

E Type **10000**.

F Tap Tab, and then type **Checking**.

G Tap Tab three times, and then type **11111-44444**.

H Tap Tab, and then type **599222043**.

3. Click **Save & Close**.

4. Click **No** in the Set Up Bank Feed window.

Take a look at your Chart of Accounts window and notice the new Checking account at the top of the list.

Edit an Account

In Chapter 3, Working with Customers, you will learn how to create items and route them to the proper account in the Chart of Accounts. For now, you will rename one of the income accounts.

5. Scroll down the Chart of Accounts, if necessary, and then single-click the **Consulting Income** account.

6. Click the **Account** menu button, and then choose **Edit Account**.

FROM THE KEYBOARD

Ctrl+e to edit the selected account

7. Follow these steps to rename the account:

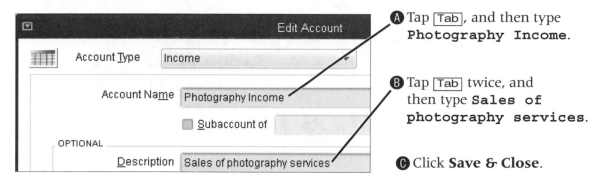

A Tap `Tab`, and then type **Photography Income**.

B Tap `Tab` twice, and then type **Sales of photography services**.

C Click **Save & Close**.

Delete an Account

8. Scroll to the bottom of the Chart of Accounts window, and then single-click the **Ask My Accountant** account.

9. Click the **Account** menu button, and then choose **Delete Account**.

10. Click **OK** in the Delete Account window.

Since you cannot undo an account deletion, QuickBooks verifies your choice.

FROM THE KEYBOARD
`Ctrl`+`d` to delete the selected account

Create Subaccounts

Guy wants to track his telephone expenses more carefully, so he has decided to use subaccounts.

11. Single-click **Telephone Expense** in the Chart of Accounts.

12. Click the **Account** menu button, and then choose **New**.

13. Follow these steps to create your new subaccount:

A Click in the circle to the left of **Expense**.

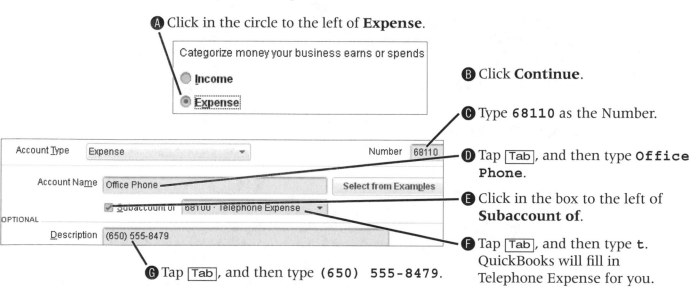

B Click **Continue**.

C Type **68110** as the Number.

D Tap `Tab`, and then type **Office Phone**.

E Click in the box to the left of **Subaccount of**.

F Tap `Tab`, and then type **t**. QuickBooks will fill in Telephone Expense for you.

G Tap `Tab`, and then type **(650) 555-8479**.

14. Click **Save & New** to add your new subaccount and leave the window open to add another one.

15. Follow step 13 C–G to add the following additional subaccounts for Telephone Expense, clicking **Save & New** after creating the first additional subaccount.

Account Number	Subaccount Name	Description
68120	Fax Line	(650) 555-4015
68130	Cell Phone	(650) 555-1011

16. Click **Save & Close** to create the last new subaccount and close the window.

17. Close the **Chart of Accounts** window.

Working with Opening Balances and Historical Transactions

If you chose a start date for your company that was not the first day you were in business, it is important to enter all of the historical transactions and opening balances in your file.

Entering and Editing Account Opening Balances

You need to make sure that you have the correct opening balances in QuickBooks for all of your accounts. There are five methods by which you can enter opening balances. The type of account that you are dealing with determines which method, or combination of methods, will work the best. The five methods available are:

- EasyStep Interview (for bank accounts only)
- Journal entries
- Forms (for individual transactions)
- Registers
- Lists (lump sums can be entered when creating entries)

Editing a Beginning Balance

If you need to correct a beginning balance that you entered, you will not be able to do it through the EasyStep Interview or the Edit Account window. In order to accomplish this task, you need to use either the account register or a journal entry. For example, if you incorrectly entered $15,000 as the opening balance for the Savings account when you created it, you will need to open the Savings account register by double-clicking the account in the Chart of Accounts and change the amount in that window.

Entering Historical Transactions for an Account

There are two ways that you can enter historical transactions into your QuickBooks file. Transactions can be entered either individually or in a summary journal entry.

Entering Historical Transactions Individually

If you wish to enter your transactions individually, you must have all of the data for each one. It is very important that you enter them in the correct order. Check out the following illustration to see the correct order for historical transaction entry.

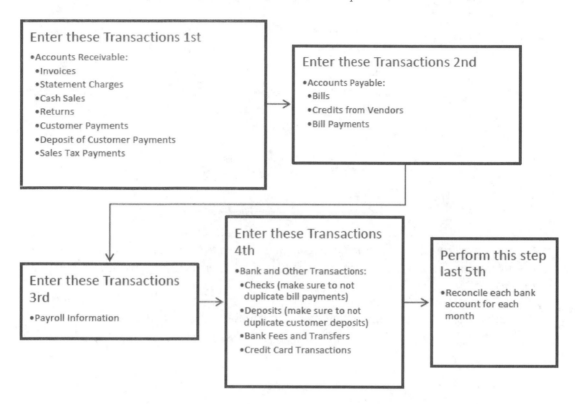

Making a Summary Journal Entry

In a summary journal entry, you will not enter the details of individual transactions; you will only enter the total amounts. In this chapter, you will edit an opening balance in a register.

QUICK REFERENCE	ENTERING HISTORICAL TRANSACTIONS
Task	**Procedure**
Edit an account opening balance	■ Open the register for the account.
	■ Drag to select the opening amount.
	■ Type the correct amount; click Record.
Enter historical transactions individually	■ Gather the information for all of the historical transactions.
	■ Enter all accounts receivable transactions and then accounts payable transactions using the proper QuickBooks forms. (Follow the order shown above.)
	■ Enter outstanding payroll information.
	■ Enter outstanding "bank and other" transactions. (Follow the order shown above.)
	■ Reconcile each bank account for each month chronologically.

QUICK REFERENCE	ENTERING HISTORICAL TRANSACTIONS (continued)
Task	**Procedure**
Make a summary journal entry to account for historical transactions	■ Gather the information for all historical transactions.
	■ Determine each account that is affected, whether the net effect is a debit or a credit, and the total amount.
	■ Choose Company→Make General Journal Entries.
	■ Enter each of the affected accounts and the amount of the debit/credit.
	■ Ensure that debits equal credits. (QuickBooks will not allow you to record the journal entry until they do!)
	■ Record the journal entry.

DEVELOP YOUR SKILLS 2-4

Deal with an Opening Balance

In this exercise, you will work with a register to deal with an adjustment to the opening balance for the Checking account, since it was not entered when you created the account. The account you will credit in this transaction is 30000•Open Balance Equity (the whole account name is cut off due to the size of the field).

1. Click the **Check Register** task icon in the Banking area of the Home page.

   There is only one bank account at this time, so the Checking register will open automatically for you.

   Check Register

2. Follow these steps to enter the opening balance for the Checking account:

   Ⓐ Type **113014** in the Date field. Ⓑ Tap ⎡Tab⎤ five times, and then type **5432.67** in the Deposit field.

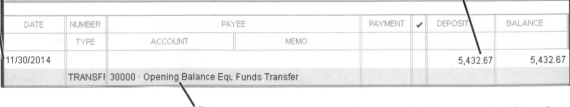

   Ⓒ Tap ⎡Tab⎤, type **3**, and then tap ⎡Tab⎤ again. QuickBooks will fill in the rest of the account for you.

   The Memo will fill in automatically when you record the transaction.

3. Click the **Record** button at the bottom of the register window.

4. Click **Yes** in the Future Transactions window, if necessary.

5. Close the **Checking** register window.

Finding Help in QuickBooks

There will be times when you will need to be able to find answers to questions you have about QuickBooks on your own. QuickBooks has a built-in help feature as well as a "coaching" feature that can come to your rescue in these circumstances.

The "Have a Question?" Window

The "Have a Question?" window is a separate window you can launch to search for help. This window is contextual, which means its contents change depending on the active window. For instance, if you choose to launch it while you have the Chart of Accounts window open, the results will relate to that window.

Type keywords here and then view the topics below. In this case, no words were necessary as the window was launched when the Chart of Accounts was the active window.

Suggested answers are presented in two categories (Answers in Help and Answers from Community).

If you click this link, you will have an options to get help by: asking a community of experts, finding a ProAdvisor, finding training, or contacting Intuit.

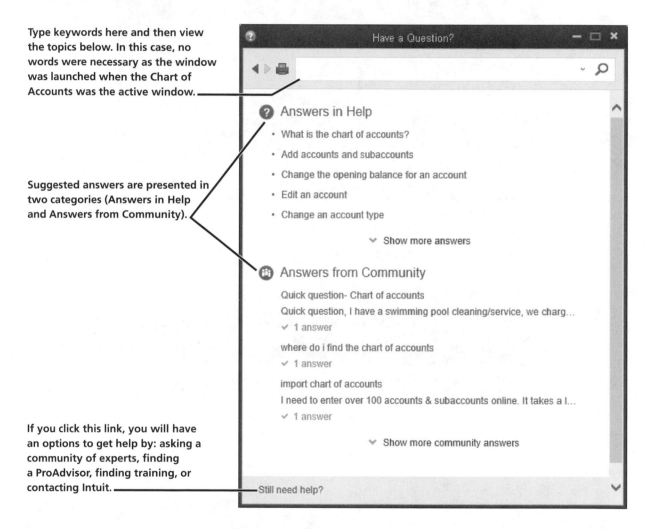

The Persistent Search Bar

The persistent search bar, which is a feature on the Icon Bar, allows you to search the company file (the results will be displayed in a Search window) or to search through help topics (the results will be displayed in the "Have a Question?" window). You will learn how to use the Search window in more detail in Chapter 3, Working with Customers.

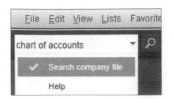

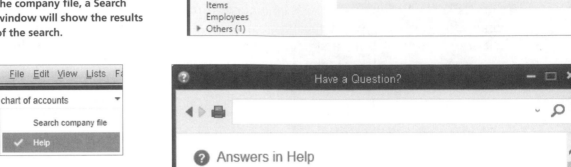

If you choose to search the company file, a Search window will show the results of the search.

File Edit View Lists F?

chart of accounts

    Search company file

  ✓ Help

If you choose to search for help, the "Have a Question?" window will display the results.

The Quick Start Center

Earlier in this chapter, you closed the Quick Start Center window that appeared after you created your new company file. This feature is available to you whenever you need it. The command to launch it can be found on the Help menu. This center helps you to perform basic tasks and is another place to access the "Visualize!" tutorials to help you learn more about working in QuickBooks.

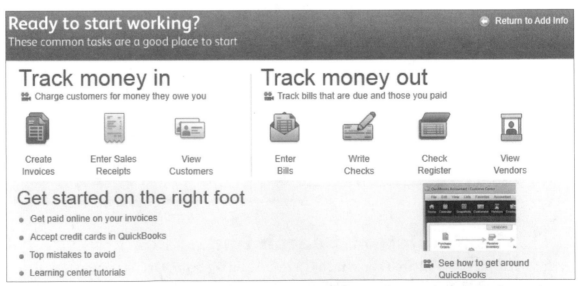

Notice that the Quick Start window is organized in sections to help you track money both coming into and leaving your business. It also features ways to start your QuickBooks experience right and to get more from the software once you are up and running.

Task	Procedure
Search for help with the "Have a Question?" window	■ Choose Help→QuickBooks Help. ■ Type the relevant keyword(s); click Search. ■ Click the desired result displayed in a Help Article window.
Search for help with the persistent search bar	■ Click in the persistent search bar; type the relevant keyword(s). ■ Choose to search for Help; click Search. ■ Click the desired result in a Help Article window.
Search your QuickBooks file with the persistent search bar	■ Click in the persistent search bar; type the relevant keyword(s). ■ Choose to Search company file; click Search.
Ask a question of another QuickBooks user	■ Choose Help→QuickBooks Help. ■ Click the Ask Community link. (An Internet browser will launch.) ■ Type your question and click Ask. ■ If you feel up to the challenge, answer a question for another user!
Print a help topic	■ Search for the desired topic; click to display it in the Help Article window. ■ Click the Print Topic button. ■ Set your printer and print options; click Print.
Open the Quick Start Center window to view a tutorial	■ Choose Help→Quick Start Center. ■ Click the hyperlink to the desired tutorial.

DEVELOP YOUR SKILLS 2-5

Search for Help

In this exercise, you will use the help feature in QuickBooks.

FROM THE KEYBOARD
F1 to open the "Have a Question?" window

1. Choose **Help→QuickBooks Help**.

   The "Have a Question?" and Help Article windows will display.

2. Follow these steps to search for a help topic:

   A Click here, and then type **user access**.

   B Click the **Search** button.

   C Click this topic.

   Your chosen topic will be displayed in the Have a Question window.

3. Scroll down to read the full article.

4. Close the **"Have a Question?"** window.

Setting Up Users

When your company grows, and you hire additional employees, you may decide that you need to allow certain employees access to your QuickBooks file.

Administrators and Users

Before you can set up any users for your QuickBooks file, you must set up an administrator who will control the access of all users. You can assign a password for each person with access to your file. The administrator controls all company preferences in the Preferences window. Users have the ability to change only their own personal preferences. QuickBooks allows you to set up unlimited users for your company file, although the number that can access the file at any one time depends on your QuickBooks license agreement.

The External Accountant user has access to all areas of QuickBooks except those that contain confidential customer information. An External Accountant can conduct reviews of your file and make changes separate from those of other users. Only an administrator can create an External Accountant user.

Restricting Access

When you decide to give employees access to your QuickBooks company file, you may not want them to see all of your company's financial information. You can choose to restrict each individual user's access to specific areas of QuickBooks.

There are nine areas for which you can give access rights to a user. Guy has asked Allison to help out at Average Guy Designs with sales and product ordering, so he will need to set

Access for user: Allison

This user has the following access rights. Click the Leave button to return.

AREA	CREATE	PRINT	REP...
Sales and Accounts Receivable	Y	Y	Y
Purchases and Accounts Payable	Y	N	N
Checking and Credit Cards	N	N	n/a
Time Tracking	N	N	N
Payroll and Employees	N	N	N
Sensitive Accounting Activities	N	N	N
Sensitive Financial Reports	N	N	n/a

her up as a user with limited access. This illustration displays those areas. In this example, Allison has access to all areas of sales and accounts receivable (creating new transactions, printing forms, and running reports) and can create new purchase and accounts payable transactions.

Setting Passwords

It is very important to make sure you have a password that is not easy for others to guess and yet that is easy for you to remember. Once you set your username and password, the Change QuickBooks Password window allows you to change your password whenever you wish (recommended every 90 days) and to set or change your secret "challenge question" that will allow you to retrieve a forgotten password. This challenge question should not have an answer with which others are familiar.

Working with QuickBooks in a Multi-User Environment

QuickBooks provides a way for more than one user to access a company file at the same time. In QuickBooks Pro and Premier, up to five users can have simultaneous access to the file. Most tasks that you usually do can be completed in multi-user mode, but there are some that must be performed in single-user mode.

You *cannot* do the following in multi-user mode:

- Create a new company file
- Set or edit a closing date
- Rebuild, clean up, or verify the file
- Create or work with accountant's copies
- Merge, delete, and sort list information
- Change company preferences
- Export and import data

Visualize!

Tab: Getting Set Up
Topic: Set up QuickBooks for multi-user

QUICK REFERENCE	SETTING UP USERS AND PASSWORDS
Task	**Procedure**
Set up an administrator name and password	■ Choose Company→Set Up Users and Passwords→Set Up Users. ■ Select Admin; click Edit User. ■ Type the username and password, entering the password twice to verify. ■ Set the challenge question and answer, if desired; click OK.
Change an administrator password	■ Choose Company→Set Up Users and Passwords→Change your password. ■ Type a complex password; retype it to verify you did it correctly. ■ Set the challenge question and answer, if desired; click OK.
Set up users	■ Choose Company→Set Up Users and Passwords→Set Up Users. ■ Click Add User. ■ Type the username and password; click Next. ■ Follow the steps in the "Set up user password and access" screens to customize the access for the user. ■ View the new user's access rights; click Finish.
Switch between multi-user/single-user modes	If you are in single-user mode and wish to switch to multi-user mode: ■ Choose File→Switch to Multi-user Mode. If you are in multi-user mode and wish to switch to single-user mode: ■ Choose File→Switch to Single-user Mode.

DEVELOP YOUR SKILLS 2-6
Set Up Users for a Company

In this exercise, you will help Guy to set up Allison as a user for the Average Guy Designs' company file. The first step is to set his own password as the administrator.

1. Choose **Company→Set Up Users and Passwords→Set Up Users**.

2. Click **Edit User**.

3. Follow these steps to set up Guy's administrator account and password:

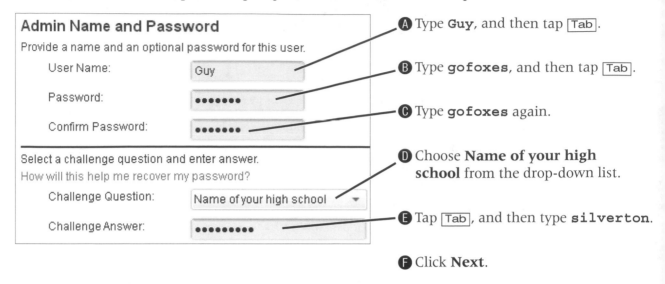

Ⓐ Type `Guy`, and then tap `Tab`.

Ⓑ Type `gofoxes`, and then tap `Tab`.

Ⓒ Type `gofoxes` again.

Ⓓ Choose **Name of your high school** from the drop-down list.

Ⓔ Tap `Tab`, and then type `silverton`.

Ⓕ Click **Next**.

4. Click **Finish**.

Notice that you do not need to change the access areas for the administrator. He has access to everything in the company file!

Add a User

Now that the administrator is set up, you can set up individual users.

5. Click the **Add User** button in the User List window; then follow these steps to add Allison as a user:

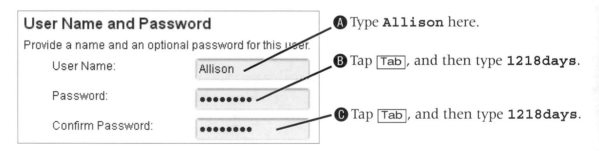

Ⓐ Type `Allison` here.

Ⓑ Tap `Tab`, and then type `1218days`.

Ⓒ Tap `Tab`, and then type `1218days`.

6. Click **Next** twice.

Each time you click Next as you move through the "Set up user password and access" screens, you can change the access for the user in one of nine areas.

7. Click to choose **Full Access** for the Sales and Accounts Receivable option; click **Next**.

8. Click in the circle to the left of **Selective Access** for Purchases and Accounts Payable.

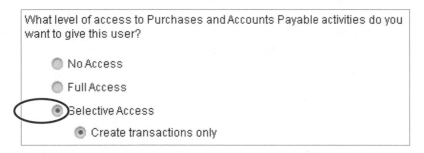

The Create transactions only option will be automatically selected.

9. Click **Finish**.

Notice that Allison has been added to the User List.

10. Click **View User**.

You will see a summary of the access you have given to Allison. You can change this at any time by opening the User List, clicking on Allison, and then clicking the Edit User button.

11. Click the **Leave** button in the View User access window.

12. Close the **User List**.

Closing the Books and Running List Reports

You will not actually close the books yet, but it is important to understand how QuickBooks deals with this task, so it will be covered now. You will, however, find the need to produce list reports early on in your QuickBooks experience. For instance, your accountant may wish to see a list of the accounts you have set up for your business to ensure all is well before you get too far down the road. QuickBooks reports can provide you with a wealth of information about your company.

Keeping the End in Mind

You are not required to "close the books" in QuickBooks, but you can choose to if you like. When you close the books, QuickBooks:

- Transfers the net income or net loss to Retained Earnings
- Restricts access to transactions prior to the closing date by requiring a password
- Allows you to clean up your data

Only the company file administrator can set a closing date and allow or restrict access to prior-period transactions by a user. For now, it is important for you to keep in mind how QuickBooks operates at the end of an accounting period.

The Report Center

There are many preset reports available for you to use in QuickBooks. They are broken into three main categories: list, summary, and transaction. The Report Center is a tool in QuickBooks that allows you to learn about different types of reports without having to create them by trial and error. It includes sample reports and descriptions of the type of information each report provides.

Contributed Reports

Contributed reports are specialized reports submitted by users that are integrated into the Report Center. You can search for specialized reports by your industry type, and you can even rate a report for other users to see how valuable it is to you.

These tabs let you view standard QuickBooks reports; your memorized, favorite, and recently displayed reports; and reports contributed by other users.

These three buttons let you change how you view Report Center information.

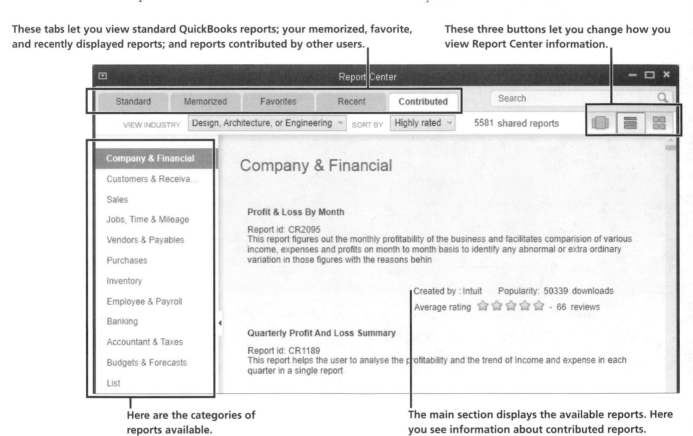

Here are the categories of reports available.

The main section displays the available reports. Here you see information about contributed reports.

Tab: Reports
Topic: Reports

List Reports in QuickBooks

One category of reports that you can access contains list reports. They simply display the information that is found in your various QuickBooks lists in an easy-to-read format.

When you view the Report Center in List View, you will see a question that the report will answer below the name of the report. This will come in handy when you are completing the Apply Your Skills exercises, where you will be expected to "answer questions with reports!"

Viewing Sample Report Images

An additional feature available in the Report Center is the ability to view what a report will look like without having to actually produce the report.

When you click the Info button for a report, a sample of what the report will look like is displayed.

Email Functionality in Reports

QuickBooks allows you to email reports from any report window. You have a chance to choose whether the recipient will receive the report as an Adobe Acrobat (PDF) or Microsoft Excel file. The report will appear the same as it would if you printed it from QuickBooks.

When you click the Email button on the toolbar, you can choose the type of file that will be attached to your email message.

QUICK REFERENCE	PRODUCING LIST REPORTS
Task	**Procedure**
Display an Account Listing report	■ Choose Reports→Report Center. ■ Choose List as the report category. ■ Scroll down; click Account Listing. ■ Click the Run report button.
Email a report from QuickBooks	■ Produce the report you wish to email. ■ Click the Email button and choose to send it as a PDF or an Excel file. ■ Using your email program, enter the recipients, and make any desired modifications to the message. ■ Send the email.

DEVELOP YOUR SKILLS 2-7

Produce a List Report

In this exercise, you will create and email a report for Guy's accountant that displays the accounts in his Chart of Accounts.

1. Choose **Reports→Report Center**.

2. Follow these steps to display the report:

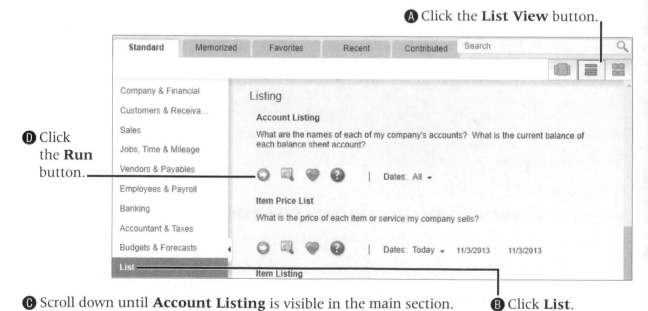

Ⓐ Click the **List View** button.

Ⓓ Click the **Run** button.

Ⓒ Scroll down until **Account Listing** is visible in the main section.

Ⓑ Click **List**.

A report displaying all of the accounts in the Chart of Accounts is displayed.

3. Close the **Account Listing** report and **Report Center** windows.

4. Choose the appropriate option for your situation:
   - If you will continue working, leave QuickBooks open.
   - If you are finished working in QuickBooks for now, choose **File→Exit**.

FROM THE KEYBOARD
Alt+F4 to exit from QuickBooks

Tackle the Tasks

Now is your chance to work a little more with Average Guy Designs and apply the skills that you have learned in this chapter to accomplish additional tasks. You will use the same company file you just created to complete the following tasks.

(If you need to reopen the file, remember that the username is "Guy" and the password for the file is "gofoxes"!)

Add Accounts	Add the following bank account: 10200•Savings Add the following income account: 48800•Print Layout Services Add the following expense account: 61500•Job Materials
Add Subaccounts	Add the following subaccounts to the Utilities account: 68610•Gas & Electric, 68620•Water
Change Account Opening Balance	Change the Savings account opening balance to $7,382.35, as of 11/30/14
Search for Help	Use the QuickBooks help feature to learn how to enter a bill from a vendor
Change Preferences	Choose to change the color scheme to Orange (hint: Desktop View/My Preferences) Turn off the two date warnings (hint: Accounting/Company Preferences)
Create a List Report	Create a list report that shows all of the Terms available (these list entries were automatically added when you created the company)

Concepts Review

To check your knowledge of the key concepts introduced in this chapter, complete the Concepts Review quiz on the Student Resource Center.

Reinforce Your Skills

Set Up a New QuickBooks Company

In this exercise, you will use Detailed Start to set up the company for Quality-Built Construction.

1. If necessary, launch **QuickBooks**.

2. Choose **File→New Company**.

3. Click the **Detailed Start** button in the QuickBooks Setup window.
   The EasyStep Interview window displays.

4. Refer to the information in the table below to complete the EasyStep Interview for Angela.

EASYSTEP INTERVIEW INFORMATION	
Field	**Data**
Company/Legal Name	Quality-Built Construction
Tax ID (Federal Employee Identification Number)	99-9999999
Address	316 Maple Street Silverton, OR 97381
Phone	(503) 555-3759
Fax	(503) 555-3758
Email	qualitybuilt@samplename.com
Industry Type	Construction General Contractor
Company Organization	S Corporation
First Month of Fiscal Year	January
Administrator Password	Build2014 (remember that passwords are case-sensitive)
File Name	RYS_Chapter02_[LastnameFirstinitial] (e.g. RYS_Chapter02_StevensA)
What Is Sold?	Services Only
Sales Tax	No
Estimates	No
Billing Statements	Yes
Invoices	Yes
Progress Invoicing	No
Bill Tracking	Yes
Time Tracking	No
Employees	No
Multiple Currencies	No (this option is not available in all versions)
Start Date	11-30-2014
Income & Expense Accounts	Start with the accounts provided

5. Once the information is entered, click **Go to Setup** to complete the interview.
   The "You've got a company file!" screen appears in the QuickBooks Setup window.

6. Click **Start working**.

7. Click the **Close** button on the Quick Start Center window.

Change Preferences

In this exercise, you will change two preferences in the file you just created for Quality-Built Construction. You will begin by turning on the account number preference so that when you create and edit accounts, you can enter the numbers.

Before You Begin: Make sure you have completed Reinforce Your Skills 2-1.

1. Choose **Edit→Preferences**.

2. Choose the **Accounting** category.

3. Click the **Company Preferences** tab.

4. Click in the box to turn on the **Use account numbers** preference.

5. Click **OK**.

Display Additional Task Icons on the Home Page

Angela would like to be able to create sales receipts in QuickBooks, so you will make the Create Sales Receipts task icon visible on the Home page.

6. Choose **Edit→Preferences**.

7. Choose the **Desktop View** category.

8. Click the **Company Preferences** tab.

9. Click in the box to the left of **Sales Receipts** in the Customers area of the window.

10. Click **OK** to change the preference, and then click **OK** again to close the window.

Work with the Chart of Accounts

In this exercise, you will add, edit, and delete accounts as well as add subaccounts in the Chart of Accounts.

Add New Accounts

Angela wants to add her company's checking account.

1. Choose **Lists→Chart of Accounts**.

2. Click the **Account** menu button, and then choose **New**.
   The account menu button can be found in the bottom-left of the Chart of Accounts window.

3. Choose **Bank** as the account type; click **Continue**.

4. Type **10000** in the Number field, tap Tab , and then type **Checking** as the Name.

5. Click **Save & New**; click **No** in the Set Up Online Services window, if necessary.

6. Choose **Income** as the account type.

7. Type **42700** in the Number field, tap Tab , and then type **Remodel Income** as the Name.

8. Click **Save & Close**.

Edit an Account

Angela wants to change the name of the Construction Income account.

9. Scroll, if necessary, and right-click on the **42600•Construction Income** account; then choose **Edit Account** from the shortcut menu.

10. Change the name of the account to **New Construction Income**, and then click **Save & Close**.

Delete an Account

Angela has decided that she doesn't want the Ask My Accountant account, so you will delete it for her.

11. Scroll down, if necessary, and single-click on account **80000•Ask My Accountant**.

12. Click the **Account** menu button, and then choose **Delete Account**.

13. Click **OK** to confirm the deletion.

Add Subaccounts

You will now add two subaccounts for the Utilities account: Gas & Electric and Water.

14. Click the **Account** menu button, and then choose **New**.

15. Choose **Expense** as the account type; click **Continue**.

16. Enter **68610** as the Number and **Gas & Electric** as the Name.

17. Make it a subaccount of **68600•Utilities**.

18. Click **Save & New**, and then create one additional subaccount for Utilities: **68620•Water**.

19. Click **Save & Close**; then close the **Chart of Accounts** window.

Produce a List Report

In this exercise, you will create an Account Listing report for Angela to show her the work that you have completed on her Chart of Accounts.

1. Choose **Reports→List→Account Listing**.

2. Take a look at the report and make sure that all of the **Chart of Accounts** work you did in the last exercise is correct.

3. Either print the report or save it as a PDF, based on your instructor's direction.

4. Submit the report based on the guidelines provided by your instructor.

5. Close the **Account Listing** report.

6. Choose the appropriate option for your situation:

   ■ If you will continue working, leave QuickBooks open.

   ■ If you are finished working in QuickBooks for now, choose **File→Exit**.

Apply Your Skills

Create and Customize a New Company File

In this exercise, you will create a QuickBooks company file for Dr. Sadie James, DVM. You should use the Express Start method to set up the company.

1. Use the following information to set up a new company file for Dr. James. Save the file in your default file location, naming it **AYS_Chapter02_ [LastnameFirstinitial]** (e.g. AYS_Chapter02_JamesS).

Company/Legal Name	Wet Noses Veterinary Clinic
Tax ID Number	99-9999999
Address	589 Retriever Drive Bothell, WA 98011
Phone	(425) 555-2939
Company Type	LLP
Fiscal Year first month	January
Industry	Medical, Dental, or Health Service
Employees	No employees yet—will have in future

Remember that with this method of new company setup, QuickBooks will automatically save the file to the default location with the default name unless you choose to change it by previewing your settings.

2. Click **Start Working** in the QuickBooks Setup window.

3. Close the **Quick Start Center** and **Accountant Center** windows.

Change Account Preferences

In this exercise, you will set preferences for Wet Noses. You will not turn on account number preferences for this company, as you will operate this company without using them.

1. Open the **Preferences** window.

2. Choose to turn off **Beep when recording a transaction**. (Hint: Look in the General category.)

3. Choose to have QuickBooks show a full list of the **To Do Notes** when you open the company file.
   Hint: Look in the Reminders category.

4. Choose to turn off **date warnings**.
   Hint: Look in the Accounting category.

5. Close the **Preferences** window.

Modify the Chart of Accounts

In this exercise, you will modify the Chart of Accounts for the company you just created.

1. Open the **Chart of Accounts**.

2. Add two new **Bank** accounts: `Checking` and `Savings`.

3. Add a new **income** account: `Boarding Income`.

4. Add a new **expense** account: `Boarding Food and Supplies`.

5. Change the name of the Vaccines and Medicines account to `Pharmaceuticals`.

6. Add two **subaccounts** for Pharmaceuticals: `Vaccines` and `Medicines`.

7. Delete the **Uniforms** account.

Answer Questions with Reports

In this exercise, you will answer questions for Dr. James by running reports. You may wish to display the Report Center in List View to help you answer the questions. Ask your instructor if you should print the reports, print (save) them as PDF files, export them to Excel, or simply display them on the screen.

1. Dr. James' accountant has asked if the Chart of Accounts has been set up correctly. Produce a report that will show all of the accounts that have been set up for the company.

2. Before Dr. James begins working with customers and vendors, her accountant asks if the proper terms have been set up for her to use on invoices and bills. Display a report that will show her what terms are currently set up for the company.

3. Submit your reports based on the guidelines provided by your instructor.

4. Choose the appropriate option for your situation:
   - If you will continue working, leave QuickBooks open.
   - If you are finished working in QuickBooks for now, choose **File→Exit**.

Extend Your Skills

In the course of working through the Extend Your Skills exercises, you will utilize various skills taught in this and previous chapters. Take your time and think carefully about the tasks presented to you. Turn back to the chapter content if you need assistance.

2-1 Sort Through the Stack

You have been hired by Arlaine Cervantes to help her with her organization's books. She is the founder of Niños del Lago, a nonprofit organization that provides impoverished Guatemalan children with an engaging educational camp experience. You have just sat down at your desk and opened a large envelope from her with a variety of documents and noticed that you have several emails from her as well. It is your job to sort through the papers and emails and make sense of what you find, entering information into QuickBooks whenever appropriate and answering any other questions in a word-processing document saved as **EYS1_Chapter02_ LastnameFirstinitial**. Remember, you are digging through papers you just dumped out of an envelope and addressing random emails from Arlaine, so it is up to you to determine the correct order in which to complete the tasks.

- An email from her accountant: Set up Chart of Accounts, use Nonprofit as industry type, and add Grant Revenue as an income account.

- A bank statement from Salem First National Bank dated 6/30/2014. Checking account #21375-01, ending balance $5,462.11; Savings account #21375-20, ending balance $18,203.54.

- A handwritten sticky note: Need for three volunteers (Bill, Karel, and Chris) to have access to entering donor revenue. How can I make sure they can do this but don't have access to other areas in QuickBooks? Will I need a password or something?

- A scrap of paper with the following written on it: Fiscal year July-June.

- A scribbled phone message from Arlaine's accountant: Make sure to use account numbers when you set up in QuickBooks.

- The following message on a sticky note: Is there a reminders list to keep me on track???

- Another email from Arlaine's accountant: Make sure to not have the starting date the day you started the organization...would be too much information to enter. How about 6/30/2014 instead since it is the end of the fiscal year?

- A copy of last year's taxes: Form 990, Federal EIN 99-9999999.

- A piece of company letterhead found is posted on the Student Resource Center.

2-2 Be Your Own Boss

Before You Begin: Complete Extend Your Skills 1-2 before starting this exercise.

In this exercise, you will create the company file that you outlined in the previous chapter. Using the information identified in Extend Your Skills 1-2 and what you have learned in this chapter, create a new company file for your business. Save the new company file as **EYS2_Chapter02_ LastnameFirstinitial** and submit it to your instructor based on the instructions provided.

2-3 Use the Web as a Learning Tool

Throughout this book, you will be provided with an opportunity to use the Internet as a learning tool by completing WebQuests. According to the original creators of WebQuests, as described on their website (http://WebQuest.org), a WebQuest is "an inquiry-oriented activity in which most or all of the information used by learners is drawn from the web." To complete the WebQuest projects in this book, navigate to the Student Resource Center and choose the WebQuest for the chapter on which you are working. The subject of each WebQuest will be relevant to the material found in the chapter.

WebQuest Subject: Working with QuickBooks in a multi-user environment

Working with Customers

CHAPTER OBJECTIVES

After studying this chapter, you will be able to:

- Use the Customer Center and Customers & Jobs List

- Create service and non-inventory items

- Create invoices and receive payment on them

- Enter sales receipts

- Correct errors in customer transactions

- Work with customer-related reports

et's face it. The best part of being in business is creating and developing relationships with customers. Intuit describes a customer as "any person, business, or group that buys or pays for the services or products that your business or organization sells or provides." When working with QuickBooks, you can consider a customer anyone who pays you funds. This simple definition will help you if you have a unique business, such as a not-for-profit organization that doesn't normally use the term "customer." The job feature is an optional aspect of QuickBooks, but the feature can be extremely helpful if you have more than one project for a customer. In this chapter, you will examine QuickBooks' lists, activities, and reports that allow you to deal with customers effectively.

CASE STUDY

Average Guy Designs

Guy has learned from his colleague Allison that the next step he needs to complete is to set up his company to track customers and sales transactions. He will begin by working on the Customers & Jobs List, which is a part of the Customer Center. Once his customers have been entered, he will be able to create transactions for them. In order to create sales transactions such as invoices and sales receipts, though, he must first create items that will be used to direct income into the proper accounts behind the scenes. Finally, Guy will create reports that will tell him about his customer-related transactions.

Guy can access the Customers & Jobs List, and all of the transactions concerning a customer, from the Customer Center. The following illustration shows the Customer Center with Evelyn Huff selected.

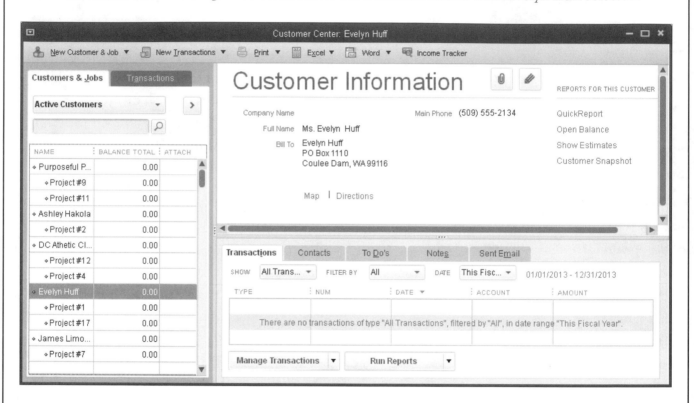

In this chapter, you will also help Guy to fix errors made when entering customer transactions.

 Tab: Tracking Money In
Topic: Sales overview; Building blocks of sales

Working with the Customer Center

When opened, the Customer Center gives you a quick look at all of your customers. If you recall from the introduction, a customer is anyone who pays you funds. This general definition is useful because it applies to all types of organizations, even those that do not have "customers" in the traditional sense, such as not-for-profits.

QuickBooks uses lists to organize your company's information. Lists allow you to store information that you can easily fill into forms by using drop-down arrows or by starting to type the entry and letting QuickBooks fill in the rest. Lists comprise the database aspect of QuickBooks. As an option, the Customers & Jobs List can be exported to contact management software such as Microsoft Outlook.

The Customer Center window provides you with the following information:

- The name of each customer and any jobs that have been created
- The balance that each customer owes
- Information for the selected customer or job
- Transactions affecting the selected customer or job

These tabs help to track information for each customer.

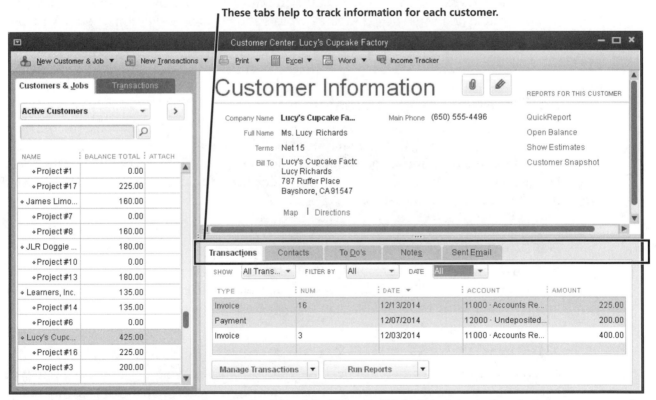

The Customer Information section displayed to the right of the Customers & Jobs List relates to the selected customer record, in this case, Lucy's Cupcake Factory.

The Customers & Jobs List tracks a lot of information for each customer and each job. This information is organized onto five tabs: Address Info, Payment Settings, Sales Tax Settings, Additional Info, and Job Info. If you have jobs assigned to a customer, you will see only four tabs. You will manage the jobs in the separate job records. If you want to track information that does not already have a field, you can create Custom Fields to customize QuickBooks for your unique business, which you will learn more about in *QuickBooks Pro 2014: Level 2*. Remember, the more information you enter for each customer, the more flexibility you will have later when you learn how to customize reports. When you utilize fields, you can sort, group, and filter your reports using those fields. You can access the Customers & Jobs List through the Customer Center.

Managing the Customers & Jobs List

List-management tasks are performed similarly for the various lists in QuickBooks. The exact procedure that you follow will depend on whether the list is integrated into a QuickBooks center (Customers & Jobs, Vendors, and Employees) or is accessible via the List option on the menu bar. The lists that are integrated into a center are not accessible separately via the menu bar.

 Centralized Info in the Customer Center

Creating a New Customer

To enter customer transactions, you must first enter your customers into the Customers & Jobs List. Customers can be entered at any time and can even be entered "on the fly" into the customer field on forms such as Create Invoices and Enter Sales Receipts; you will then have to select Quick Add or Setup from the pop-up window. Once you have added a customer to the list, you can create individual jobs for that customer.

Editing an Existing Customer

Once you have created a customer, you can always go back and edit that customer through the Customer Center. The one item that cannot be edited after you have created and saved a new customer is the opening balance (it must be adjusted through the customer register). When you change the information for a customer, including the customer's name, it will be reflected in both future and past transactions.

Deleting a Customer

You can delete a customer or job from the Customers & Jobs List *as long as you have not used it in a transaction*. If you have used it in a transaction, you can make it inactive, but you cannot delete it until after you close the books for a period and clean up your company's data.

Allowing List Entries to Fill In

When your insertion point is in a field that draws from a list, you can simply begin to type the entry that you want to choose from the list. QuickBooks will search down the list and fill in the entry for you. This fill-in feature is not case-sensitive, so you can type in lowercase even though the list entry will fill in with the proper capitalization (if you entered it with proper capitalization in the list).

Adding/Editing Multiple List Entries

You can manage the customer, vendor, and item lists all in one location. You can also choose to type the list entries or paste them from Microsoft Excel. In this chapter, you will add one entry at a time in the Customers & Jobs List. In *QuickBooks Pro 2014: Level 2,* you will work with the Add/Edit Multiple List Entries feature.

The Income Tracker

The Income Tracker is a new feature in QuickBooks 2014 that allows you to view all of your customer-related transactions in one convenient place.

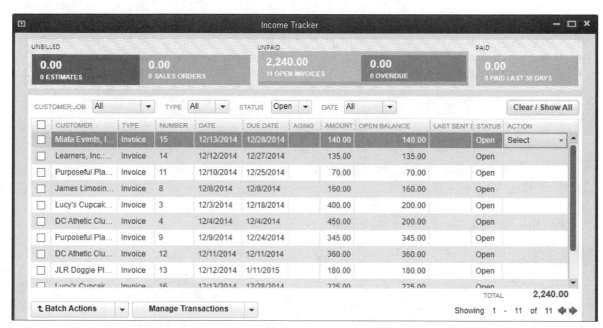

In the Income Tracker, you can easily see and manage all customer-related transactions. You can also perform actions on transactions in batches from this window.

The QuickBooks Lead Center

The QuickBooks Lead Center is a feature that provides you with a tool to track potential sales leads. Within the Lead Center, you can track outstanding tasks, contact information for the leads, location information, and notes related to your interactions and knowledge of the sales lead.

Working with Nonprofit Organizations

You use QuickBooks to work with nonprofit organizations just as you do with for-profit companies. Intuit also offers a specialized QuickBooks Premier edition designed especially for nonprofits. In this book you have been and will continue to work with a nonprofit organization, Niños del Lago, in the Extend Your Skills exercises.

When working with nonprofits in QuickBooks, take care with the term "customer." QuickBooks defines a customer as anyone who pays you funds. So, with a nonprofit, donors are customers.

They should be entered in the Customers & Jobs List. You can also use the customer and vendor profile lists in creative ways to track aspects of a nonprofit organization.

QUICK REFERENCE	MANAGING THE CUSTOMERS & JOBS LIST
Task	**Procedure**
Edit an existing customer/job	▪ Open the Customer Center; double-click the desired customer or job. ▪ Make the change(s) in the field(s); click OK.
Add a new customer	▪ Open the Customer Center; click the New Customer & Job button, and then choose New Customer. ▪ Enter all of the customer's information; click OK.
Add a new job	▪ Open the Customer Center; single-click the desired customer. ▪ Click the New Customer & Job button, and then choose Add Job. ▪ Enter all of the information for the job; click OK.
Delete a customer/job	▪ Open the Customer Center; single-click the desired customer/job. ▪ Choose Edit→Delete Customer:Job; click OK to confirm.
Make a list entry inactive	▪ Open the center in which the list entry is located. ▪ Right-click the desired list entry, and then choose Make Inactive.
Merge list entries	▪ Open the center in which the list entries are located. ▪ Double-click the list entry you wish to merge with another. ▪ Change the name of the entry to exactly match the entry into which you wish to merge; click OK.
Access the Income Tracker	▪ Choose Customers→Income Tracker.
Access the Lead Center	▪ Choose Customers→Lead Center.

Manage the Customers & Jobs List

In this exercise, you will manage the Customers & Jobs List. The first step is to open QuickBooks, and then either open a company file or restore a portable company file.

Intuit provides maintenance releases throughout the lifetime of the product. These updates may require you to update your student exercise files before you work with them. Please follow the prompts on the screen if you are asked to update your company file to the latest QuickBooks release.

1. Start **QuickBooks 2014**.

   If you downloaded the student exercise files in the portable company file *format, follow Option 1 below. If you downloaded the files in the* company file *format, follow Option 2.*

Option 1: Restore a Portable Company File

2. Choose **File→Open or Restore Company**.

3. Restore the **DYS_Chapter03 (Portable)** portable company file from your file storage location, placing your last name and first initial at the end of the filename (e.g., DYS_Chapter03_MarshallG).

   It may take a few moments for the portable company file to open. Once it does, continue with step 5.

Option 2: Open a Company File

2. Choose **File→Open or Restore Company**, ensure that **Open a regular company file** is selected, and then open the **Average Guy Designs** company file for this chapter from your file storage location.

   The QuickBooks company file will open.

3. Click **OK** to close the QuickBooks Information window. Click **No** in the Set Up External Accountant User window, if necessary.

4. Close the **Reminders** window.

Edit an Existing Customer

The first step in performing any Customers & Jobs list management task is to open the Customer Center.

FROM THE KEYBOARD

Ctrl+j to open the Customer Center

5. Click the **Customers** button located in the Customers area of the Home page.

CUSTOMERS

6. Single-click to select **DC Athetic Club LLC** in the Customers & Jobs List.

   You must first select the customer you wish to edit, and yes, it is spelled incorrectly—you will be fixing it!

7. Click the **Edit Customer** button in the Customer Information area of the Customer Center.

   The Edit Customer window will open for the selected customer.

8. Correct the name to read **DC Athletic Club LLC**.

   You will need to correct this in four separate places in the Edit Customer window.

> **TIP**
> In QuickBooks, you can use the same text editing techniques you use in word-processing programs. Simply select the text to be replaced by clicking and dragging the mouse pointer over it and then type the replacement. You can also use the Delete or Backspace keys on your keyboard.

9. Click **OK** to accept the change.

Add a New Customer

Now you will add a new customer to the Customers & Jobs List.

10. Click the **New Customer & Job** button, and then choose **New Customer**.

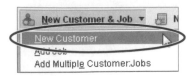

11. Follow these steps to fill in the information on the Address Info tab:

A Type **Dance a Little**.   **B** Tap [Tab] three times, and then type **Dance a Little** again.

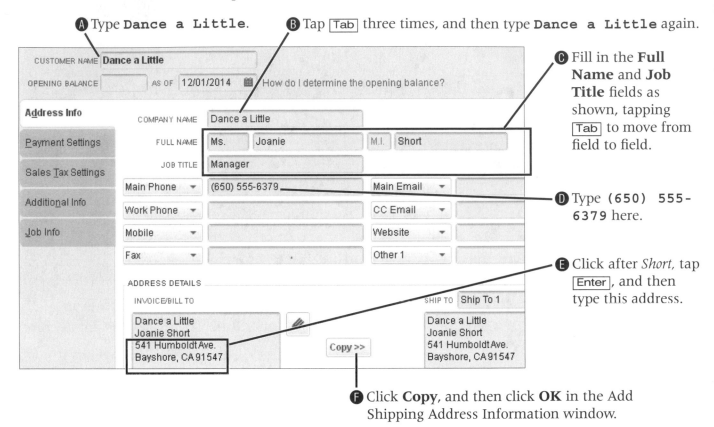

C Fill in the **Full Name** and **Job Title** fields as shown, tapping [Tab] to move from field to field.

D Type **(650) 555-6379** here.

E Click after *Short,* tap [Enter], and then type this address.

F Click **Copy**, and then click **OK** in the Add Shipping Address Information window.

Since you are not entering an opening balance, you do not need to worry about the date displayed for it.

12. Click the **Payment Settings** tab, and then follow these steps to add information:

A Type **GD-54** here.

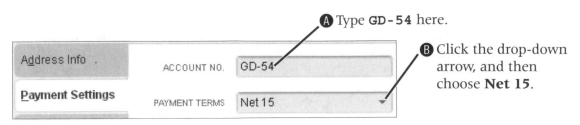

B Click the drop-down arrow, and then choose **Net 15**.

13. Click the **Additional Info** tab.

14. Click the Customer Type drop-down arrow and choose **From advertisement**.

15. Click **OK** to complete the new customer record.

Add a Job

16. Ensure **Dance a Little** is selected, click the New Customer & Job button, and then choose **Add Job**.

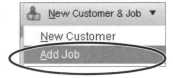

17. Type **Project #19** as the Job Name; click **OK**.

In the next step, you will close the Customer Center window within QuickBooks. Do not click the Close button for the QuickBooks window, as it will exit the program rather than simply close the center window!

18. Close the **Customer Center** window.

Understanding and Creating Items

Before you can create an invoice, you must create items to be included on the invoice. You will now learn how to create items for service and non-inventory items. An item is defined in QuickBooks as something that a company buys, sells, or resells in the course of business.

When you create a new item, you need to provide QuickBooks with very important information. When an item is sold, it directs the sales to the proper income account based on the information you entered when you created the item. The Item List will be studied in more depth in *QuickBooks Pro 2014: Level 2*, when you begin to work with inventory. In this chapter, you will access the Item List through the Home page.

This search feature can come in handy if you have many items through which you may need to look to find a specific item.

This column shows the item names. This is what you will enter into a form to choose the item.

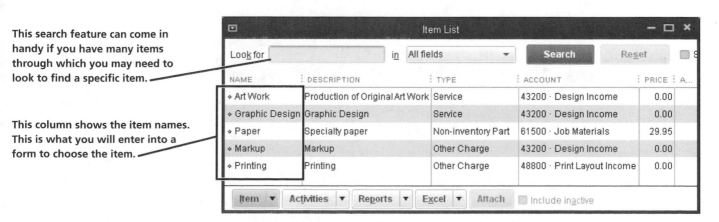

TYPES OF ITEMS	
Item Type	Description
Service	For services you charge for or purchase (e.g., specialized labor, consulting hours, or professional fees)
Non-inventory Part	For goods you buy but don't track (e.g., office supplies) or materials for a specific job that you charge back to the customer
Inventory Part	For goods you purchase, track as inventory, and resell
Other Charge	For miscellaneous labor, material, or part charges (e.g., delivery charges, setup fees, or service charges)
Subtotal	Totals all items above it on a form up to the last subtotal; to apply a percentage discount or surcharge to many items
Group	Quickly enters a group of individual items on an invoice
Discount	Subtracts a percentage or fixed amount from a total or subtotal; do not use for an early payment discount
Payment	Records a partial payment at the time of sale; reduces the amount owed on an invoice
Sales Tax Item	Calculates a single sales tax at a specific rate that you pay to a single tax agency
Sales Tax Group	Calculates and individually tracks two or more sales tax items that apply to the same sale; customer sees only the total sales tax

Service Items

Service items are used in QuickBooks to track services that you both sell to others and purchase from them. They can be used to track time that employees spend on a certain customer's project and then be easily passed on to a customer using the QuickBooks time tracking feature. This use of service items will be covered in *QuickBooks Pro 2014: Level 2*.

Non-Inventory Items

Non-inventory part items are for things that a business buys but doesn't stock as inventory. You can use purchase orders to obtain non-inventory items if you wish to track items that are used in your business but not resold to customers, such as papers and printer ink. You will learn more about purchase orders in *QuickBooks Pro 2014: Level 2*. You can also purchase non-inventory items through the Enter Bills window by utilizing the Items tab. In order to track both purchase and sales information for an item, you need to identify that the item is "used in assemblies or is purchased for a specific customer: job" in the New or Edit Item window.

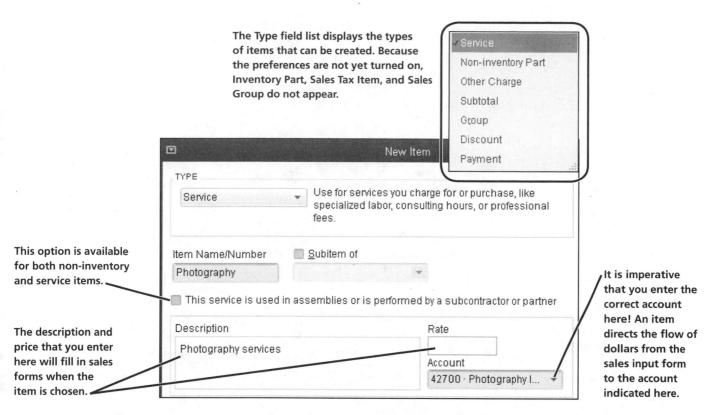

The Type field list displays the types of items that can be created. Because the preferences are not yet turned on, Inventory Part, Sales Tax Item, and Sales Group do not appear.

This option is available for both non-inventory and service items.

The description and price that you enter here will fill in sales forms when the item is chosen.

It is imperative that you enter the correct account here! An item directs the flow of dollars from the sales input form to the account indicated here.

When you enter an item on a QuickBooks form, you can override the price that you have recorded in the Item List. If you don't have standard pricing and find that you enter specialized pricing more than you use a default price, you may wish to leave the Price field blank in the Item List and fill it in on each form created.

Introducing Sales Tax Items

In some states, sales tax is collected on services provided. However, this is the exception rather than the rule. In this book, dealing with sales tax will be introduced in *QuickBooks Pro 2014: Level 2*, when you begin to work with the inventory tracking and product resale. In order to charge sales tax on a sales form, it must first be set up as an item.

Make sure that when you deal with sales tax, you take some time to learn about how the sales tax laws are set up in your jurisdiction. Some states do not collect sales tax at all. For states that do, there is variation among what is taxed. What it comes down to is that you must know the sales tax laws where you do business before you set up sales tax for your company.

Using Subitems

If you wish to track your items in a more detailed fashion, you can use subitems. They can be created for any item on your Item List and can be useful on reports to determine aspects of your business such as profitability. You might use subitems in your company file to:

- Differentiate between broad categories of products and services and individual items within them
- Manage pricing levels for volume discounts
- Differentiate between measurements (see the following figure)
- Track multiple vendors for an item

When using subitems, you state an item with no price for the main item, and then list prices for the subitems beneath it.

 Tab: Getting Set Up
Topic: Add the products and services you sell

QUICK REFERENCE	CREATING ITEMS
Task	**Procedure**
Create a new item	■ Open the Item List. ■ Click the item menu button, choose New, and then choose the desired item type. ■ Enter an item name, description, and price. ■ Select the account (income for a service item, expense, or cost of goods sold for a non-inventory item) to which you want the purchase of the item directed.
Turn on the QuickBooks sales tax feature	■ Choose Edit→Preferences. ■ Click the Sales Tax category; click the Company Preferences tab. ■ Click in the circle to the left of Yes in the "Do you charge sales tax?" section. ■ Select your most common sales tax item. If necessary, create the sales tax item. ■ Select when you owe sales tax and how often you must pay it; click OK.
Create a sales tax item	■ Open the Item List, click the Item menu button, and then click New. ■ Choose Sales Tax Item as the type of item (the sales tax preference must be set up first). ■ Type the name and description for the item. ■ Set the tax rate and agency to which you pay the tax; click OK.

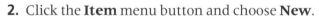 DEVELOP YOUR SKILLS 3-2

Create Items

In this exercise, you will create both a service and a non-inventory item.

1. Click the **Items & Services** task icon in the Company area of the Home page.

2. Click the **Item** menu button and choose **New**.

3. Tap `Tab`, and the default service item type, **Service**, is chosen automatically.

Items & Services

FROM THE KEYBOARD

`Ctrl`+`n` to open a New Item window from the Item List

4. Follow these steps to create a new service item:

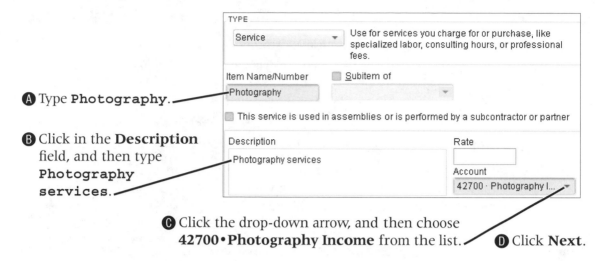

A Type **Photography**.

B Click in the **Description** field, and then type **Photography services**.

C Click the drop-down arrow, and then choose **42700•Photography Income** from the list.　　**D** Click **Next**.

The new item will be added to the Item List, and the New Item window will remain open so you can create another item. You have left the rate field blank as you will enter the price on each sales form based on what you quoted to your customers.

Set Up a Non-Inventory Item

5. Follow these steps to create a new non-inventory part:

A Click the drop-down arrow, and then choose **Non-inventory Part**.

B Tap Tab , and then type **Paper**.

C Click in the **Description** field, and then type **Specialty paper**.

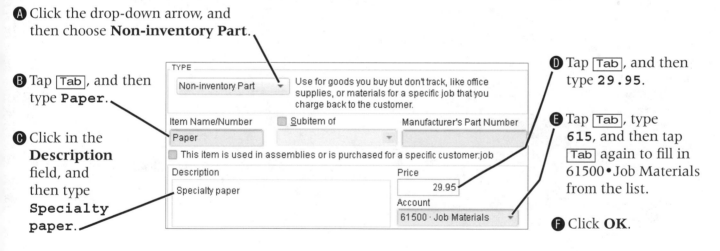

D Tap Tab , and then type **29.95**.

E Tap Tab , type **615**, and then tap Tab again to fill in 61500•Job Materials from the list.

F Click **OK**.

6. Close the **Item List** window.

Creating Invoices

Once you have set up your initial Customers & Jobs List, you can begin to enter sales transactions. In this section, you will learn to create invoices and use Accounts Receivable, which is the account debited when invoices are created. When you create an invoice, you *must* specify a customer because Accounts Receivable (along with the customer's individual sub-register) will be debited by the transaction.

Invoicing a customer is also known as a customer making a purchase "on account."

After you select your customer from the drop-down list at the top of the form, all of the relevant information you entered in that customer's record will fill into the appropriate fields on the Create Invoices window.

This menu shows all entries in the Customers & Jobs list from which you may choose.

This menu shows the available invoice templates. You can customize the existing templates or create your own templates from scratch.

This column section of the invoice deals specifically with the items the customer purchases.

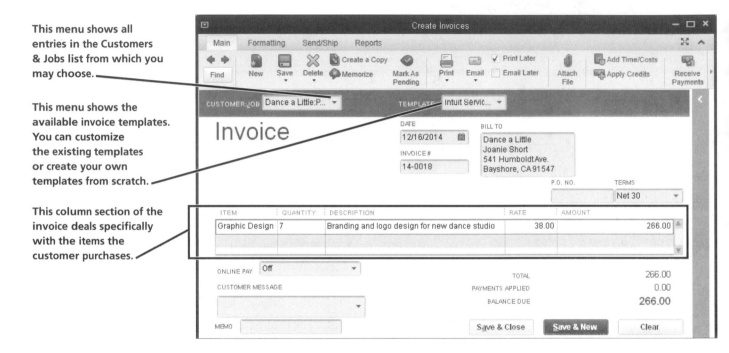

 Tab: Tracking Money In
Topic: Create an invoice

When you created your customer records, you entered a lot of information about each customer that will automatically fill into invoices when the customer is chosen. You have the option of changing that information when you create an invoice, though. If you change a customer's information in the Create Invoices window, QuickBooks will ask if you want to make the change permanent before recording the transaction.

If you click Yes, QuickBooks will change the customer information in the Customers & Jobs List.

If you click No, the new information will appear on the current invoice, but the Customers & Jobs List record will remain unchanged.

If you click Cancel, QuickBooks will return you to the Create Invoices window.

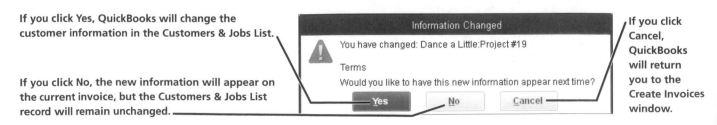

Entering Customers Not Already on the Customers & Jobs List

When you type a new entry into a field that draws from a list, QuickBooks gives you the opportunity to add the record to the list. You can choose to Quick Add the new record (the name will be entered into the list without accompanying information, which you can add at a later date) or to complete a full setup (a New Customer window appears in which you can type all of the relevant information).

Tab: New to QuickBooks?
Topic: Using forms

Understanding Payment Terms

Payment terms dictate an agreement between buyer and seller as to when and how much is to be paid for a product or service. In the case of "Net 30" payment terms, the net (or entire) amount of the invoice is due in thirty days. There are also discount payment terms (discussed in *QuickBooks Pro 2014: Level 2*) that allow for a discount to be taken if the invoice is paid quickly. For instance, 2% 10 Net 30 means that the buyer can take a 2 percent discount off of the total amount of the invoice if it is paid within 10 days, or the net amount is due to the seller in 30 days.

By default, if payment terms are not stated for a customer or on an invoice, QuickBooks will set the payment due date to be ten days from the date of sale.

Emailing Invoices

For the majority of companies, email is one of the primary ways they do business nowadays. QuickBooks allows you to easily email invoices to customers, rather than having to send them via "snail mail" or fax. To indicate that you wish to send invoices and other forms to your customers via email, use the Additional Info tab of either the New or Edit Customer window. If you choose to email an invoice to a customer, that customer will receive it as a PDF file attached to the email along with a message that you set in the Preferences window.

Customer Send Method

The customer send method is the way that you primarily send invoices and other forms to a customer. You can change this on each transaction for the customer if it is not always the same method. In the Preferences window, you can customize both personal and company preferences for this feature.

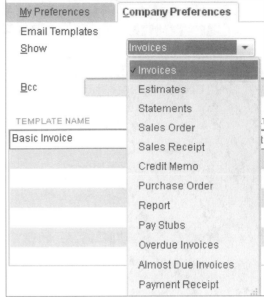

In the Send Forms category of the Preferences window, you can set preferences for both yourself and the company (if you are the administrator). The administrator controls how the email message sent with the invoice (or other type of form) to customers will appear.

Form Templates

When you first install QuickBooks, Intuit provides you with various templates, such as the Intuit Service Invoice, Intuit Product Invoice, Intuit Professional Invoice, and Intuit Packing Slip. You can continue to use these invoices as they are, create custom invoices to meet your specific needs, or download templates from the QuickBooks website. In this section, you will work with one of the default invoice forms—the Intuit Service Invoice. The creation and customization of form templates will be covered in *QuickBooks Pro 2014: Level 2*.

Going Behind the Scenes

If you recall in Chapter 1, Introducing QuickBooks Pro, there is a special feature in this book that allows you to take a peek at the accounting that QuickBooks is doing for you when you enter information into forms. In the following illustration, you will find the first instance of the "Behind the Scenes" feature. Remember that the names used in this feature are the account names QuickBooks uses, not traditional accounting nomenclature. If you would like to learn more about basic accounting principles and what the "behind the scenes stuff" is all about, you may want to check out another Labyrinth Learning book, *Accounting Basics: An Introduction for Non-Accounting Majors*.

When creating invoices, QuickBooks takes care of all of the accounting for you. Following is an illustration of the accounting that goes on behind the scenes for the first invoice you will create in the following exercise.

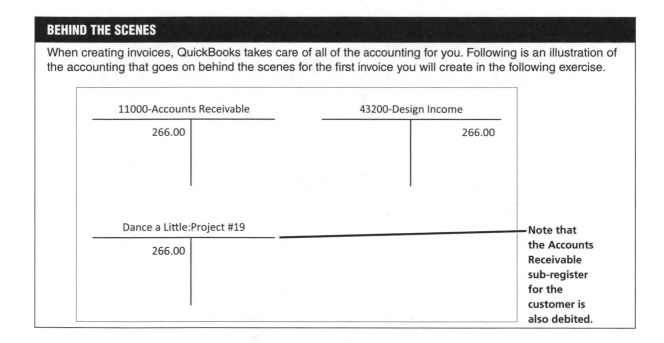

11000-Accounts Receivable	43200-Design Income
266.00	266.00

Dance a Little:Project #19	
266.00	

Note that the Accounts Receivable sub-register for the customer is also debited.

Behind the Scenes (BTS) Brief

This book includes an additional feature to help you further understand the accounting that occurs behind the scenes. Labeled "BTS Brief," these accounting notes will appear within Develop Your Skills exercises. As an example (though not associated with an exercise), the BTS Brief for the transaction described in the Behind the Scenes table above is shown here.

BTS BRIEF

11000•Accounts Receivable DR 270.00; **43200•Design Income CR <270.00>**

In this feature, DR indicates a debit and CR indicates a credit. CR amounts display with brackets.

QUICK REFERENCE	CREATING INVOICES
Task	**Procedure**
Create an invoice	■ Open the Create Invoices window.
	■ Choose an existing customer or type a new customer.
	■ Choose the correct date and terms.
	■ Fill in the item(s) for which you wish to bill your customer, including the correct quantity for each item.
	■ Choose a customer message, if desired; click Save & Close or Save & New.

Create Invoices

Joanie Short has just emailed you to ask you to do a job for her company, Dance a Little. You have agreed to a rate of $38/hour and to grant her terms of "Net 30," which means that her bill will be due in 30 days. In this exercise, you will create invoices for customers.

FROM THE KEYBOARD
Ctrl+I to open the Create Invoices window

1. Click the **Create Invoices** task icon in the Customers area of the Home page.

2. Click the **Customer:Job** field drop-down arrow at the top of the window, and then choose **Dance a Little:Project #19** from the Customers & Jobs List.

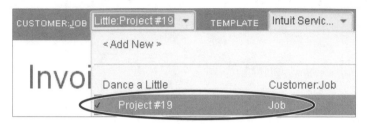

Notice that the customer's address and terms fill in for you from the underlying list.

3. Tap [Tab] two times, type **121614**, and then tap [Tab].

When you type in a date field, you do not need to include the slash marks. QuickBooks will format the date properly for you once you move to the next field.

4. Type **14-0018** as the Invoice #.

5. Follow these steps to complete the invoice:

Ⓐ Click the drop-down arrow, and then choose **Net 30**.

Ⓑ Tap [Tab], and then type **g**. Ⓒ Tap [Tab], and then type **7**. Ⓓ Tap [Tab] twice, and then type **38.**

Once you select the item, the description, rate, and amount information fill in for you from the Item List. QuickBooks automatically calculates the total amount by multiplying the quantity by the rate. In this case, you had to type in the rate since it was not entered in the Item List. QuickBooks recalculates the amount once you move your insertion point to another field on the invoice form after changing the rate.

BTS BRIEF

11000•Accounts Receivable DR 266.00; **43200•Design Income CR <266.00>**

6. Click the **Save & New** button; click **Yes** in the Name Information Changed window.

A Name Information Changed window appeared since you changed the terms for the customer.

Create an Invoice for a New Customer

A new customer, Mary Jones, has stopped by Average Guy Designs' new office to pick up a project you just completed for her. You will add her as a new customer "on the fly" while creating the invoice for her. Your insertion point should be in the Customer:Job field at the top of a new invoice. If this is not the case, choose Customers→Create Invoices.

7. Type **Mary Jones**, and then tap Tab.

   The Customer:Job Not Found window will be displayed.

8. Click **Quick Add** in the Customer:Job Not Found window.

FROM THE KEYBOARD

+ to increase the date by one day at a time

- to decrease the date by one day at a time

t in a Date field to enter today's date

9. Tap Tab to go to the Date field, and then tap + until the date reads **12/18/2014**.

10. Follow these steps to complete the invoice:

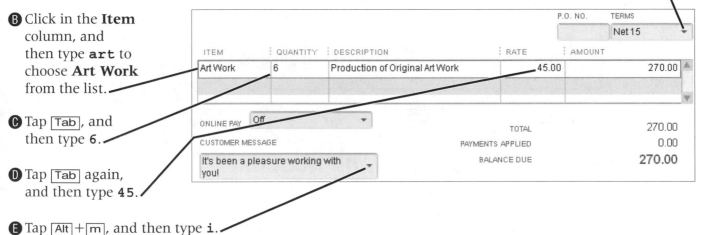

Ⓐ Click the drop-down arrow and choose **Net 15**.

Ⓑ Click in the **Item** column, and then type **art** to choose **Art Work** from the list.

Ⓒ Tap Tab, and then type **6**.

Ⓓ Tap Tab again, and then type **45**.

Ⓔ Tap Alt+m, and then type **i**.

When you see a field name that has an underlined letter, you can tap the Alt key as well as the underlined letter to move to that field quickly.

FROM THE KEYBOARD

Alt+m to move to the Customer Message field

BTS BRIEF

11000•Accounts Receivable DR 270.00; **43200•Design Income CR <270.00>**

---

11. Click **Save & Close**; click **Yes** in the Name Information Changed window.

Receiving Payments

Once you have created invoices, you need to be able to accept the payments on them from your customers. In QuickBooks, you will use the Receive Payments window to credit Accounts Receivable and the appropriate customer sub-register. The other half of the equation (the account that will be debited) depends on how you treat the payments you receive.

It is very important to use the payments received window to enter payments received from invoiced customers. If you don't, the invoices will remain open, and your income and the amounts in accounts receivable will be overstated.

Options for Accepting Payments

There are many different customer payment types that you can record in QuickBooks, just as you will likely allow your customers multiple ways to pay you.

In the Receive Payments window, you can choose from a variety of popular payment methods, or choose to set up your own.

The Undeposited Funds Account

If you typically collect payments from more than one source before making a deposit, you will want to choose to group all payments in QuickBooks using the Undeposited Funds account. QuickBooks automatically creates this Other Current Asset account for you.

The default setting is for all payments received and cash sales to be placed in the Undeposited Funds account. You can change this preference in the Payments category of the Edit Preferences window.

Once you are ready to make a deposit to the bank, you will use the Make Deposit window, where you can select the payments in the Undeposited Funds account that you wish to deposit. You will learn about making deposits in QuickBooks in the next chapter.

Tab: Tracking Money In
Topic: Receiving and depositing payments

Let's look at accounting scenarios that result when you receive payments.

11000-Accounts Receivable		12000-Undeposited Funds	
Bal. 2,485.00	70.00	70.00	
2,415.00			

Purposeful Playtime:Project #11	
	70.00

Using the Undeposited Funds account when receiving a customer payment

11000-Accounts Receivable		10000-Checking	
Bal. 2,485.00	70.00	70.00	
2,415.00			

Receiving a customer payment directly into a bank account

QUICK REFERENCE	RECEIVING PAYMENTS
Task	**Procedure**
Receive a payment	■ Open the Receive Payments window.
	■ Choose the customer from whom you are receiving a payment.
	■ Enter the correct date and the amount received.
	■ Choose the correct payment method and enter any reference or check number information.
	■ Apply the payment to the correct invoice(s).
	■ Click Save & Close or Save & New.

Receive Payments

In this exercise, you will deal with payments received from invoiced customers. You have just received a credit card payment from Purposeful Playtime for Project #11.

1. Click the **Receive Payments** task icon in the Customers area of the Home page.
   The Receive Payments window opens with the insertion point in the Received From field.

Receive Payments

2. Follow these steps to enter a customer payment:

Ⓐ Click the drop-down arrow and choose **Purposeful Playtime:Project #11**.

Ⓑ Tap [Tab], and then type **70**.

Ⓒ Tap [Tab], and then type **121814** as the Date.

Ⓓ Click the **Credit Debit** button.

Ⓔ Choose **Visa**, tap [Tab], and then type **8977554621339666**.

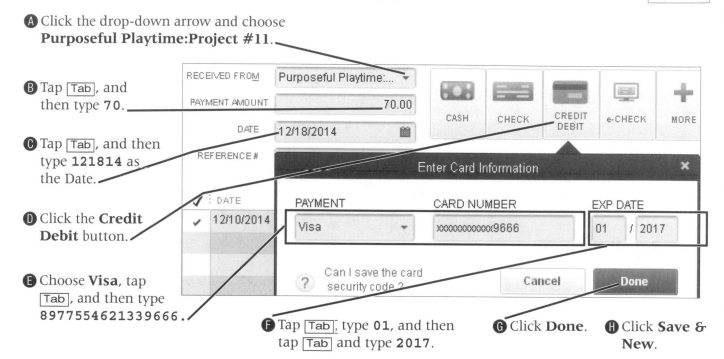

Ⓕ Tap [Tab], type **01**, and then tap [Tab] and type **2017**.

Ⓖ Click **Done**.

Ⓗ Click **Save & New**.

Notice that when you typed the amount, QuickBooks automatically applied it to the invoice listed. If you had multiple invoices displayed, QuickBooks would first apply the payment to the invoice that was for the exact amount. If no invoices matched the amount, it would be applied to invoice(s) beginning with the oldest one.

BTS BRIEF

12000•Undeposited Funds DR 70.00; **11000•Accounts Receivable CR <70.00>**

Receive a Partial Payment

Guy just received a check from Lucy's Cupcake Factory for $100 to apply to the outstanding invoice for Project #16. You will receive this payment.

3. Choose **Lucy's Cupcake Factory:Project #16**, and then tap [Tab].

4. Follow these steps to complete the payment receipt:

Ⓐ Type **100** in the **Payment Amount** field.

Ⓑ Tap ⎡Tab⎤, and then tap ⎡+⎤ to change the date to 12/19/14.

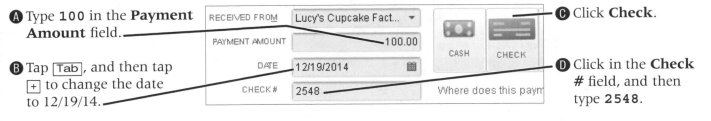

Ⓒ Click **Check**.

Ⓓ Click in the **Check # field**, and then type **2548**.

QuickBooks applies the payment to the outstanding invoice. The next time you select Lucy's Cupcake Factory:Project #16 as the customer in the Receive Payments window, QuickBooks will show that there is a balance due of $125.00. Notice that QuickBooks gives you an option as to how to deal with underpayments on invoices while you're still in the Receive Payments window.

BTS BRIEF

12000•Undeposited Funds DR 100.00; **11000•Accounts Receivable CR <100.00>**

5. Click **Save & Close** once you have ensured that you have entered all information correctly.

Entering Sales Receipts

As discussed earlier, you can use either of two forms to enter sales transactions. You have already learned how to create invoices and about the effect that they have behind the scenes. Now you will learn how to enter sales when payment is received up front.

A company does not have to choose one method of recording sales transactions and stick with it. Both forms can be used for the same company, depending on the situation at hand. When entering a sales receipt, you do not have to enter a customer (as accounts receivable is not affected) although you may want to enter customers to produce more meaningful sales reports. You have the option of adding a customer "on the fly" in the Enter Sales Receipts window just as you do when creating invoices.

As with the Receive Payments window, you can set a preference in order to be able to choose whether to group your payment with other funds waiting to be deposited or directly deposit it in the bank. The default option is to place all payments in the Undeposited Funds account. If you change the preference, you will need to choose into which account to deposit each payment.

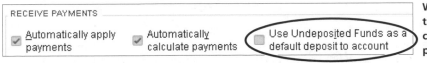

When this option is deselected in the Preferences window, you can choose which asset account the payment will go to.

You should notice how the Enter Sales Receipt form differs from the Create Invoices form and is essentially a combination of the Create Invoices and Receive Payments windows.

 Tab: Tracking Money In
Topic: Sales receipts

Choosing the Correct Form

In a previous section, you learned about invoices. There are other ways of recording customer sales and charges. The following table describes the three main forms you can use.

COMPARING CUSTOMER FORMS	
Form	**When to Use**
Invoices	Use this when a customer does not make a payment at the time of service and/or receipt of product. The invoice amount is held in Accounts Receivable.
Sales Receipts	Use this when a customer makes a payment at the time of service and/or receipt of product. Accounts Receivable is not affected. You will learn more about sales receipts later in this chapter.
Statements	Use this to leave a balance in the customer's Accounts Receivable account without creating an invoice. For example, if you have a customer for whom you do multiple jobs throughout the month, you can gather the charges and send one statement for all of them. You will learn more about statements in *QuickBooks Pro 2014: Level 2*.

"JIT" Customer and Transaction History

There are two tabs on the history panel that allow you to view information about the active transaction. The history panel allows you to view information just when you need it ("just in time"), without your having to leave the transaction and go to the Customer or Vendor Center to find it.

The Customer tab displays information specific to the active customer only.

You can hide the history panel by clicking this button.

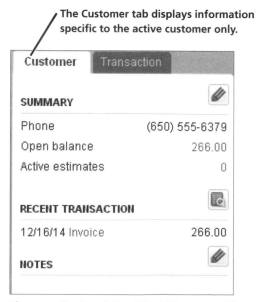

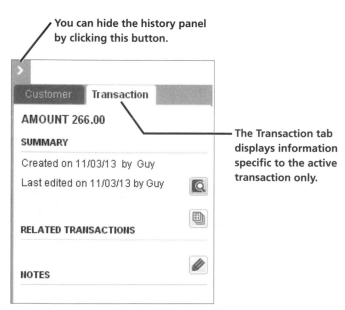

The Transaction tab displays information specific to the active transaction only.

These are the two tabs of the history panel for Invoice #14-0018 associated with Lucy's Cupcake Factory. They allow you to view information quickly or "just in time" without your having to search through your company file. You can use the hyperlinks to view a transaction, edit a list entry, enter a note, or create a report.

The behind the scenes accounting that occurs when you enter cash sales is a hybrid of the two previous transactions (Creating Invoices and Receiving Payments) with the elimination of the middleman—Accounts Receivable.

10000-Checking, or 12000-Undeposited Funds		43200-Design Income	
180.00			180.00

Task	Procedure
Enter a cash sale	■ Open the Enter Sales Receipts window and choose a customer, if desired.
	■ Enter the date of the transaction, payment method, and reference/check number.
	■ Enter the items and quantity sold.
	■ Select a message for the customer, if desired.
	■ Click Save & Close or Save & New.

DEVELOP YOUR SKILLS 3-5

Enter Cash Sales

In this exercise, you will receive payment at the time of the sale. Ashley was in the area so she stopped by your office to pick up the art work you created for her. Since she is prepared to pay with cash, you will enter a sales receipt instead of an invoice.

1. Click the **Create Sales Receipts** task icon in the Customers area of the Home page.

   The Enter Sales Receipts window opens with the insertion point in the Customer:Job field.

Create Sales Receipts

2. Follow these steps to complete the sale:

Ⓐ Choose **Ashley Hakloa:Project #18**.

Ⓑ Click in the **Date** field, and then use ⊞ to change the date to **12/20/14**.

Ⓒ Click the **Cash** button.

Ⓓ Click in the **Item** column, and then type **art**.

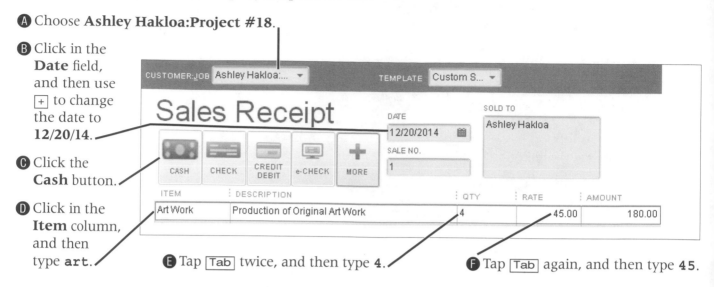

Ⓔ Tap ⌷Tab⌷ twice, and then type **4**.

Ⓕ Tap ⌷Tab⌷ again, and then type **45**.

3. Click **Save & New**.

Your insertion point should be in the Customer:Job field of a new Enter Sales Receipt window.

Record a Sales Receipt Without a Specified Customer

Since Accounts Receivable is not affected when you enter a cash sale, you can create a sales receipt without choosing a customer. This may come in handy if you sell something to someone just once and don't need that customer listed in your Customers & Jobs List or if you provide services in a different capacity. In this exercise, Guy worked with another photographer to take photos at a Christmas party.

4. Click in the date field and tap ⊞ until the date reads **12/22/2014**.

5. Follow these steps to complete the sales receipt:

Ⓐ Click the **Check** button.

Ⓑ Click in the **Check No.** field, and then type **1894**.

Ⓒ Tap ⌷Tab⌷, and then type **ph**.

Ⓓ Tap ⌷Tab⌷ three times, and then type **200**.

Ⓔ Click **Save & Close**.

This transaction will debit Undeposited Funds and credit Photography Income, but there will be no customer tracked. The purpose of selecting a customer for a sales receipt is to ensure that you can produce meaningful customer reports, such as Sales by Customer Summary, if they are important to your business.

Dealing with Oops in Customer Transactions

It is inevitable that you will need to deal with either errors or modifications to transactions in QuickBooks. It is very important that you do this properly to ensure that everything behind the scenes is correct.

Editing an Existing Transaction

To edit an existing transaction in QuickBooks, you simply open the window where the transaction is recorded and make the changes. You do need to think about the implications of any modifications that you make, though. Many transactions are tied to others, and a change to one can affect another. For instance, if an invoice has been paid, both the invoice and the payment are linked in QuickBooks.

Voiding vs. Deleting Transactions

QuickBooks allows you to either void or delete a transaction you no longer need recorded. In most cases, you will want to void a transaction so that you can keep a record of it. This will remove everything from behind the scenes and yet leave evidence that the transaction existed.

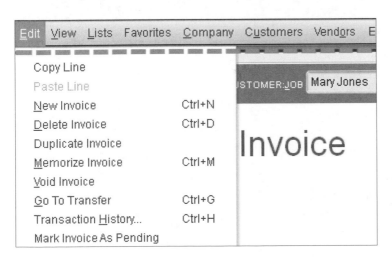

The Edit menu on the Create Invoices window provides options that allow you to work with the currently active transaction (in this case, an invoice for Mary Jones).

Locating Transactions in QuickBooks

QuickBooks provides two methods for you to choose from in order to locate transactions in your company file.

QuickBooks Find Feature

QuickBooks provides a Find feature that helps you to locate a transaction if you don't know all of the information about it. This can save you a lot of time when you have a company file with a large number of transactions. The two options within Find are:

FROM THE KEYBOARD
Ctrl+f to open the Find window

- **Simple** to perform basic searches
- **Advanced** to perform more complex searches, utilizing filters to help to sort through all of your data

QuickBooks Search Feature

With QuickBooks, you have the ability to perform searches based on text you enter throughout your company file and the menu commands. This feature is much more powerful than the Find feature and is similar to a search that you might perform on the Internet with any search engine. QuickBooks allows you to search for the following types of information:

- Forms/transactions (invoices, estimates, and so on)
- People and companies (customers, vendors, employees, and other names)
- List entries (items, tax items, and so on)
- Amounts and dates
- Menu commands (QuickBooks opens the menu and highlights the command for you)
- Specific text within notes, descriptions, memos, and transactions

You learned about the search feature and how to access it through the persistent search bar in Chapter 2, Creating a Company. You will explore it more in this chapter, and you will use it to locate a transaction to edit.

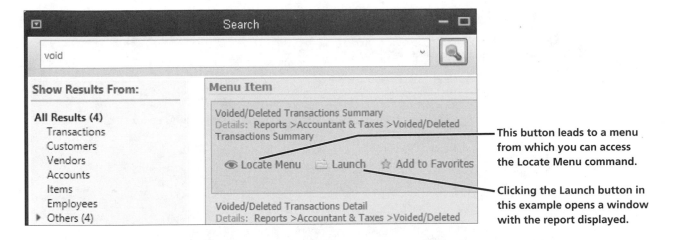

This button leads to a menu from which you can access the Locate Menu command.

Clicking the Launch button in this example opens a window with the report displayed.

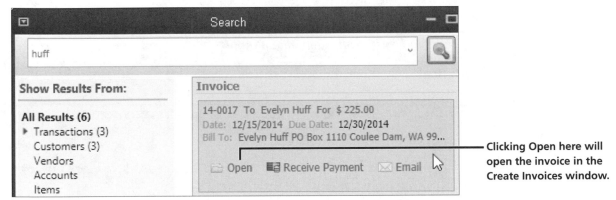

Clicking Open here will open the invoice in the Create Invoices window.

A search on *void* brings up menu items (one displayed here). A search on *huff* brings up the entry in the Customers & Jobs List and the customer invoices. The buttons below the invoice and menu items appear when you move your mouse pointer over the entries.

Fixing Errors

The following table outlines a common customer-related error, the effects of the error behind the scenes, and how to correct the error. You will see a similar table throughout the book when dealing with errors in other areas of QuickBooks.

A COMMON ERROR AND ITS FIX

Error	Effect Behind the Scenes	The Fix
An invoice is entered but the Receive Payments window is not used when the payment is deposited	Your income will be double-stated and Accounts Receivable for the customer is not "cleared out"	Delete the deposit and then enter the transaction properly using the Receive Payments window

FLASHBACK TO GAAP: PRUDENCE

Remember that if you need to choose between two solutions, pick the one that is less likely to overstate assets and income.

QUICK REFERENCE	FINDING AND SEARCHING FOR INFORMATION
Task	**Procedure**
Find a transaction in QuickBooks	■ Choose Edit→Find. ■ Choose either the Simple or the Advanced tab. ■ Enter as much information as possible about the transaction; click Find.
Search for text in the QuickBooks file and menu commands	■ Choose Edit→Search. ■ Type in the keyword on which you wish to base your search; tap Enter.

Correct Customer Transactions

In this exercise, you will search for and edit an invoice. You will also collect a customer payment incorrectly and then fix it. First, you will help Guy to edit an invoice on which he charged a customer the wrong hourly rate.

1. Choose **Edit→Search**; choose to update search information, if necessary.

FROM THE KEYBOARD
F3 to launch the Search feature

2. Type **joanie**, and then tap Enter.

3. Move your mouse pointer over the invoice transaction displayed for **Dance a Little** until the buttons appear, and then click **Open**.

4. Change the rate for the graphic design work to **35**.

5. Click **Save & Close**; click **Yes** to record the transaction with the changes.

6. Close the **Search** window.

Do It the Wrong Way – Receive Payment for an Invoice

Guy has just received a check from Mary Jones for $270. Now you will enter the payment incorrectly for the purpose of learning how to fix the error and do it correctly.

7. Choose **Banking→Make Deposits**.

8. Close the **Payments to Deposit** window.

   You will learn how to work with this window in Chapter 5, Banking with QuickBooks.

9. Follow these steps to enter the check:

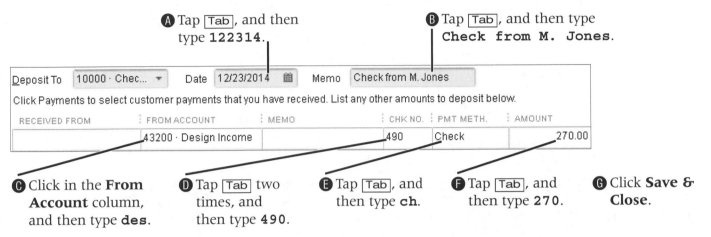

Ⓐ Tap [Tab], and then type **122314**.

Ⓑ Tap [Tab], and then type **Check from M. Jones**.

Ⓒ Click in the **From Account** column, and then type **des**.

Ⓓ Tap [Tab] two times, and then type **490**.

Ⓔ Tap [Tab], and then type **ch**.

Ⓕ Tap [Tab], and then type **270**.

Ⓖ Click **Save & Close**.

Think about this transaction. What is wrong with it? By entering the check for an invoice in the Make Deposits window, you have stated income twice and have not cleared the amount from Accounts Receivable.

BTS BRIEF

10000•Checking DR 270.00; 43200•Design Income CR <270.00>

Do It the Right Way – Receive Payment for an Invoice

To fix the deposit that was handled improperly, you must delete it and reenter the payment using the Receive Payments window.

10. Choose **Banking→Make Deposits**; close the **Payments to Deposit** window.

11. Click the **Previous** button until the deposit you just made is displayed.

You can look for a transaction by using the Previous and Next buttons, if you believe the transaction to be easy to locate. If not, use the Find or Search feature.

12. Choose **Edit→Delete Deposit**; click **OK** in the Delete Transaction window.

FROM THE KEYBOARD
[Ctrl]+[d] to delete the selected transaction

13. Close the **Make Deposits** window.

14. Click the **Receive Payments** task icon in the Customers area of the Home page.

15. Follow these steps to enter the payment correctly:

Ⓐ Type **m** for QuickBooks to fill **Mary Jones** in for you.

Ⓑ Tap Tab, and then type **270**.

Ⓒ Tap Tab, and then type **122314**, if necessary.

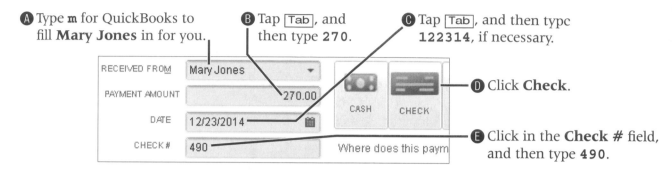

Ⓓ Click **Check**.

Ⓔ Click in the **Check #** field, and then type **490**.

BTS BRIEF

12000•Undeposited Funds DR 270.00; **12000•Accounts Receivable CR <270.00>**

---

16. Click **Save & Close**.

Before moving on, think about what you have just completed and make sure you understand the "why" behind it. You have deleted the overstated income by deleting the deposit and have "cleared out" Accounts Receivable by receiving the payment correctly.

Working with Customer-Related Reports

You learned in the last chapter that there are many preset reports you can run to display QuickBooks company information. Now we will look at reports related to customer- and company-related transactions.

The Report Window Toolbar

When viewing other reports, you may also see additional buttons specific to certain reports.

Some of the basic functions that the toolbar buttons allow you to do include:

- Change and memorize the settings for the report
- Print or email the report; clicking the Print button will also allow you to choose to preview how the report will appear in printed form before you issue the command to print it
- Export the report to Microsoft Excel
- Share the report with other users as a template

QuickReports

A QuickReport can be run from the various center windows. They show all transactions recorded in QuickBooks for a particular list record. You will use this report to get a quick snapshot of all customer transactions for James Limousine Service in the Develop Your Skills exercise.

FLASHBACK TO GAAP: TIME PERIOD

Remember that it is implied that the activities of the business can be divided into time periods.

QUICK REFERENCE	PRODUCING CUSTOMER AND QUICKREPORTS
Task	**Procedure**
Produce a customer-related report using the Report Center	■ Choose Reports→Report Center. ■ Choose Customers & Receivables as the report category. ■ Click on the report you wish to produce in the main section of the Report Center. ■ Click the Display report button.
Produce a QuickReport	■ Open the center with the record on which you wish to run the report. ■ Click the list entry. ■ Click the QuickReport link at the right of the center window. ■ Set the correct date range.

DEVELOP YOUR SKILLS 3-7

Produce Customer-Related Reports

In this exercise, you will help Guy to create customer reports. QuickBooks provides a report for you that displays all unpaid invoices. You will produce this for Average Guy Designs, but first you will produce a QuickReport for Dance a Little.

1. Click the **Customers** button on the Icon Bar.

2. Single-click **James Limousine Service** to select it.

You must always select the list item on which you wish to run a QuickReport.

3. Click the **QuickReport** link at the right of the Customer Center window.

If you cannot see the QuickReport link, use the sizing arrows to make the window wider.

4. Change the date range to **All** by typing **a** to select All from the Dates list.

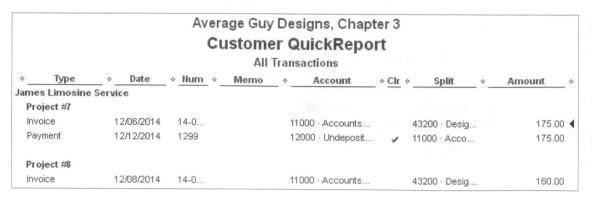

A customer QuickReport will display all transactions for a selected customer within a designated date range.

When you first display a report, the Dates field is selected. Typing *a* chooses All from the Dates list.

5. Close the **QuickReport** and the **Customer Center** windows.

Create an Open Invoices Report

6. Choose **Reports→Report Center**.

7. Follow these steps to create an Open Invoices report:

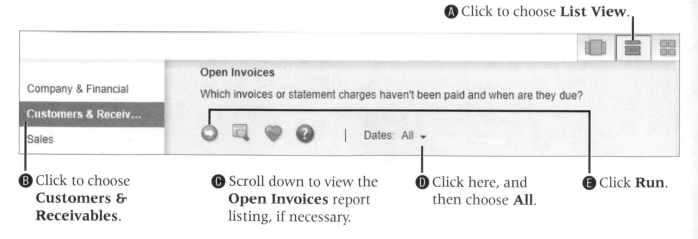

Ⓐ Click to choose **List View**.

Ⓑ Click to choose **Customers & Receivables**.

Ⓒ Scroll down to view the **Open Invoices** report listing, if necessary.

Ⓓ Click here, and then choose **All**.

Ⓔ Click **Run**.

QuickBooks will display the Open Invoices report, which shows all unpaid invoices.

8. Close the **Open Invoices** report and the **Report Center**.

9. Choose the appropriate option for your situation:
   - If you will continue working, leave QuickBooks open.
   - If you are finished working in QuickBooks for now, choose **File→Exit**.

Tackle the Tasks

Now is your chance to work a little more with Average Guy Designs and apply the skills that you have learned in this chapter to accomplish additional tasks. You will use the same company file you used in the Develop Your Skills exercises throughout this chapter. Enter the following tasks, referring back to the concepts in the chapter as necessary.

Add Customers	Add the following customers: Olivia York, 1021 Miller St., Medford, OR 97504 • 541-555-8921 • Referral • Due on Receipt • Job: Project #20 Masters Manufacturing, James McDonald, 575 Industrial Way, Eureka, CA 95501 • 707-555-6722 • From Advertisement • Net 15 • Job: Project #21 Tim's BBQ Palooza, Tim Laughlin, 8 College Drive, Berkeley, CA 94608 • 510-555-4419 • Referral • Net 30 • Job: Project #22
Create Items	Service item: Print • Print Layout Services • $40 • 48800•Print Layout Income. Service item: Video • Basic Video Editing Services • $55 • 48900•Video Editing Income (you will need to set up a new account). Service item: Adv Video • Advanced Video Editing Services • $75 • 48900•Video Editing Income. Service item: Branding • Comprehensive Branding Plan • $400 • 43200•Design Income.
Create Invoices	Olivia York:Project #20 • 12/23/14 • 5 hours of Print Layout Services Masters Manufacturing:Project #21 • 12/26/14 • 8 hours of Basic Video Editing Services Tim's BBQ Palooza:Project #22 • 12/27/14 • Comprehensive Branding Plan
Receive Payments (remember to choose the correct job)	Receive full payment for invoice #14-0018 from Joanie Short of Dance a Little, Check #1632, 12/27/14 Receive full payment for invoice #14-0013 from JLR Doggie Playhouse, Check #872, 12/29/14 Receive $200 payment for invoice #14-0003 from Lucy's Cupcake Factory, Check #341, 12/29/14 Receive $50 payment for invoice #14-0014 from Learners, Inc., MasterCard # 9565332412894455, exp 03/2015, 12/30/14
Generate Reports	Create a report that will show the contact information for all of your customers.

Concepts Review

To check your knowledge of the key concepts introduced in this chapter, complete the Concepts Review quiz on the Student Resource Center.

Reinforce Your Skills

Angela Stevens has just relocated her company, Quality-Built Construction, from California to Silverton, Oregon. You will be working with a QuickBooks Sample Company File in this exercise as it will allow you to run full payroll in a future chapter without having to purchase a payroll subscription.

Before you begin the Reinforce Your Skills exercises, complete one of these options:

- Open **RYS_Chapter03** from your file storage location.

- Restore **RYS_Chapter03 (Portable)** from your file storage location. For a reminder of how to restore a portable company file, see Develop Your Skills 3-1. Add your last name and first initial to the end of the filename.

Manage Your Customers & Jobs List

In this exercise, you will create, edit, and delete Customers & Jobs List entries for Angela.

1. Choose **Customers→Customer Center**.

2. Double-click **Campbell, Heather** to open it for editing.

3. Change the customer's name to **Escalona, Heather**.

   You will have to change the name in five separate locations. You can use the Copy button to copy the Bill to Address to the Ship to Address field. This customer's name will change in all of the transactions that Heather was involved in, as well as in all of her future transactions.

4. Click **OK** to accept the change.

Add a New Customer

5. Click the **New Customer & Job** button, and then choose **New Customer**.

6. Use the following information to set up the new customer, making sure to select the correct tab to enter each piece of information.

Name	Hector Ramirez
Mailing Address	PO Box 7762, Mt. Angel, OR 97362
Shipping Address	1738 Church Avenue, Mt. Angel, OR 97362
Phone	(503) 555-4431
Type	Referral
Terms	Net 15

7. Click **OK** to accept the new record.

Add a Job to a Customer

8. Single-click the new customer you just created, **Hector Ramirez** to select it.

9. Choose **Edit→Add Job.**

10. Type **New Home** as the name of the job; click **OK.**

11. Close the **Customer Center** window.

REINFORCE YOUR SKILLS 3-2

Create a New Service Item

In this exercise, you will create a subitem for an existing service item so you can use it on a sales form.

1. Choose **Lists→Item List.**

2. Click on **01 Plans & Permits,** and then choose **Edit→New Item.**

3. Use this figure to create a new service subitem:

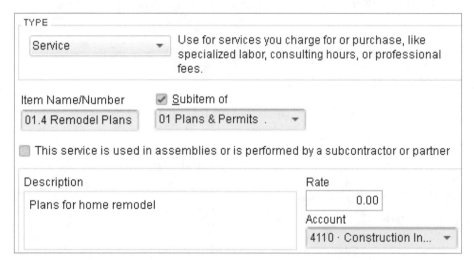

4. Click **OK** to accept the new item and close the window.

5. Close the **Item List.**

REINFORCE YOUR SKILLS 3-3

Enter Sales Transactions

In this exercise, you will create invoices for Quality-Built Construction.

1. Choose **Customers→Create Invoices.**

2. Choose **Ramirez, Hector:New Home** as the Customer: Job.

3. Set the date to read **12/16/2018,** and then choose to use the **Intuit Service Invoice Template.**

4. Click in the **Item** column of the invoice and choose **01.1 Plans** as the item.

5. Tap [Tab], type **15**, tap [Tab] again, and type **New Home** in front of "Plans."

6. Tab [Tab], and then type **80** in the **Rate** column.

7. Select **We appreciate your prompt payment** in the Customer Message field.

8. Click **Save & Close** to record the transaction and close the **Create Invoices** window.

Enter a Job "On the Fly" for a Customer in an Invoice
Now you will enter a new job for a customer while creating an invoice.

9. Choose **Customers→Create Invoices**.

10. Type **Escalona, Heather:Remodel** in the Customer: Job field; choose to Quick Add the new job.

11. Set the date to read **12/18/2018**.

12. Click the **Item** column of the invoice and choose **01.4 Remodel Plans** as the item.

13. Enter **9** as the quantity and **$80** as the rate.

14. Click **Save & Close** to record the transaction and close the Create Invoices window.

REINFORCE YOUR SKILLS 3-4

Receive Payments

In this exercise, you will receive the payment for the invoice you created earlier.

1. Choose **Customers→Receive Payments**.

2. Choose **Ramirez, Hector:New Home** from the Received From field.

3. Enter **1200** for the amount.

4. Set the date to read **12/24/2018**.

5. The payment was submitted by check number **1574**.

6. Click **Save & Close**.

Find and Edit a Transaction

Angela realized that the number of hours recorded on the invoice for Heather Escalona was incorrect, and she needs to edit the transaction. In this exercise, you will use the QuickBooks Find feature to locate the transaction.

1. Choose **Edit→Find**.

2. Choose **Invoice** as the Transaction Type, and **Escalona, Heather** as the Customer:Job.

   All of the invoices for the customer will be displayed in the bottom of the window. Note that previous invoices created for Heather Campbell have been updated with the new name.

3. Double-click the invoice dated **12/18/2018** in the bottom portion of the window.

   The Create Invoices window will open; leave it open for the next step.

Edit a Transaction

4. Change the quantity on the invoice to **8**.

5. Save and close the transaction; close the **Find** window.

Run Customer-Related Reports

In this exercise, you will run three reports for Angela, beginning with a QuickReport.

1. Open the **Customer Center**.

2. Single-click **Ramirez, Hector** to select it.

3. Click the **QuickReport** link at the far right of the window.

4. Set the date range to **All**.

   You will see a report that shows all of the transactions for Hector Ramirez.

5. Choose **Window→Close All**.

Create a List Report and Edit a Customer Record

6. Choose **Reports→Customers & Receivables→Customer Phone List**.

7. Double-click **Ramirez, Hector**.

   QuickBooks will open an Edit Customer window, from where you can make any changes to the customer's information.

8. Change Hector's phone number to **(503) 555-8037**; click **OK**.

9. Choose **Window→Close All**.

10. Choose the appropriate option for your situation:
    - If you will continue working, leave QuickBooks open.
    - If you are finished working in QuickBooks for now, choose **File→Exit**.

Apply Your Skills

Before you begin the Apply Your Skills exercises, complete one of these options:

- *Open* **AYS_Chapter03** *from your file storage location.*

- *Restore* **AYS_Chapter03 (Portable)** *from your file storage location. For a reminder of how to restore a portable company file, see Develop Your Skills 3-1. Add your last name and first initial to the end of the filename.*

APPLY YOUR SKILLS 3-1
Set Up a Customers & Jobs List

In this exercise, you will work on the Customers & Jobs List for Wet Noses. If you wish, you may explore the Add/Edit Multiple List Entries feature and use it to complete this exercise. It will be introduced fully in QuickBooks Pro 2014: Level 2.

1. Open the **Customer Center**.

2. Set up the following customers for Wet Noses Veterinary Clinic:

Name	Edison York	LaShonda Reeves	Ellie Sanders
Address	7931 NE 176th St. Bothell, WA 98011	11908 100th Pl. NE Kirkland, WA 98034	302 Northshore Blvd. Bothell, WA 98011
Phone	425-555-4401	425-555-3953	425-555-7731
Type	From advertisement	Referral	From advertisement
Terms	Due on receipt	Due on receipt	Due on receipt
Account Number	D22	C94	D34

3. Close the **Customer Center**.

Set Up Items

In this exercise, you will set up service and non-inventory items.

1. Set up the following service items:

Item Name	Boarding	Dental
Description	Overnight Boarding	Dental Cleaning
Rate	35.00	45.00
Account	Nonmedical Income	Fee for Service Income

2. Set up the following non-inventory item:

Item Name	Treats
Description	Treats for patients—by the box
Rate	18.43
Account	Boarding Food & Supplies

3. Close the **Item List** window.

Work with Customer Transactions

In this exercise, you will complete sales transactions and receive payments for Wet Noses' customers.

Record Sales Transactions

You will start by helping Dr. James to record invoices and cash sales. Enter the sales information and update the Additional Info tab for the job to capture the custom field information for each pet.

1. On 6/1/14, Emily Dallas brought her dog, Cowboy, in for an Exam, Vaccine Injection Fee, and Rabies Vaccine. Invoice her for these services. Terms are Net 15; choose to save the new terms for the customer.

2. On 6/2/14, Kimberly Wurn brought her cat, Princess, in for a New Patient Exam, Vaccine Injection Fee, Feline DHC, and FIV/FeLV. She paid cash, so you will need to create a sales receipt for her.

3. On 6/3/14, Becky Todd brought her dog, Jedi, in for an Exam requiring Venipuncture, ACTH Stimulation Test, CBC Chem, and a Kennel fee. Create an invoice for her.

4. On 6/4/14, Millie Schumann brought her kitten, Smelly, in for an Exam and Pre-A Blood Work. She paid cash, so create a sales receipt for her.

Accept Customer Payments

You will now receive the payments for customer invoices that have been recorded.

5. On 6/7/14, you received check #773 for $56.90 from Emily Dallas as payment for invoice #173.

6. On 6/8/14, you received check #2310 for $284.21 from the County Animal Shelter as payment for invoice #163.

Answer Questions with Reports

In this exercise, you will answer questions for Dr. James by running reports. You may wish to display the Report Center in List View to help you to answer the questions. Ask your instructor if you should print the reports, print (save) them as PDF files, export them to Excel, or simply display them on the screen.

1. Are there any unpaid invoices and, if so, when are they due?

2. Would you please provide a summarized list of all customers with a balance?

3. What transactions has Wet Noses had with each customer during June 2014?

4. Would you please produce a report that lists the contact information and current balance for each customer?

5. What are the prices for each item?

   Hint: One report will show them all.

6. Submit your reports based on the guidelines provided by your instructor.

7. Choose the appropriate option for your situation:

   ■ If you will continue working, leave QuickBooks open.

   ■ If you are finished working in QuickBooks for now, choose **File→Exit**.

Extend Your Skills

In the course of working through the following Extend Your Skills exercises, you will be utilizing various skills taught in this and previous chapter(s). Take your time and think carefully about the tasks presented to you. Turn back to the chapter content if you need assistance.

3-1 Sort Through the Stack

Before You Begin: Restore the EYS1_Chapter03 (Portable) file or open the EYS1_Chapter03 company file from your storage location.

You have been hired by Arlaine Cervantes to help her with her organization's books. She is the founder of Niños del Lago, a nonprofit organization that provides impoverished Guatemalan children with an engaging educational camp experience. You have just sat down at your desk and opened a large envelope from her with a variety of documents and noticed that you have several emails from her as well. It is your job to sort through the papers and emails and make sense of what you find, entering information into QuickBooks whenever appropriate and answering any other questions in a word-processing document saved as **EYS1_Chapter03_ LastnameFirstinitial**. Remember, you are digging through papers you just dumped out of an envelope and addressing random emails from Arlaine, so it is up to you to determine the correct order in which to complete the tasks.

- Sticky note: We now also receive donations from the Hanson Family Trust. Would we set them up as a customer? The information for the trust is 900 SE Commercial St., Salem, OR 97306; (503) 555-9331; contact, Richard Hanson.

- A handwritten note: We will be providing cultural competency training to schools and organizations to raise additional funds for the organization. Can we set up a service item directed to 47250•Service to Outside Orgs? (You will need to set this account up as a subaccount for 47200•Program Income.) Set the amount to zero as it will be entered at the time of "sale."

- Note: How would we set up the students who participate in our program? They don't pay us money, so are they customers or is there another list we can include them on? Enter the following students when you find an answer: Diego Margarita, Maria Prentice, Felipe Valdez, and Rosa Batres.

- Scribbled on a scrap of paper: Provided a Cultural Competency 3-day workshop on 7/9/2014 at St. Martin's Catholic School, received check #3821 for $4,500. Can we enter this receipt of cash into QuickBooks?

- A letter from the House Foundation: They will be providing a $5,000 grant (not yet received) to the organization to complete construction on the dormitories. Set up the new customer, who is located at 552 Sheridan Avenue, Macon, GA 31205.

- Handwritten invoice dated 7/10/2014: Cultural competency workshop to be held at Lakeside Christian School on 7/27/2014 for $1,500. Due Net 15. (They have agreed to pay 50% upfront.)

- Scribbled note from Arlaine: Can you produce a report for me that shows all of the donors and customers for Niños del Lago?

- Photocopy of check #1826 from Lakeside Christian School for $750 (50% deposit for upcoming training), with a note of "deposited into checking account on 7/15/2014."
- A handwritten question: I don't have customers, but I do have donors and grants… How do I set them up if QuickBooks just has customers?

3-2 Be Your Own Boss

Before You Begin: Complete Extend Your Skills 2-2 before starting this exercise.

In this exercise, you will build on the company file that you outlined and created in previous chapters. If you have created a file for your actual business, enter your customers and customer transactions that have occurred since your start date. If you are creating a fictitious company, enter fifteen customers and at least one transaction for each customer. You will make up the names and information for this exercise.

Create Customer Transaction List and Transaction List by Customer reports and submit them to your instructor based on the instructions provided.

Open the company file you created in Extend Your Skills 2-2 and complete the tasks outlined above. When you are finished, save it as a portable company file, naming it as **EYS2_ Chapter03_LastnameFirstinitial (Portable)**, and submit it to your instructor based on the instructions provided.

3-3 Use the Web as a Learning Tool

Throughout this book, you will be provided with an opportunity to use the Internet as a learning tool by completing WebQuests. According to the original creators of WebQuests, as described on their website (http://WebQuest.org), a WebQuest is "an inquiry-oriented activity in which most or all of the information used by learners is drawn from the web." To complete the WebQuest projects in this book, navigate to the Student Resource Center and choose the WebQuest for the chapter on which you are working. The subject of each WebQuest will be relevant to the material found in the chapter.

WebQuest Subject: Charging sales tax for services and different types of payment receipt options

Working with Vendors

CHAPTER OBJECTIVES

After studying this chapter, you will be able to:

■ Work with the Vendor Center and List

■ Enter and pay bills

■ Write and print checks

■ Correct errors in vendor transactions

■ Produce vendor and profit & loss reports and QuickBooks graphs

Tracking expenses properly is very important for your financial statements as well as for keeping your vendors happy! A vendor is essentially anyone to whom you pay money. However, this does not include employees. A vendor could be the electric company, the organization to which you pay taxes, a merchandise supplier, or subcontractors you pay to do work for your customers. QuickBooks allows you to produce 1099 tax forms for subcontractors at the end of the year. In this chapter, you will examine the QuickBooks lists, activities, and reports that allow you to effectively deal with vendors.

CASE STUDY

Average Guy Designs

Now that Guy Marshall has set up his customers and entered transactions related to them, he needs to set up the Vendor List for Average Guy Designs before he can track his expenses by entering bills, paying bills, and writing checks. Once he has established the list of vendors, he will be able to choose them from drop-down lists in the various vendor forms. Guy will also learn how to produce reports that will provide relevant vendor information as well as a profit & loss report.

Guy can access the Vendor List and activities (entering and paying bills) from the Vendor Center, pictured below. In total, there are four centers: Customer, Vendor, Employee, and Report. As you saw in the last chapter, centers allow you to view a snapshot of information; in this case, it's an all-in-one look at an individual vendor's information, bills, and payments. You can also initiate a new transaction for the selected vendor from the center.

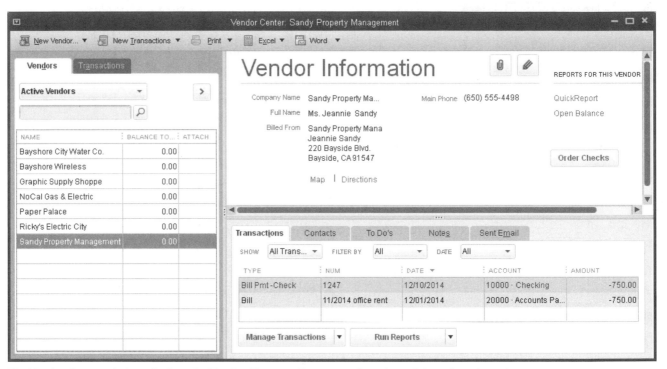

The Vendor Center window displays the Vendor List as well as a snapshot view of the selected vendor.

Exploring the Vendor Center

In Chapter 1, Introducing QuickBooks Pro, you were introduced to the four types of tasks you will work with in QuickBooks throughout this book (lists, activities, company setup, and reports). Information is stored in QuickBooks through the use of lists. Lists allow you to store information that can easily be filled into forms by using drop-down arrows or by beginning to type the entry and letting QuickBooks fill in the rest. Lists comprise the database aspect of QuickBooks; the Vendor List can even be exported to contact management software such as Microsoft® Outlook.

 Visualize! **Tab:** Tracking Money Out
Topic: Expenses overview; Building blocks of recording expenses

Each individual vendor record tracks information organized into five tabs: Address Info, Payment Settings, Tax Settings, Account Settings, and Additional Info. In addition, you can customize eight different contact fields. Keep in mind that the more information you enter for each vendor, the better prepared you will be later when you learn how to customize reports because you can sort, group, and filter your reports using the information in the vendor records.

Here you can add vendors to the list. Here you can create transactions for the selected vendor. The Attach button lets you attach files to the selected vendor record. This button opens the Edit Vendor window so you can modify information.

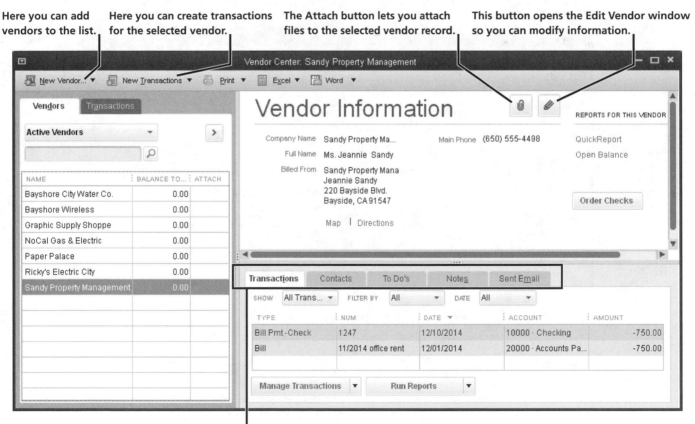

The tabs allow you to see transactions, contacts, to do's, and notes from the main vendor center window.

 Visualize! **Tab:** New to QuickBooks?
Topic: Using Centers

Managing the Vendor List

The list management techniques that you learned about in Chapter 3, Working with Customers are very similar for the Vendors List as well as the Employees List. The next three concepts will serve as a review of creating, editing, and deleting Customers & Jobs, Vendors, and Employees List entries.

Creating a New Vendor

To start entering vendor transactions, you must first enter your vendors into the Vendor List. You can enter vendors directly into the list in the Add/Edit Multiple List Entries window (which you will learn more about in *QuickBooks Pro 2014: Level 2*) or "on the fly" in forms such as Enter Bills and Write Checks and then select Quick Add or Setup from the pop-up window. Remember that subcontractors should be set up as vendors, not as employees.

Editing an Existing Vendor

Once created, the vendor can always be edited through the Vendor Center. The only item that cannot be edited after you have created and saved a new vendor is the opening balance (it must be adjusted through the accounts payable register). When you change the information for a vendor, including the vendor's name, it will be reflected in both future and past transactions.

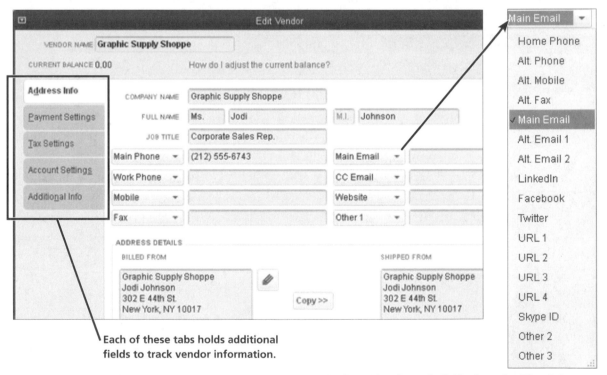

Each of these tabs holds additional fields to track vendor information.

The Edit Vendor window allows you to enter a large amount of information for an individual vendor. The eight contact fields are highly customizable by simply clicking the drop-down arrow, as seen by the list displayed.

Deleting a Vendor

You can delete a vendor from the Vendor List *as long as you have not used it in a transaction*. If you have used it in a transaction, you can make it inactive, but you cannot delete it until after you close the books for a period and clean up your company's data.

Making a List Entry Inactive

If you have a customer, vendor, or employee with whom you are no longer working, you cannot delete him from the associated list if he has been involved in any transactions. What you can do is make him inactive. The benefit of making list entries inactive is that they will no longer clutter your lists. If you find you need a list entry again, you can reactivate it.

Merging List Entries

Occasionally, you may find that you have two records created for the same list entry. QuickBooks allows you to merge these duplicated entries into one. You perform the merge by editing one of the entries and changing its name to match the other exactly. The two entries will permanently become one once you complete the merge. All prior transactions with the merged list entry will reflect the change in name.

Merging list entries *cannot* be undone!

 Tab: Getting Set Up
Topic: Add the people you do business with

QUICK REFERENCE	MANAGING THE VENDOR LIST
Task	**Procedure**
Edit an existing vendor	■ Open the Vendor Center. ■ Double-click the vendor you need to edit. ■ Make the desired changes; click OK.
Add a new vendor	■ Open the Vendor Center. ■ Click the New Vendor button on the toolbar. ■ Enter the necessary information; click OK.
Delete a vendor	■ Open the Vendor Center. ■ Click the vendor you wish to delete. ■ Choose Edit→Delete Vendor; click OK.

DEVELOP YOUR SKILLS 4-1
Manage the Vendor List

In this exercise, you will manage the Vendor List for Average Guy Designs. The first step is to open QuickBooks, and then either open a company file or restore a portable company file.

1. Start **QuickBooks 2014**.

   If you downloaded the student exercise files in the portable company file *format, follow Option 1 below. If you downloaded the files in the* company file *format, follow Option 2 below.*

Option 1: Restore a Portable Company File

2. Choose **File→Open or Restore Company**.

3. Restore the **DYS_Chapter04 (Portable)** portable file for this chapter from your file storage location, placing your last name and first initial at the end of the filename (e.g., DYS_Chapter04_MarshallG).

It may take a few moments for the portable company file to open. Once it does, continue with **step 4**.

Option 2: Open a Company File

2. Choose **File→Open or Restore Company**, ensure that **Open a regular company file** is selected, and then open the **DYS_Chapter04** company file from your file storage location.

The QuickBooks company file will open.

3. Click **OK** to close the QuickBooks Information window. If necessary, click **No** in the Set Up External Accountant User window.

Edit an Existing Vendor

The first step in modifying a vendor record is to open the Vendor Center so you can view the Vendor List. You did not enter the address and phone number for Graphic Supply Shoppe when you created the vendor, so you will add it now.

FROM THE KEYBOARD
Ctrl+e to open the selected list item to edit

4. Click the **Vendors** button in the Vendors area of the Home page.

5. Double-click **Graphic Supply Shoppe** to open it for editing.

When you double-click a record on the Vendor List, QuickBooks opens it for editing. You could also single-click the vendor you wish to open and then click the Edit Vendor button.

6. Follow these steps to edit the vendor information:

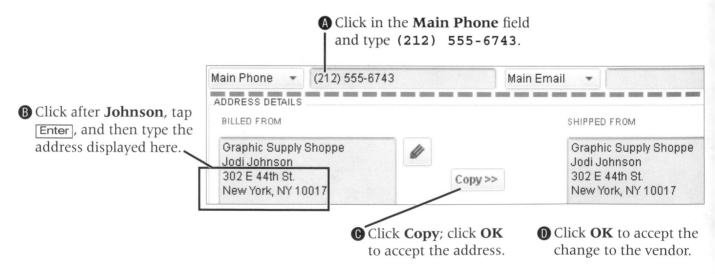

Ⓐ Click in the **Main Phone** field and type **(212) 555-6743**.

Ⓑ Click after **Johnson**, tap Enter, and then type the address displayed here.

Ⓒ Click **Copy**; click **OK** to accept the address.

Ⓓ Click **OK** to accept the change to the vendor.

Add a New Vendor

Next you will help Guy to add a new vendor to the list.

7. Click the **New Vendor** button on the toolbar, and then choose **New Vendor** from the menu.

8. Follow these steps to enter the information for the vendor:

You will not need to change the Opening Balance date unless you enter an amount for the opening balance, as the information is used only when accompanied by an amount.

A Type `Popelka Broadband`.   **B** Tap Tab three times, and then type `Popelka Broadband`.

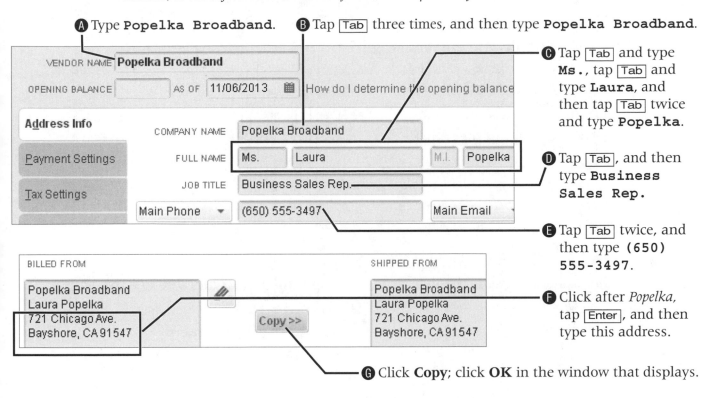

C Tap Tab and type `Ms.`, tap Tab and type `Laura`, and then tap Tab twice and type `Popelka`.

D Tap Tab, and then type `Business Sales Rep.`

E Tap Tab twice, and then type `(650) 555-3497`.

F Click after *Popelka*, tap Enter, and then type this address.

G Click **Copy**; click **OK** in the window that displays.

Tapping Enter in a field with multiple lines (such as the Billed From Address field) takes you to the next line. Tapping Enter while working in a single line field (such as Name or Phone) is equivalent to clicking the default button in the window (the blue button)—in this case, the OK button.

9. Follow these steps to add the additional vendor information:

A Click the **Payment Settings** tab.

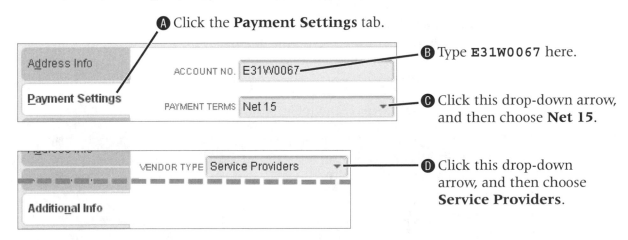

B Type `E31W0067` here.

C Click this drop-down arrow, and then choose **Net 15**.

D Click this drop-down arrow, and then choose **Service Providers**.

10. Click **OK** to complete the new vendor record.

Delete a Vendor

Guy has not purchased anything from Paper Palace yet, and the company has just gone out of business. You will now delete this company from the Vendor List.

11. Single-click the **Paper Palace** record in the Vendor List to select it.

12. Choose **Edit→Delete Vendor**.

QuickBooks asks you to confirm the deletion. QuickBooks wants to ensure that you don't delete anything by accident; it will always ask you to confirm deletions.

13. Click **OK** to confirm the deletion.

14. Close the **Vendor Center** window.

Make a List Entry Inactive

Customer Mary Jones was a "one time" customer with whom you do not believe you will do business again. You can make her inactive so her name will no longer appear in the Customers & Jobs List (unless you choose to show the customers who are inactive).

15. Choose **Customers→Customer Center**.

16. Right-click on **Mary Jones**, and then choose **Make Customer:Job Inactive**.

You will no longer see Mary displayed on the Customers & Jobs List.

17. Click the **View** drop-down arrow, and then choose **All Customers**.

Notice that when you choose to view all customers, you see the inactive customers listed with an "X" next to their names and jobs.

18. Click the **View** drop-down arrow again, and then choose **Active Customers**.

Merge List Entries

Customer Ashley Hakola has been entered twice by mistake. You will now help Guy to merge the two list entries into one. The problem you will encounter, however, is that a job has been created under the incorrect name. You will need to move the job to the correct customer first, and then merge the list entry.

19. Follow these steps to move the Job to another customer:

Ⓐ Place your mouse pointer over the diamond to the left of **Project #18** until you see a move pointer.

Ⓑ Click and drag down until you see the two-way arrow below **Project #2** and release.

◆ Ashley Hakloa	0.00
✛ Project #18	0.00
◆ Purposeful Playti...	345.00
◆ Project #9	345.00
◆ Project #11	0.00
Ashley Hakola	0.00
◆ Project #2	0.00
◆ DC Athletic Club L...	560.00

20. Double-click the list entry for **Ashley Hakloa**.

You must always open the incorrect entry (or the one that is "going away") for editing when you are merging list entries.

21. Type **Ashley Hakola** in the Customer Name field.

You must type the name exactly as it appears in the list or it will not merge into the other entry! You only need to change the name in the Customer Name field, not elsewhere in the Edit Customer window in order to perform the merge (however, you will want to correct the rest of the information as well for your company file).

22. Click **OK**.

QuickBooks displays a message asking if you would like to merge the duplicate list entries. Remember, clicking Yes is a permanent action! If you did not receive the Merge pop-up window, check your spelling. You must enter the name you want it to merge into perfectly.

23. Click **Yes** to permanently merge the two entries

Ashley Hakloa will no longer be displayed on the Customers & Jobs List, and any transactions for her will appear with Ashley Hakola displayed as the customer.

24. Close the **Customer Center**, leaving the Home page displayed.

Entering Bills

Once you have set up your initial Vendor List, you can begin to enter spending transactions. In this section, you will learn to enter bills and use accounts payable, which is the account credited when bills are entered. When you enter a bill, you *must* specify a vendor because accounts payable will be credited by the transaction.

Entering Vendor Information on Bills

After you select your vendor from the drop-down list at the top of the form, QuickBooks automatically fills the relevant information for that vendor into the appropriate fields on the Enter Bills window. If you wish to enter a bill for a new vendor not yet entered into the Vendor List, QuickBooks will allow you to create the new record "on the fly," just as you did for customers.

When entering bills, you need to decide if the expenditure is for an expense or items that you will add to your inventory. The following illustration displays the primary features of the Enter Bills window.

In this chapter you will deal only with expenses. You will learn about QuickBooks' inventory features in *QuickBooks Pro 2014: Level 2*.

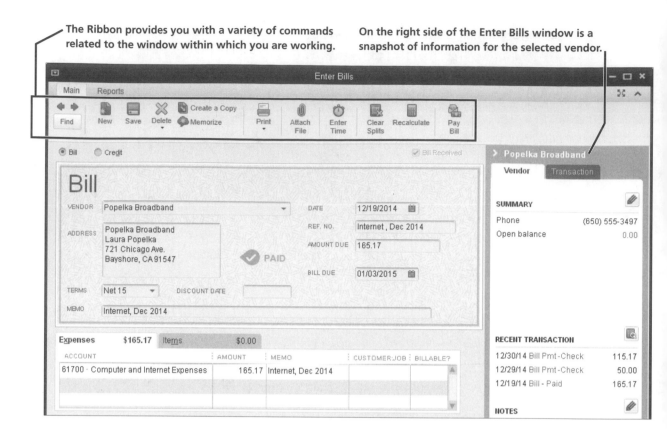

The Ribbon provides you with a variety of commands related to the window within which you are working.

On the right side of the Enter Bills window is a snapshot of information for the selected vendor.

Importance of Entering Reference Numbers and Memos

When entering a bill, it is very important to enter reference information or the bill number in the Ref. No. field and notes in the Memo fields. This information displays in reports and can aid you if you are looking for a duplicate bill number.

Making Changes to Vendor Information on Forms

Whenever you make a change to a vendor's information on a form such as the Enter Bills window, QuickBooks asks if you want to make that change permanent. If you choose Yes, QuickBooks will change the vendor's record. If you choose No, the new information will appear only on the current form; the permanent record remains unchanged.

Entering a Vendor "On the Fly"

You can enter customers "on the fly" in sales forms just as you did with vendors in the last chapter by simply typing them into the Vendor field. Once you enter the customer that is not in the Vendors List, you will have an option to Quick Add or Setup the new vendor before completing the rest of the form.

Choosing Accounts to Prefill Information

In QuickBooks, when you set up a vendor, you have the option to choose up to three expense accounts for which information will fill in when you make a payment. By setting up expense account information to be prefilled, you can make tracking expenses easier and faster.

When you enter a vendor's name in the Enter Bills, Write Checks, or Enter Credit Card Charges windows, QuickBooks fills in the expense account names for you. This allows you to then enter the amounts to be debited to each expense account. By prefilling information, you can make sure that you use the same expense account(s) each time you use a particular vendor. You can always choose to override the default accounts that are filled in by changing them in the individual transaction window. If there are fewer than three expense accounts for a vendor, just leave the additional account prefill fields blank.

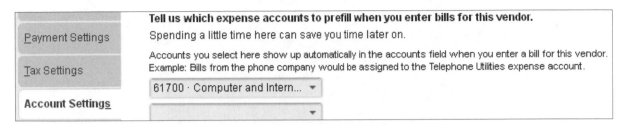

Editing a Vendor Record from a Form

You do not have to return to the Vendor Center (or Customer Center if you are dealing with a customer-related transaction) in order to make a change to a vendor's record. In the history pane there is an edit button that will allow you to go directly to an Edit Vendor window so that you can make any necessary changes.

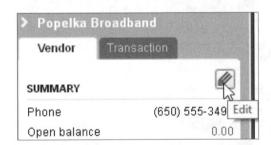

Notice the Edit button in the history panel of the Enter Bills window.

Passing On Expenses to Customers

When you enter a bill, you may be purchasing equipment or supplies for which you wish to pass on the expense to the customer. QuickBooks allows you to easily indicate which expenses are to be billed to a customer by providing a "Billable?" column in the Enter Bills window. Simply ensure that there is a checkmark in the column; it will be easy to create a customer invoice for the item(s).

The Cost of Goods Sold comprises expenses that are directly related to the manufacture of products or services that the company sells. Some expenses that might be considered Cost of Goods Sold are labor, raw materials, depreciation, and overhead. You cannot pass on the Cost of Goods Sold to a customer (it is instead incorporated into the final price of the product), so make sure that you use the proper type of account (expense) if the costs are to be billed to your customer. You will have an opportunity to create an invoice for billable costs later in this lesson.

FLASHBACK TO GAAP: COST

Remember that when a company purchases assets, it should record them at cost, not fair market value. For example, if you bought an item worth $750 for $100, the item should be recorded at $100.

When entering bills, QuickBooks takes care of all of the accounting for you. Here is an illustration of the accounting going on behind the scenes.

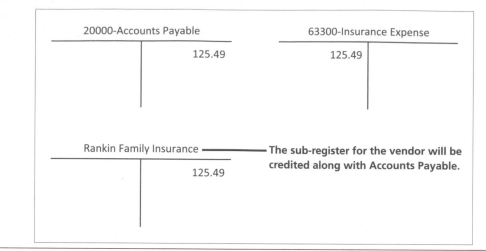

20000-Accounts Payable	63300-Insurance Expense
125.49	125.49

Rankin Family Insurance ——— **The sub-register for the vendor will be credited along with Accounts Payable.**

125.49

BTS BRIEF

63300•Insurance Expense DR 125.49; **20000•Accounts Payable CR <125.49>**

QUICK REFERENCE	ENTERING BILLS
Task	**Procedure**
Enter a bill for an existing vendor	■ Open the Enter Bills window; select a vendor.
	■ Enter the amount of the bill; ensure that the terms are correct.
	■ Expense the bill.
	■ If desired, select a customer to whom you wish to pass on the expense; click OK.
Enter a bill for a vendor not on the Vendor List	■ Open the Enter Bills window, fill in the Vendor field, and choose to Quick Add or Set Up.
	■ Enter the amount of the bill and the terms for the vendor.
	■ Expense the bill.
	■ If desired, select a customer to whom you wish to pass on the expense; click OK.

DEVELOP YOUR SKILLS 4-2

Enter Bills

In this exercise, you will enter bills and track expenses. First you will enter the broadband internet bill that Guy just received into QuickBooks.

1. Click the **Enter Bills** task icon in the Vendors area of the Home page.

Enter Bills

2. Click the **Vendor** drop-down button, and then choose **Popelka Broadband**.

Look at the form and notice that the vendor's terms fill in for you from the underlying list and that the due date is calculated.

3. Tap Tab to move to the date field, and then follow these steps to create a bill for Popelka Broadband:

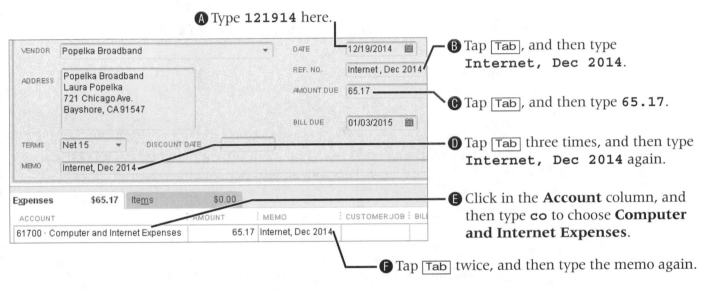

A Type **121914** here.

B Tap Tab, and then type **Internet, Dec 2014**.

C Tap Tab, and then type **65.17**.

D Tap Tab three times, and then type **Internet, Dec 2014** again.

E Click in the **Account** column, and then type **co** to choose **Computer and Internet Expenses**.

F Tap Tab twice, and then type the memo again.

When you typed "co," QuickBooks filled in Computer and Internet Expenses *from the underlying list for you (in this case, the Chart of Accounts).*

You know that all bills for Popelka Broadband will use the same expense account , so you will now edit the vendor and set the account pre-fills right from the Enter Bills window.

4. Click the **Edit** button in the history panel of the **Enter Bills** window.

The Edit Vendor window will be displayed.

5. Click the **Account Settings** tab, and then click the drop-down arrow and choose **61700 • Computer and Internet Expenses**.

6. Click **OK** to save the changes to the vendor record, and then click the **Save & New** button.

   QuickBooks records your bill transaction by crediting Accounts Payable and debiting the expense(s) you chose in the Account column (in this case, 61700•Computer and Internet Expense). The Enter Bills window stays open for the next step.

BTS BRIEF

61700•Computer and Internet Expense DR 65.17; **20000•Accounts Payable CR <65.17>**

Enter a Bill for a Vendor Not on the Vendor List

When you enter a vendor name that is not on the Vendor List, QuickBooks allows you to add it to the Vendor List.

7. Make sure the insertion point is in the Vendor field at the top of a new bill. Type **Rankin Family Insurance**, and then tap Tab .

   A Vendor Not Found window will appear.

8. Click **Set Up**.

9. Follow these steps to create the new vendor:

Ⓐ Tap Tab three times, and then type **Rankin Family Insurance** again.

Ⓑ Tap Tab ; fill in the **Full Name** and **Job Title** fields as shown, tapping Tab to move from field to field.

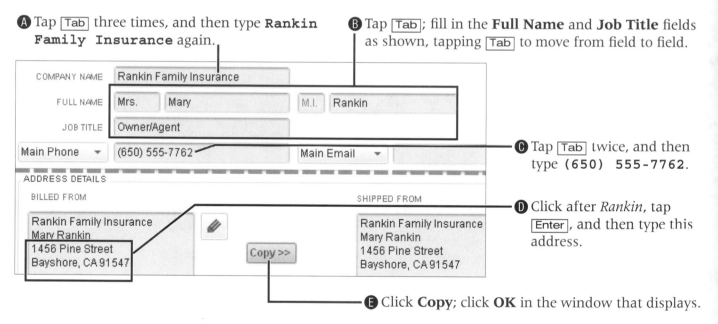

Ⓒ Tap Tab twice, and then type **(650) 555-7762**.

Ⓓ Click after *Rankin*, tap Enter , and then type this address.

Ⓔ Click **Copy**; click **OK** in the window that displays.

10. Click **OK** to accept the information for the new vendor.

    You could also Quick Add the vendor, in which case you would need to return to the Vendor List later and edit the entry to include all of the vendor information in your company file.

11. Follow these steps to finish entering the bill:

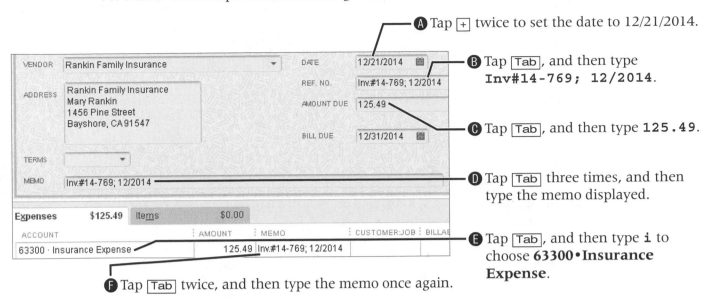

Ⓐ Tap ⊞ twice to set the date to 12/21/2014.

Ⓑ Tap [Tab], and then type **Inv#14-769; 12/2014**.

Ⓒ Tap [Tab], and then type **125.49**.

Ⓓ Tap [Tab] three times, and then type the memo displayed.

Ⓔ Tap [Tab], and then type **i** to choose **63300•Insurance Expense**.

Ⓕ Tap [Tab] twice, and then type the memo once again.

TIP

Rather than typing the information for the reference number and memo fields three times, you can drag to select the information in the Ref. No. field, copy it, and then paste it in the two Memo fields.

BTS BRIEF

63300•Insurance Expense DR 125.49; **20000•Accounts Payable CR <125.49>**

---

12. Click **Save & Close** to record the bill.

Paying Bills

Once you have entered your bills, you will need to pay them in a timely manner. In QuickBooks you use the Pay Bills window to debit accounts payable. The other half of the equation (the account that will be credited) depends on the account from which you withdraw funds (or charge, in the case of bill payment by credit card). The Pay Bills window shows all bills due in chronological order by due date. If you wish, you can choose Due on or before and set a date by which to arrange the list. You also have the option to pay only a portion of what you owe on a particular bill by editing the value in the Amt. To Pay column.

WARNING

When you have used the Enter Bills window, make sure you use the Pay Bills window to issue the payment—*not* the Write Checks window! If you use the Write Checks window, you will expense the purchase twice and not "clear out" the entry in the accounts payable account.

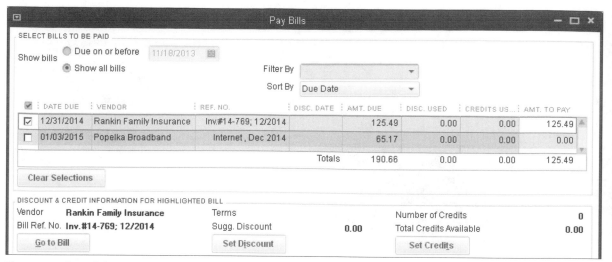

The top portion of the Pay Bills window lets you choose which bills to pay as well as notes any discount and credit information for the selected bill.

 Visualize! **Tab:** Tracking Money Out
Topic: Entering and paying bills

Payment Details

At the bottom of the Pay Bills window, you must make three important choices regarding your payment: Payment Date, Payment Method, and Payment Account.

QuickBooks allows you to choose the payment options for each bill.

- **Payment Date**—Make sure you select the date you want the payment to be reflected in your bank and Accounts Payable accounts.

- **Payment Method**—You can choose how you will pay the bill. If you choose to pay by check, you must select whether you will print the check or write it by hand. You will learn how to print checks in the Writing Checks section. You can also choose to pay your bill by credit card. In order to pay by credit card, you must have a credit card account set up. Then you can choose it from the Payment Method drop-down list.

- **Payment Account**—You can select to pay the bill from any bank account you have set up. When you select an account, QuickBooks will show you the ending balance for the account so you can ensure you have enough money to pay the bill. Make sure to select the proper account, as it will be credited behind the scenes!

The Payment Summary Window

Once you have chosen to pay the selected bills in the Pay Bills window, QuickBooks will display a Payment Summary window. There are three options made available to you from this window: pay another bill, print checks, or close the window.

Making Other Forms of Payment

You can also choose to pay your bills using additional forms of payment such as by credit card or by electronic check. You will have an opportunity to pay a bill with a credit card in Chapter 5, Banking with QuickBooks. If you use electronic checks to pay your bills, it will be treated similar to a debit card, which you will also have a chance to work with in the next chapter.

BEHIND THE SCENES

Let's look at the accounting scenario that results when you pay bills.

20000-Accounts Payable		10000-Checking	
125.49	Bal. 290.66		125.49
	Bal. 165.17		

Rankin Family Insurance ———	QuickBooks debits the sub-register for the vendor along with Accounts Payable.
125.49	

QUICK REFERENCE	PAYING BILLS
Task	**Procedure**
Pay a bill	■ Open the Pay Bills window; select the desired bill.
	■ Select the account from which you wish to make the payment, along with the payment method and date.
	■ Click Pay & Close or Pay & New.
Pay a partial amount on a bill	■ Open the Pay Bills window; select the desired bill.
	■ Enter the bill amount in the Amt. To Pay column.
	■ Select the account from which you wish to make the payment, along with the payment method and date.
	■ Click Pay & Close or Pay & New.

Pay Bills

In this exercise, you will pay bills that have been entered into QuickBooks.

Guy is ready to pay his bills and will pay the bills that were entered in the last exercise, although he will enter a partial payment for one of them. He will complete this task by using the Pay Bills window because the bills were originally entered in the Enter Bills window and, therefore, are "sitting" in Accounts Payable.

1. Click the **Pay Bills** task icon on the Home page.

   The Pay Bills window opens with the Show All Bills option selected at the top of the window.

   Pay Bills

2. Follow these steps to pay the insurance bill:

Ⓐ Click in the box beside the bill due for **Rankin Family Insurance**.

Ⓑ Click the calendar button in the Payment Date field, and then click to choose **12/29/2014**.

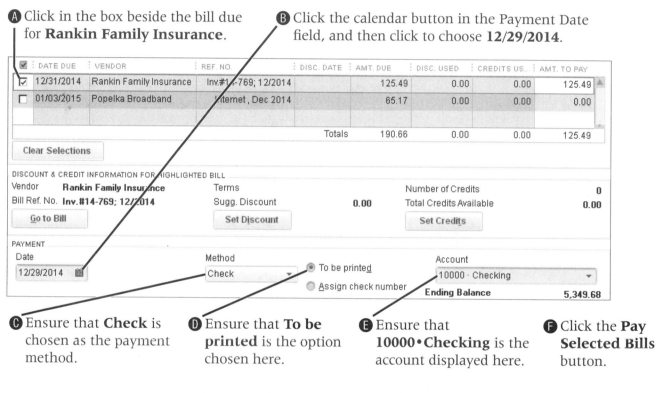

Ⓒ Ensure that **Check** is chosen as the payment method.

Ⓓ Ensure that **To be printed** is the option chosen here.

Ⓔ Ensure that **10000•Checking** is the account displayed here.

Ⓕ Click the **Pay Selected Bills** button.

BTS BRIEF

20000•Accounts Payable DR 125.49; **10000•Checking CR <125.49>**

---

3. Click **Pay More Bills** in the Payment Summary window.

Pay a Partial Amount on a Bill

You will now help Guy to pay a partial amount of a bill due.

4. Follow these steps to pay a portion of the Popelka Broadband bill:

A Click to place a checkmark for the **Popelka Broadband** bill.   **B** Drag to select the total amount in the **Amt. To Pay** column and type **50**.

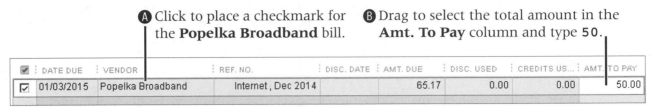

	DATE DUE	VENDOR	REF. NO.	DISC. DATE	AMT. DUE	DISC. USED	CREDITS US...	AMT. TO PAY
☑	01/03/2015	Popelka Broadband	Internet , Dec 2014		65.17	0.00	0.00	50.00

5. Click the **Pay Selected Bills** button to complete the transaction.

6. Click **Pay More Bills** in the Payment Summary window.

   Take a look at the current bills to be paid. Notice that the bill for Popelka Broadband is still on the list, but only for the remaining amount due of $15.17.

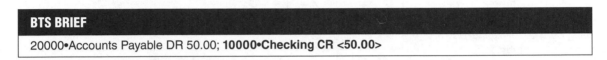

BTS BRIEF

20000•Accounts Payable DR 50.00; **10000•Checking CR <50.00>**

7. Close the **Pay Bills** window.

Writing and Printing Checks

If you are using the cash basis of accounting, you do not have to use the enter bills and pay bills features of QuickBooks—even though they are useful features for managing cash flow. Instead, you can simply write a check to pay for your expenditures when they are due and expense them properly.

Remember that if you use the Enter Bills feature, you must use the Pay Bills feature for the bills you have entered! If you don't, your expenses will be overstated, and you will have funds "hanging out" in Accounts Payable and getting you into trouble.

As with the Pay Bills window, you must decide from which account to issue the check and whether to print or handwrite the check.

The following illustration displays the primary features of the Write Checks window.

Notice that a check number displays if one has been
assigned and the Print Later option is not checked.

You can choose from which account
to write the check, if applicable.

This area looks like a typical
check. The "Pay to the Order
of" field will draw from all of
your name lists.

On this tab you can expense
your purchase just as you did
in the Enter Bills window. You
can also pass on expenses to
customers or jobs.

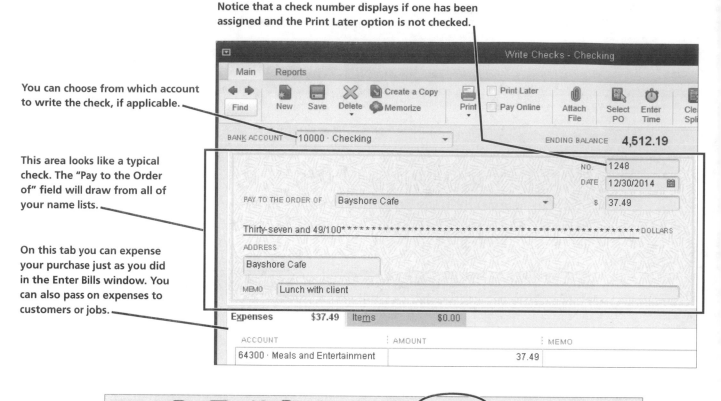

If you choose to Print Later, the check number will be set "to print."

 Tab: Paying Money Out
Topic: Write checks

Printing Checks

When you choose to print your checks in the Pay Bills and Write Checks windows, QuickBooks
will "hold" all of them in a queue until you are ready to print a batch of them. You can issue the
command to print a batch of checks from the menu bar, or you can click the Print Checks task
icon in the Banking area of the Home page.

Select Checks to Print

| Bank Account | 10000 · Checking ▾ | First Check Number | 1251 |

Select Checks to print, then click OK.
There is 1 Check to print for $750.00.

✓	DATE	PAYEE	AMOUNT
✓	12/30/2014	Sandy Property Management	750.00

From this window, you can choose exactly which checks from your batch to print.

BEHIND THE SCENES

The behind the scenes accounting that occurs when you write a check is a hybrid of the two previous transactions (Enter Bills and Pay Bills), with the elimination of Accounts Payable, the middle man.

67100-Rent Expense	10000-Checking
750.00	750.00

QUICK REFERENCE — WRITING CHECKS

Task	Procedure
Write a check to be printed	<ul><li>Open the Write Checks window; choose the payee.</li><li>Type the check amount; ensure the Print Later box is checked.</li><li>Select the proper expense account(s) on the Expense tab; select a customer if you wish to pass on the expense.</li><li>Click Save & Close or Save & New.</li></ul>
Record a handwritten check	<ul><li>Open the Write Checks window; choose the payee.</li><li>Type the amount of the check; ensure there is *not* a checkmark in the Print Later box.</li><li>Type the check number in the "No" field at the top of the window.</li><li>Select the proper expense account(s) on the Expense tab; select a customer if you wish to pass on the expense.</li><li>Click Save & Close or Save & New.</li></ul>
Print a batch of checks	<ul><li>Choose File→Print Forms→Checks.</li><li>Select the checks you wish to print from the Select Checks to Print window; click OK.</li><li>Select the correct options in the Print Checks window, ensuring the correct first check number is entered; click OK.</li></ul>

Write and Print Checks

In this exercise, Guy will pay for expenses with both printed and handwritten checks.

1. Click the **Write Checks** task icon in the Banking area of the Home page.

2. Follow these steps to complete the check:

Write
Checks

(A) Ensure the **Print Later** box is checked.

Find | New | Save | Delete | Create a Copy | Memorize | Print | ☑ Print Later | ☐ Pay Online | Attach File | Select PO | Enter Time | Cl Sp

DATE 12/30/2014

(B) Tap Tab, and then type **123014** here.

PAY TO THE ORDER OF Sandy Property Management $ 750.00

(C) Tap Tab, and then type **s**.

Seven hundred fifty and 00/100**DOLLARS

ADDRESS

Sandy Property Management
Jeannie Sandy
220 Bayside Blvd.
Bayside, CA 91547

(D) Tap Tab, and then type **750** here.

MEMO Rent for January 2015

(E) Tap Tab twice, and then type the memo displayed.

Expenses $750.00   Items $0.00

ACCOUNT	AMOUNT	MEMO
67100 · Rent Expense	750.00	

(F) Tap Tab, and then type **r** for the account.

BTS BRIEF

67100•Rent Expense DR 750.00; **10000•Checking CR <750.00>**

---

3. Click **Save & New** to record this check and leave the Write Checks window open.

Record a Handwritten Check

You may not always be at your computer when you wish to write a check. In this situation, Guy has taken his checkbook shopping and needs to record the handwritten check.

4. Click to remove the checkmark from the **Print Later** box.

The check number field can be edited once this checkmark is removed.

Print ☐ Print Later

5. Follow these steps to record the handwritten check:

Ⓐ Tap Tab, and then type **1248**.

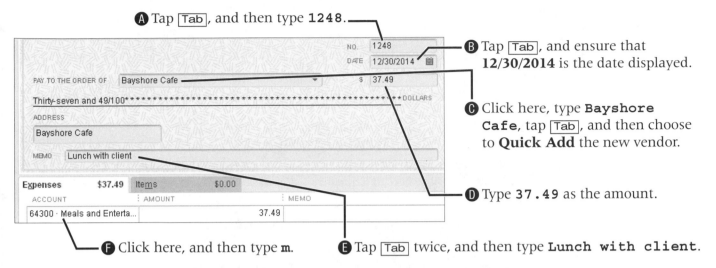

Ⓑ Tap Tab, and ensure that **12/30/2014** is the date displayed.

Ⓒ Click here, type **Bayshore Cafe**, tap Tab, and then choose to **Quick Add** the new vendor.

Ⓓ Type **37.49** as the amount.

Ⓕ Click here, and then type **m**.

Ⓔ Tap Tab twice, and then type **Lunch with client**.

> **BTS BRIEF**
>
> 64300•Meals and Entertainment DR 37.49; **10000•Checking CR <37.49>**

6. Click the **Save & Close** button to complete the transaction.

Print a Batch of Checks

Once you have indicated that checks are to be printed, you need to issue a separate command to print them.

7. Click the **Print Checks** task icon in the Banking area of the Home page.

Print Checks

> ⚠ **NOTE** If you don't see the Print Checks task icon, use the sizing arrow to make the Home page larger or choose File→Print Forms→Checks.

8. Tap Tab, and then type **1249** as the first check number.
By default, all of the checks will be selected.

9. Click the checkmark to the left of the **Sandy Property Management** to deselect it.

10. Click **OK**.
The Print Checks window will appear.

If you wish to be "green," you can choose to not physically print the checks in the next step by choosing to print to PDF or to just preview how they would appear if printed.

11. Ensure that **Voucher** is chosen as the check style, and then click **Print**.

    QuickBooks will display a Print Checks - Confirmation window. Here you have the opportunity to reprint any checks that did not print correctly or to troubleshoot the order in which your checks printed.

12. Click **OK** in the Print Checks - Confirmation window.

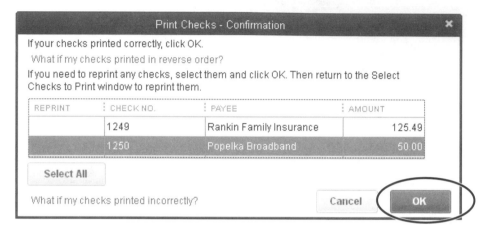

Notice that there are links to help you if your checks do not print correctly.

Dealing with Oops in Vendor Transactions

In Chapter 3, Working with Customers, you learned how to deal with errors related to customer-related transactions. Now we will look at those associated with transactions related to vendors.

QuickBooks tries very hard to make sure you don't make errors that will affect what happens behind the scenes, as shown by the Open Bills Exist window that is displayed. However, it seems that users still end up making errors that need to be corrected!

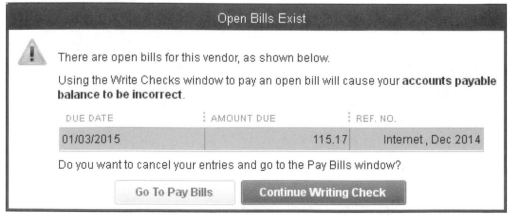

The Open Bills Exist window is displayed when you try to write a check to a vendor for whom you have an outstanding bill.

Fixing Errors

The following table outlines a common vendor-related error as well as an error that occurs in the Write Checks window, the effects of the errors behind the scenes, and how to correct them.

COMMON ERRORS AND FIXES

Error	Effect Behind the Scenes	The Fix
A bill is entered but the Pay Bills window is not used when the payment is made.	Your expenses will be double-stated and Accounts Payable for the vendor is not "cleared out".	Delete the check or credit card payment for the expense and then enter the transaction properly using the Pay Bills window.
A "regular" check was cut to pay payroll or sales tax liabilities.	The liability accounts are not cleared out; QuickBooks payroll essentially has a second set of books that are affected only when you pay the liabilities through the proper method.	Void the "regular" check and then process the payment through the proper method (Pay Payroll Liabilities or Pay Sales Tax).

FLASHBACK TO GAAP: PRUDENCE

Remember that if you need to choose between two solutions, pick the one that is less likely to overstate assets and income.

You will learn how to process liability payments properly in *QuickBooks Pro 2014: Level 2* as they must be treated differently since QuickBooks keeps a separate set of books behind the scenes for payroll.

DEVELOP YOUR SKILLS 4-5

Correct Vendor Transactions

In this exercise, you will find and edit a bill. Then you will execute a task incorrectly and fix it.

Use the Find Feature to Edit a Bill
You will help Guy to edit the bill for Popelka Broadband, as it should have been for $165.17 rather than $65.17.

1. Choose **Edit→Find**.

2. Follow these steps to locate the bill and then go to it:

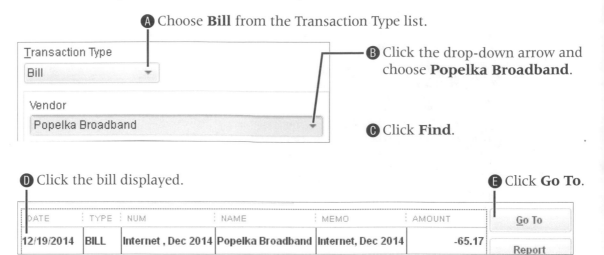

A Choose **Bill** from the Transaction Type list.

B Click the drop-down arrow and choose **Popelka Broadband**.

C Click **Find**.

D Click the bill displayed.

E Click **Go To**.

DATE	TYPE	NUM	NAME	MEMO	AMOUNT	Go To
12/19/2014	BILL	Internet , Dec 2014	Popelka Broadband	Internet, Dec 2014	-65.17	Report

3. Change the **Amount Due** on the bill to **165.17**.

4. Click **Save & Close**; click **Yes** to record the transaction with the changes.

5. Close the **Find** window.

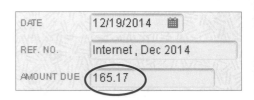

BTS BRIEF

61700• Computer and Internet Expense DR 100.00; **20000•Accounts Payable CR <100.00>**

Do It the Wrong Way – Pay a Bill with a Check

Guy has decided to pay the bill due for Popelka Broadband. Now you will enter the payment incorrectly for the purpose of learning how to fix the error and do it correctly.

6. Choose **Banking→Write Checks**.

7. Follow these steps to begin to create the check:

A Click to choose to **Print Later**.

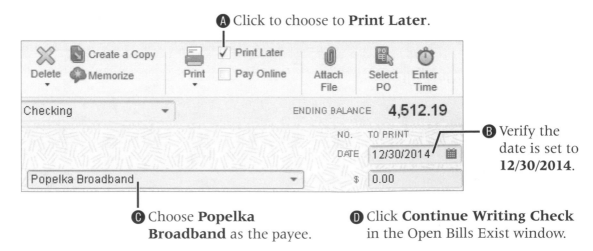

B Verify the date is set to **12/30/2014**.

C Choose **Popelka Broadband** as the payee.

D Click **Continue Writing Check** in the Open Bills Exist window.

8. Tap `Tab`, and then type `115.17`; click **Save & Close** to record the check.

Think about this transaction. What is wrong with it? By writing a check for an outstanding bill in the Write Checks window, you have stated income twice and have not cleared the amount from Accounts Payable.

> **BTS BRIEF**
>
> 61700• Computer and Internet Expense DR 115.17; **10000•Checking CR <115.17>**

Do It the Right Way – Pay a Bill Using the Pay Bills Window

To fix the bill that was paid improperly, you must delete the check and reenter the payment using the Pay Bills window.

9. Choose **Banking→Write Checks**.

10. Click the **Previous** button until the check you just entered is displayed.

   You can look for a transaction by using the Previous and Next buttons, if you believe the transaction to be easy to locate. If not, use the Find or Search feature.

11. Choose **Edit→Delete Check**; click **OK** in the Delete Transaction window.

12. Close the **Write Checks** window.

13. Choose **Vendors→Pay Bills**.

14. Follow these steps to enter the payment correctly:

Ⓐ Click to select the **Popelka Broadband** bill.

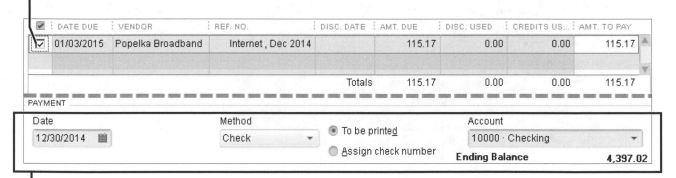

	DATE DUE	VENDOR	REF. NO.	DISC. DATE	AMT. DUE	DISC. USED	CREDITS US...	AMT. TO PAY
✓	01/03/2015	Popelka Broadband	Internet , Dec 2014		115.17	0.00	0.00	115.17
				Totals	115.17	0.00	0.00	115.17

PAYMENT

Date	Method		Account	
12/30/2014	Check	● To be printed ○ Assign check number	10000 · Checking	
			Ending Balance	4,397.02

Ⓑ Ensure the payment details match what is displayed.

Ⓒ Click **Pay Selected Bills**.

> **BTS BRIEF**
>
> 10000•Checking DR 115.17; **61700•Computer and Internet Expense CR <115.17>**
> 20000•Accounts Payable DR 115.17; **10000•Checking CR <115.17>**

15. Click **Done** in the payment summary window.

   Before moving on, think about what you have just completed and make sure you understand the "why" behind it. You have deleted the overstated expenses by deleting the check and have "cleared out" Accounts Payable for Popelka Broadband by processing the payment correctly.

Producing Vendor and P&L Reports

Once you have recorded your vendor-related transactions, QuickBooks has many reports that you can produce to view your data. In Chapter 2, Creating a Company, you learned about list reports. The other two general types of reports are listed below:

- Summary reports subtotal your data and provide a summary.
- Transaction reports show each transaction that makes up the subtotal found in a summary report.

If you wish to see all transactions grouped by vendor, there are two different reports you can run. The Vendor Balance Detail report (found in the Vendors & Payables category) shows only those transactions affecting Accounts Payable (transactions entered and paid as "bills"). The Expense by Vendor reports (both summary and detail, found in the Company & Financial category) show transactions made by all payment methods.

QuickZoom

QuickBooks has a great feature called QuickZoom. This feature allows you to zoom through underlying sub-reports until you reach the form where the data was originally entered. This can be extremely useful if you have questions as to where a figure in a report comes from. You can even edit the source transaction once you have QuickZoomed to it, if you desire.

The zoom pointer indicates that you can double-click to dive deeper into your data. The number of layers to zoom through depends on the type of report (or graph) with which you started. Here, a double click would open the Write Checks window with the transaction for Bayshore Café displayed.

The Profit & Loss Report

Now that you have recorded both income and expenses for December, you will be able to run a meaningful profit and loss (P&L) report. It is important to make sure all income and expense transactions are entered so that income is matched to expenses for the period you are reporting. A P&L is a financial report that can be found in the Company & Financial category of the Report Center window. The P&L report will reflect all transactions that have affected income and expense accounts.

FLASHBACK TO GAAP: MATCHING

Remember that expenses need to be matched with revenues.

Visualize!

Tab: Reports
Topic: Profit & Loss statement

QUICK REFERENCE	CREATING VENDOR-RELATED REPORTS
Task	**Procedure**
Produce a vendor-related report using the Report Center	■ Choose Reports→Report Center. ■ Choose Vendors & Payables as the report category. ■ Click the report you wish to produce in the main section of the Report Center. ■ Click the Display report button.
Print or preview a report	■ Display the report you wish to print or preview. ■ Click the Print button on the toolbar. ■ Click Preview or Print.
Produce a profit & loss report	■ Choose Reports→Company & Financial→Profit & Loss Standard.

DEVELOP YOUR SKILLS 4-6

Produce Vendor and P&L Reports

In this exercise, you will produce a vendor summary report, a vendor detail report, and a profit & loss report.

Create a Vendor Detail Report and Use QuickZoom

You will now create a report that shows what you owe all vendors. Then you will use QuickZoom to see the details of where a balance originated.

1. Choose **Reports→Vendors & Payables→Vendor Balance Detail**.

    You can generate reports through the Report Center or the menu bar with the same result. The report will be displayed with the date range of All selected, as it is the default for this particular report.

2. Place your mouse pointer over the amount due for Popelka Broadband until you see the zoom pointer, and then double-click.

◇ Type ◇	Date ◇	Num ◇	Account ◇	Amount ◇	Balance
Popelka Broadband					
Bill	12/19/2014	Intern...	20000 · Accounts...	165.17	165.17
Bill Pmt -Check	12/29/2014	1250	20000 · Accounts...	-50.00	115.17
Bill Pmt -Check	12/30/2014	1253	20000 · Accounts...	-115.17	0.00
Total Popelka Broadband				0.00	0.00

A Customer Transaction Detail Report will be displayed that shows the transactions leading to the balance for Popelka Broadband.

3. Place your mouse pointer over the Bill date 12/19/2014 that you entered for this vendor until you see the zoom pointer, and then double-click.

	Type	Date	Num	Name
▶	Bill	12/19/2014	Intern...	Popelka Broadband
	Bill Pmt -Check	12/29/2014	1250	Popelka Broadband
	Bill Pmt -Check	12/30/2014		Popelka Broadband

The Enter Bills window will open with the bill that you entered for this vendor earlier in this chapter. If need be, you could edit the transaction at this point.

4. Choose **Window→Close All**.

Click No if asked to memorize any of the reports displayed.

Display a Vendor Summary Report

Now you will create a report that shows a summary of all expenses by vendor, regardless of payment method

5. Choose **Reports→Company & Financial→Expenses by Vendor Summary**.

6. Tap a to set the date range to **All**.

The Expenses by Vendor Summary report will be displayed, listing the total amount ever paid or accrued for each active vendor.

7. Close the report, clicking **No** when asked if you want to memorize it.

Create a Profit and Loss Report

Guy would now like to see if the company had a net income or loss for December based on the transactions entered.

8. Choose **Reports→Company & Financial→Profit & Loss Standard**.

Remember, you can display all reports available through the Report Center via the menu bar as well.

9. Follow these steps to set the correct date range:

Ⓐ Tap Tab to reach the **From** field, and then type **120114**.

Ⓑ Tap Tab, type **123114**, and then tap Tab again.

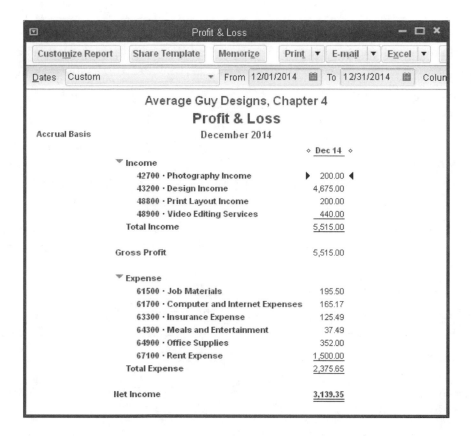

You will see a report that shows your total income and expenses for the time period along with the resulting net income (or loss). The income portion of your report should match the illustration. Notice that the date range is set to Custom on the toolbar. QuickBooks gives you the option to set the exact date range you desire in your reports.

10. Close the **Profit & Loss** report, choosing not to memorize it.

Working with QuickBooks Graphs

QuickBooks provides several graphs along with the preset reports. QuickBooks graphs are accessible through the Reports option on the menu bar or through the Report Center.

Types of QuickBooks Graphs

Following are the six graphs provided by QuickBooks. If you can't find a graph that suits your needs, you always have the option of exporting a report to Microsoft Excel and using the Excel charting features to create additional charts and graphs.

The graphs provided in QuickBooks include:

- Income and Expense
- Net Worth
- Accounts Receivable
- Sales
- Accounts Payable
- Budget vs. Actual

The Graph Toolbar

The Graph toolbar displays different buttons depending on which graph you have created. Once you have created your graph, you can use the Graph toolbar to do a variety of tasks such as:

- Customize your graph by date
- Choose how to view your data
- View your next group of information
- Print your graph
- Refresh the data contained within your graph (if you have made changes to your data since the graph was created)

For some graphs, there are also buttons at the bottom of the window that allow you to choose how to view the pie chart data at the bottom of the window (e.g., by Income or by Expense).

QuickZooming with Graphs

The QuickZoom feature you used previously in this chapter for reports is also available with graphs. You simply double-click on a portion of a graph (when you see the QuickZoom pointer) to zoom in and see where the data comes from.

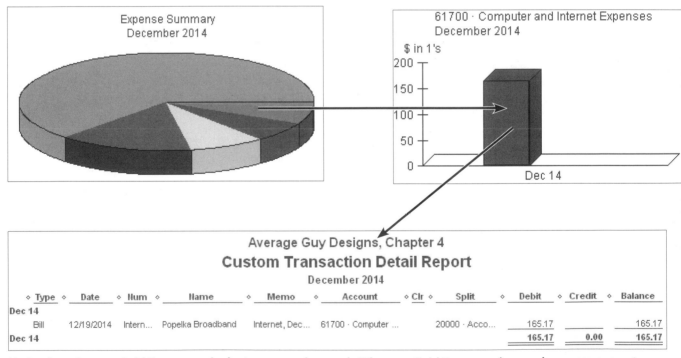

Notice that when you QuickZoom on a pie chart, you see a bar graph. When you QuickZoom on a bar graph, you see a report showing where the data originated.

DEVELOP YOUR SKILLS 4-7

Create QuickBooks Graphs

In this exercise, you will create a graph that will depict the information you already viewed on the profit & loss report—income and expenses. You will use QuickZoom to drill down to the source of the data for one vendor.

1. Choose **Reports→Company & Financial→Income & Expense Graph**.

2. Follow these steps to set the date for the graph:

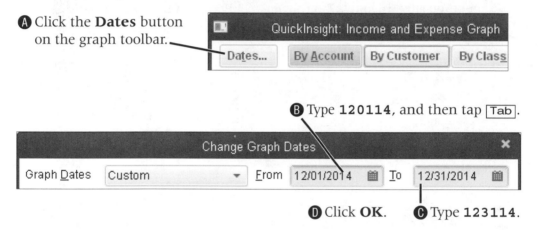

Ⓐ Click the **Dates** button on the graph toolbar.

Ⓑ Type **120114**, and then tap ⎡Tab⎤.

Ⓓ Click **OK**.   Ⓒ Type **123114**.

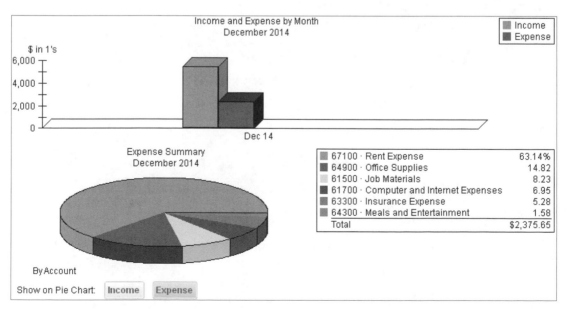

The Income & Expense graph will display data from December 2014.

3. Place your mouse pointer over the green slice that shows the rent expense, and then hold down the right mouse button.

   Holding down the mouse button allows you to see the dollar amount corresponding to the "pie slice."

4. Double-click on the pie slice for **Computer and Internet Expenses**.

   A bar graph will appear showing just the amount for the selected expense account.

5. Double-click on the bar graph showing the amount of computer and Internet expenses.

   A Custom Transaction Detail Report will be displayed.

6. Double-click on the bill dated 12/19/14 for Popelka Broadband.

   The Enter Bills window will be displayed. This is as far as QuickZoom will go!

7. Choose **Window→Close All**.

8. Choose **Company→Home Page**.

9. Choose the appropriate option for your situation:

   - If you will continue working, leave QuickBooks open.
   - If you are finished working in QuickBooks for now, choose **File→Exit**.

Tackle the Tasks

Now is your chance to work a little more with Average Guy Designs and apply the skills that you have learned in this chapter to accomplish additional tasks. You will use the same company file you used in the Develop Your Skills exercises throughout this chapter. Enter the following tasks, referring back to the concepts in the chapter as necessary.

Add a Vendor	Enter the following vendor: Professional Software Distributors 6439 Washington Square, Wausau, WI 54401 Contact: Abby Gibbs, Manager, (715) 555-9922 Acct #: PR203X, Type: Supplies, Terms: Net 15
Enter Bills	Enter the following bills: Professional Software Distributors; Dated: 12/31/2014; Amt. $563.27; Memo: Inv. #17-222; Acct: 61700•Computer and Internet Expenses Handyman by the Bay; Dated: 1/2/2015; Amt. $239.44; Memo: Inv. #15-001; Acct: 67200•Repairs and Maintenance NoCal Gas & Electric; Dated: 1/2/2015; Amt. $82.37; Memo: NGE Jan 2015; Acct: 68610 Gas & Electric Bayshore City Water Co.; Dated: 1/5/2015; Amt. $48.22; Memo: BC Inv. #9435D1; Due: 1/17/2015; Acct: 68620•Water
Pay Bills	Pay all bills due on or before 1/13/2015 on 1/7/2015; Acct.: Checking; checks to be printed Pay $200 towards the bill for Professional Software Distributors on 1/9/2015; Acct.: Checking; check to be printed
Write and Print Checks	Write a check on 1/3/2015 to Allen Brothers Grocery for $36.21 for Office Supplies, check #1251 Print all checks waiting in the queue on 1/9/2015, first check #1252
Display Reports	Display reports that will answer the following questions: Which bills are due? What is my company's current balance with each vendor? What is the contact information and current balance for each vendor? Did I have a profit or a loss during December?

Concepts Review

To check your knowledge of the key concepts introduced in this chapter, complete the Concepts Review quiz on the Student Resource Center.

Reinforce Your Skills

Angela Stevens has just relocated her company, Quality-Built Construction, from California to Silverton, Oregon. You will be working with a QuickBooks Sample Company File in this exercise as it will allow you to run full payroll in a future chapter without having to purchase a payroll subscription.

Before you begin the Reinforce Your Skills exercises, complete one of these options:

- Open **RYS_Chapter04** from your file storage location.
- Restore **RYS_Chapter04 (Portable)** from your file storage location. For a reminder of how to restore a portable company file, see Develop Your Skills 3-1. Add your last name and first initial to the end of the filename.

REINFORCE YOUR SKILLS 4-1
Manage the Vendor List

In this exercise, you will work with the Vendor List for Quality-Built Construction. You will edit an existing vendor, create a new vendor, and delete a vendor.

To begin, Valley Insurance Company has changed its name to Vista Insurance Company. You will help Susie to make that change in QuickBooks.

1. Choose **Vendors→Vendor Center**.
2. Scroll down and double-click **Doors Galore** to open it for editing.
3. Change the vendor's name to **Coast Doors**.

    You will have to change the name in four separate places, including on the Payment Settings tab. This new name will be reflected in all transactions that deal with this vendor—past and present.

4. Click **OK** to accept the change.

Add a New Vendor

Angela has begun to purchase job supplies from a new vendor in Oregon. You will set up the company as a vendor.

5. Click the **New Vendor** button, and then choose **New Vendor**.
6. Enter the following information to create a new vendor.

Company Name	Valley Building Supply
Contact Name	Ms. Carmela Hutch, Owner
Address	525 E. Valley Road Salem, OR 97305
Phone	503-555-9438
Fax	503-555-9455
Type	Suppliers
Terms	Net 15
Account #	84-976

7. Click **OK** to accept the new vendor record.

Delete a Vendor

8. Click **Abercrombie Fence Co** to select it.

9. Choose **Edit→Delete Vendor**.

10. Click **OK** to confirm the deletion.

11. Close the **Vendor Center** window.

Enter and Pay Bills

In this exercise, you will enter a bill Angela just received. You will also pay all bills due by a certain date for Angela.

1. Choose **Vendors→Enter Bills**.

2. Click the drop-down arrow and choose **Ruff Postage Machines** as the Vendor.

3. Set the date to **12/19/2018**, and then enter `Postage, Dec 2018` as the memo and ref. no.

4. Type **$100.00** as the amount, and choose **6610•Postage and Delivery** as the account.

5. Click the **Save & Close** button to enter the transaction and close the window.

Pay a Bill

6. Open the Pay Bills window by choosing **Vendors→Pay Bills**.

7. Choose all bills that are due on or before **12/31/2018** (you should find one).

8. Set the date to **12/23/2018**, and choose to print the check.

9. Click **Pay Selected Bills** to record the payment and close the window.

10. Click **Done** in the Payment Summary Window.

Write and Print Checks

In this exercise, you will write a check for an expense and print the checks you have created.

1. Choose **Banking→Write Checks**.

2. Set the check to print later.

3. Set the date to **12/26/2018**.

4. Type **Marion County** into the Pay to the Order of field and choose to **Quick Add** it to the Vendor List.

5. Type **$250** as the amount and **Business License, 2019** as the memo.

6. Select **6090•Business License & Fees** as the account.

7. Click **Save & Close** to accept the transaction and close the window.

Print a Batch of Checks

8. Choose **File→Print Forms→Checks**.
   Notice that, by default, QuickBooks selects all checks; you can change this if you need to.

9. Ensure that **Checking** is the bank account and type **11353** as the first check number.

10. Click **OK** to move to the Print Checks window.
    At this point you can verify that the correct printer and check style are selected. Now, either "stay green" and print the checks to a PDF file or physically print the checks using an available printer.

11. Click **Print** once you have chosen how you will print the checks.

12. Click **OK** in the Print Checks - Confirmation window.

Find and Edit a Transaction

Angela received an adjusted amount for the December phone bill. Rather than clicking the Previous button over and over again, in this exercise, you will use the QuickBooks Find feature to locate the transaction.

1. Choose **Edit→Find**.

2. Choose **Bill** as the Transaction Type and **Western Telephone Company** as the Vendor.

3. Enter the date range as **12/1/2018** to **1/15/2019**, and then click **Find**.
   The bill you are looking for will be displayed in the bottom of the window.

4. Double-click the bill dated **1/2/2019** in the bottom portion of the window.
   The Enter Bills window will open; leave it open for the next step.

Edit a Transaction

5. Change the amount of the bill to **329.77** and choose to record the change to the transaction.

6. Save and close the transaction; close the **Find** window.

Create Vendor and P&L Reports

In this exercise, you will run vendor and profit & loss reports for Quality-Built Construction.

1. Choose **Reports→Vendors & Payables→Vendor Balance Summary**.

2. Submit the report based on the guidelines provided by your instructor.

3. Choose **Reports→Company & Financial→Profit & Loss Standard**.

4. Type **a** to set the date range to **All**.

5. Submit the report based on the guidelines provided by your instructor.

6. Choose **Window→Close All**, choosing not to memorize either.

7. Choose the appropriate option for your situation:

   ■ If you will continue working, leave QuickBooks open.

   ■ If you are finished working in QuickBooks for now, choose **File→Exit**.

Apply Your Skills

Before you begin the Apply Your Skills exercises, complete one of these options:

- Open **AYS_Chapter04** from your file storage location.

- Restore **AYS_Chapter04 (Portable)** from your file storage location. For a reminder of how to restore a portable company file, see Develop Your Skills 3-1. Add your last name and first initial to the end of the filename.

Work with the Vendor List

In this exercise, you will manage the Vendor List for Wet Noses.

1. Using the following information, create three new **Vendor List** entries.

Name	Casey's Consulting	Take a Walk	Billy's Van Service
Address	902 Creekview Dr. Kirkland, WA 98034	13602 75th Ave NE Seattle, WA 98132	9501 NE 182nd Pl Bothell, WA 98011
Phone	425-555-9569	206-555-9433	425-555-4477
Fax	425-555-9568	206-555-9434	425-555-4478
Contact Name	Ms. Casey Scripps	Ms. Shannon High	Mr. Billy Ranch
Job Title	Owner	Walker	President
Type	Consultant	Service Providers	Service Providers
Terms	Due on Receipt	Net 15	Net 15
Account Number	JR154	VET87	BB23

2. Edit the **Puget Sound Power Company** vendor record to display **Shaunda Jones** as the contact.

3. Add the following vendor types to the existing vendor records, adding a new entry to the **Vendor Type List** when necessary:
   - Wyland Broadband: Service Providers
   - Northshore Water Company: Utilities
   - Oberg Property Management: Service Providers
   - Puget Sound Power Company: Utilities
   - Seattle Vet Supply: Suppliers
   - Whoville Office Supplies: Supplies
   - Brian's Pet Taxi: Service Providers

Enter and Pay Bills

In this exercise, you will deal with expenses incurred by Wet Noses.

1. On 7/2/2014, Dr. James received a bill from Seattle Vet Supply for $3,813.58. It should be broken down by account as follows: $1,773.25 for medical supplies, $1,056.92 for vaccines, and $983.41 for medicines. The ref. no./memo is: Inv. #77-9-56.

2. Enter a bill received on 7/8/2014 from Northshore Water Company for **$210.67**.

3. The ref. no./memo is **Water Bill, 7/2014**.

4. On 7/18/2014, a bill was received from Puget Sound Power Company for **$241.33**.

5. The ref. no./memo is **Power Bill, 7/2014**.

6. Enter a bill received on 7/21/2014 from Wyland Broadband for **$159.44**. It should be broken down by account as follows: $55.99 for internet service and $103.45 for telephone service.

7. The ref. no./memo is **Int/Phone July 2014**.

8. On 7/21/2014, Sadie decided to sit down and pay her bills. Pay all of the bills due on or before 7/22/2014. You will print the checks later.

9. Choose **Done** in the Payment Summary window.

Write and Print Checks

In this exercise, you will write and print checks for Dr. James. You will need to use your best judgment to determine the account to use for each transaction.

1. Dr. James took all of her employees out for a working lunch at Laura's Café on 7/21/2014. The total cost was **$84.35**. She wrote a check at the restaurant, using check number 1418.

2. Sadie received a bill from Animal Lovers for an advertisement for $135.00 on 7/22/2014. Since she just paid her bills she has decided to just enter a check for the expense that she will print next.

3. Print all checks in the queue using 1419 as the first check number.

Find and Edit a Transaction

Dr. James received an adjusted amount for the bill from Patrick Janitorial Service. Rather than clicking the Previous button over and over again, in this exercise, you will use the QuickBooks Find feature to locate the transaction.

1. Using the QuickBooks Find feature, locate the **Patrick Janitorial Service** bill dated **6/30/2014**.

2. Open the bill and change the amount of it to $**505.00**.

   Since you have already paid this bill for the initial amount, this vendor will have a negative amount (debit balance) until you receive the next bill from them.

3. Save and close the transaction; close the **Find** window.

Answer Questions with Reports

In this exercise, you will answer questions for Dr. James by running reports. You may wish to display the Report Center in List View to help you answer the questions. Ask your instructor if you should print the reports, print (save) them as PDF files, export them to Excel, or simply display them on the screen.

1. Are any of the bills overdue?

2. Is there a way to see all of the transactions for each vendor for the month of July 2014?

3. I would like to have a list of the phone numbers for all of the vendors. Can you create one for me?

4. Can I see a graph of the total amount owed and the amount by vendor as of July 31, 2014?

5. Submit your reports based on the guidelines provided by your instructor.

6. Choose the appropriate option for your situation:
   - If you will continue working, leave QuickBooks open.
   - If you are finished working in QuickBooks for now, choose **File→Exit**.

Extend Your Skills

In the course of working through the following Extend Your Skills exercises, you will be utilizing various skills taught in this and previous chapter(s). Take your time and think carefully about the tasks presented to you. Turn back to the chapter content if you need assistance.

4-1 Sort Through the Stack

Before You Begin: Restore the EYS1_Chapter04 (Portable) file or open the EYS1_Chapter04 company file from your storage location.

You have been hired by Arlaine Cervantes to help her with her organization's books. She is the founder of Niños del Lago, a nonprofit organization that provides impoverished Guatemalan children with an engaging educational camp experience. You have just sat down at your desk and opened a large envelope from her with a variety of documents and noticed that you have several emails from her as well. It is your job to sort through the papers and emails and make sense of what you find, entering information into QuickBooks whenever appropriate and answering any other questions in a word-processing document saved as **EYS1_Chapter04_ LastnameFirstinitial**. Remember, you are digging through papers you just dumped out of an envelope and addressing random emails from Arlaine, so it is up to you to determine the correct order in which to complete the tasks.

- Sticky note: New source for cultural competency books—enter Woods Publishing Company as a vendor: 921 Pamela Lake Drive, Pittsburg, KS 66762; (620) 555-2211; Terms—Net 30; Contact—Pam Woods.
- Bill: From Network Links (for website hosting), dated 7/3/2014, for $34.57, due 7/13/2014.
- Canceled check: Written to USPS for stamps on 7/2/2014 for $25.10, number 1003.
- Sticky note: There are some checks that can be used with the printer. Could you please print checks for any bills that I didn't write a check for?
- Note: Would like to track employee anniversaries. How can I do that?
- Scribbled on a scrap of paper: I need a report that shows all of the bills that have been entered into QuickBooks.
- Packing slip and bill: Materials received for a cultural competency seminar; need to enter the bill for $124.32, payable to Chandler Distributors, dated 7/1/2014, terms Net 15. (Arlaine is not tracking inventory in QuickBooks.)
- Carbon copies of checks: Used to pay Network Links (#1004, 7/7/2014, for full amount) and Hernandez Catering (#1005, 7/15/2014, for full amount).
- Note: We have donors who are referred to us by a local service organization. Can we include them in the customer type list?
- Bill: From Child Play, Inc. for supplies for the camp, dated 7/5/2014, for $1,212.65, due 7/15/2014.
- Printed email message from accountant: Please send a report that shows the amount owed to each vendor as of 7/10/2014.
- Bill: From Hernandez Catering for food provided at a fundraising event in California, dated 7/8/2014, payment due on receipt, for $167.21.

4-2 Be Your Own Boss

Before You Begin: Complete Extend Your Skills 3-2 before starting this exercise.

In this exercise, you will build on the company file that you outlined and created in previous chapters. If you have created a file for your actual business, then enter your vendors and vendor-related transactions that have occurred since your start date. If you are creating a fictitious company, then enter ten vendors and at least one transaction for each vendor. You will make up the names and information for this exercise.

Create Vendor Transaction List and Transaction List by Vendor reports and submit them to your instructor based on the instructions provided.

Open the company file you worked on in Extend Your Skills 3-2 and complete the tasks outlined above. When you are done, save it as a portable company file, naming it as **EYS2_Chapter04_ LastnameFirstinitial (Portable)** and submit it to your instructor based on the instructions provided.

4-3 Use the Web as a Learning Tool

Throughout this book, you will be provided with an opportunity to use the Internet as a learning tool by completing WebQuests. According to the original creators of WebQuests, as described on their website (http://WebQuest.org), a WebQuest is "an inquiry-oriented activity in which most or all of the information used by learners is drawn from the web." To complete the WebQuest projects in this book, navigate to the Student Resource Center and choose the WebQuest for the chapter on which you are working. The subject of each WebQuest will be relevant to the material found in the chapter.

WebQuest Subject: Working with web-based vendor information

Banking with QuickBooks

CHAPTER OBJECTIVES

After studying this chapter, you will be able to:

- Create bank accounts
- Make deposits into bank accounts
- Transfer funds
- Manage debit and credit card transactions
- Reconcile accounts
- Create banking reports
- Use online banking with QuickBooks

Any business must be able to work with bank accounts and the funds contained within to be able to operate effectively. If you utilize debit and credit cards for your business, you will need to know how to work with them as well. In this chapter, you will learn all about dealing with bank and credit card accounts in QuickBooks, from creating them to running reports about them. You will also have an opportunity to explore a little about banking online with QuickBooks.

CASE STUDY

Average Guy Designs

Guy has been getting comfortable performing the basic vendor and customer transactions in QuickBooks. One of the individuals whom he often contracts with, Allison Fox, is now going to take over the books because Guy has gotten quite busy with his design work customers and marketing his new company. Allison will take over creating bank accounts, tracking banking transactions, dealing with credit card transactions, and reconciling both the bank and credit card accounts.

In addition, Allison is interested in exploring how online banking with QuickBooks works.

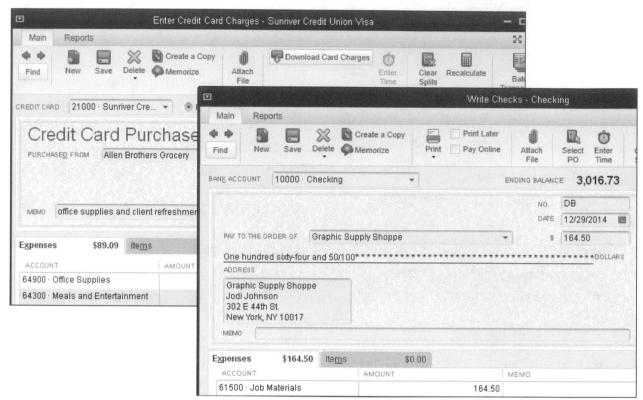

You use the Enter Credit Card Charges window to enter credit card purchases and the Write Checks or Bill Payment window to enter debit card transactions.

Creating Bank Accounts

The accounts you will work with in this chapter are assets (bank accounts) and liabilities (credit cards). There are two types of bank accounts you will deal with: Checking and Savings. Petty cash accounts will be covered in *QuickBooks Pro 2014: Level 2*.

Accessing Banking Activities in QuickBooks

The Banking area on the Home page displays task icons for many of the activities you will perform in this chapter. The rest of the activities can be accessed via the menu bar.

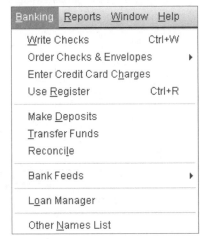

Notice that you can begin the reconciliation process by either clicking the task icon in the Banking area of the Home page or by choosing an option from the menu bar. However, to transfer funds and work with the bank feeds feature, you must use the menu bar.

The Chart of Accounts

Remember from Chapter 2, Creating a Company that the Chart of Accounts is composed of all of the asset, liability, equity, income, and expense accounts your company utilizes. In that chapter, you learned how to create new accounts, edit existing accounts, and delete unused accounts. QuickBooks responds differently when you double-click items in the Chart of Accounts, depending on the type of account, as explained in the following table.

DOUBLE-CLICKING ACCOUNTS AND QUICKBOOKS RESPONSES	
When you double-click this type of account...	**QuickBooks responds by...**
Any balance sheet account (asset, liability, or equity)	Opening an account register for that account (Exception: The Retained Earnings account, which is a specially created account without a register; you will get a QuickReport when you double-click this account)
Any income or expense account	Creating an account QuickReport

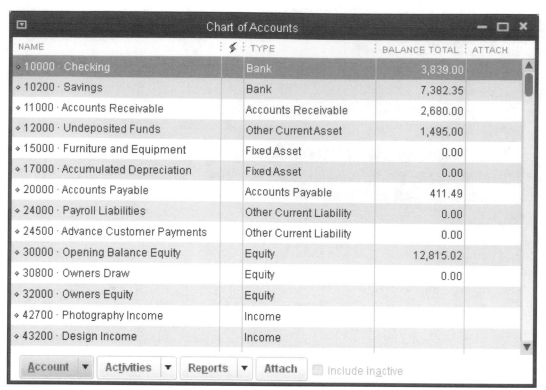

The Chart of Accounts window displays all accounts for a company. It shows balances for all balance sheet accounts but not for income, cost of goods sold, and expense accounts. Accounts are listed alphabetically by type (unless you manually rearrange them). The highlighted account (Checking here) will be affected if you issue any command.

Creating and Editing Accounts

You have already learned the basics regarding creating and editing accounts in the Chart of Accounts. In this chapter, you will look specifically at the basic accounts used in banking: Bank and Credit Card. Remember that you will use the same editing techniques used in a word-processing program to edit account information.

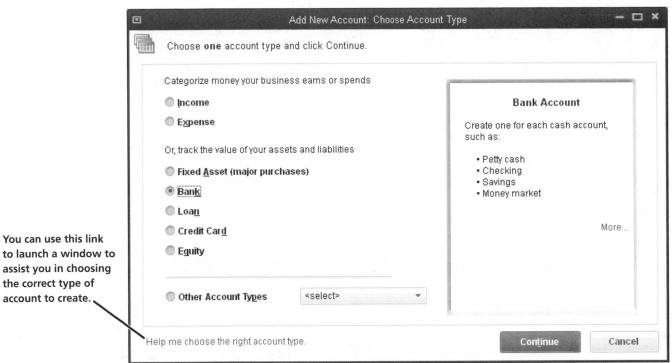

You can use this link to launch a window to assist you in choosing the correct type of account to create.

The Add New Account window will help to ensure that you choose the correct type of account when creating a new one. Notice how, when an account type is selected on the left, you see a description of how it is used on the right to assist you in choosing the correct type.

 Visualize! **Tab:** Getting Set Up
Topic: Add your bank accounts

Working with an Account Register

Each balance sheet account (except for Retained Earnings) has its own register, which is a record of all transactions pertaining to the account. A QuickBooks register looks like the check register you may already keep for your personal checking account. The running balance automatically recalculates as you record each new transaction.

When you double-click within a transaction in a register, QuickBooks takes you to the source of the transaction (similar to the QuickZoom feature). For instance, if you double-click the transaction for Handyman by the Bay in the following illustration, QuickBooks opens the Bill Payments (Check) - Checking window with all information for the transaction displayed.

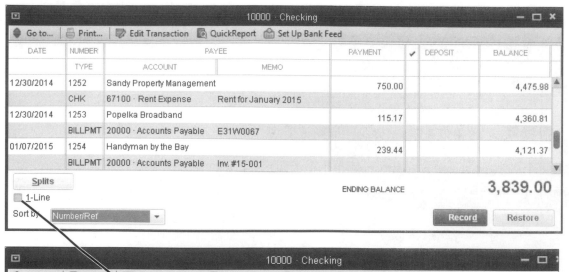

Notice that by default each transaction in the register includes two lines. The header at the top consists of two lines and describes what is found in each field.

If you choose the 1-Line option, your register will be displayed in a more condensed fashion, and you will not have a Memo field available to you.

QUICK REFERENCE	WORKING WITH BANKING ACCOUNTS
Task	**Procedure**
Open an account register	■ Open the Chart of Accounts. ■ Double-click the balance sheet account for the register you wish to view.

Work with Banking Accounts

In this exercise, you will help Allison to work with banking accounts and view a register. The first step is to open QuickBooks, and then either open a company file or restore a portable company file.

1. Start **QuickBooks 2014**.

   If you downloaded the student exercise files in the portable company file *format, follow Option 1 below. If you downloaded the files in the* company file *format, follow Option 2 below.*

Option 1: Restore a Portable Company File

2. Choose **File→Open or Restore Company**.

3. Restore the **DYS_Chapter05 (Portable)** portable file for this chapter from your file storage location, placing your last name and first initial at the end of the filename (e.g., DYS_Chapter05_FoxA).

   It may take a few moments for the portable company file to open. Once it does, continue with step 4.

Option 2: Open a Company File

2. Choose **File→Open or Restore Company**, ensure that **Open a regular company file** is selected, and then open the **DYS_Chapter05** company file from your file storage location. *The QuickBooks company file will open.*

3. Click **OK** to close the QuickBooks Information window. If necessary, click **No** in the Set Up External Accountant User window.

Edit an Existing Account

4. Click the **Chart of Accounts** task icon in the Company area of the Home page.

   A Single-click **10200•Savings**.

   B Click the **Account** menu button.

   C Choose **Edit Account** from the menu.

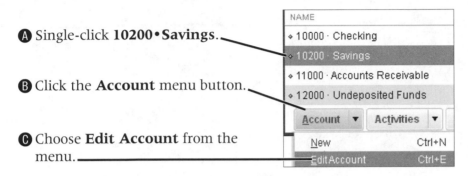

5. Follow these steps to edit the account:

   D Click in the **Bank Acct No** field and type **22222-55555**.

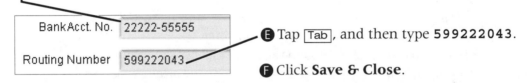

   E Tap [Tab], and then type **599222043**.

   F Click **Save & Close**.

Create a New Account

You will now create a new credit card account that will be used later in this chapter. The Chart of Accounts window should still be open. If it isn't, choose Lists→Chart of Accounts.

6. Click the **Account** menu button, and then choose **New**.

7. Follow these steps to create the new credit card account:

   A Click to choose the **Credit Card** type.

   B Click **Continue**.

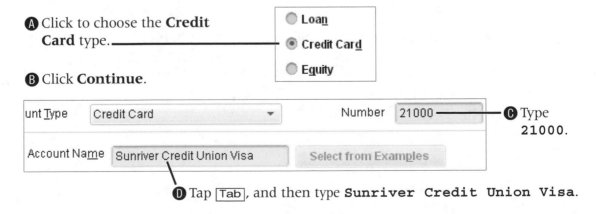

   C Type **21000**.

   D Tap [Tab], and then type **Sunriver Credit Union Visa**.

8. Click **Save & Close**; click **No** in the Set Up Online Services window.

Open and View a Register

FROM THE KEYBOARD

Ctrl+r to open a register

9. Double-click **10000•Checking** in the Chart of Accounts window, scrolling up if necessary.

10. Scroll up, and then double-click anywhere within the two lines of the **1/7/2015 Handyman by the Bay** transaction.

DATE	NUMBER	PAYEE		PAYMENT	✔	DEPOSIT	BALANCE
	TYPE	ACCOUNT	MEMO				
12/30/2014	1253	Popelka Broadband		115.17			4,360.81
	BILLPMT	20000 · Accounts Payable	E31W0067				
01/07/2015	1254	Handyman by the Bay		239.44			4,121.37
	BILLPMT	20000 · Accounts Payable	Inv. #15-001				

QuickBooks will take you to the Bill Payments (Check) – Checking window.

11. Choose **Window→Close All**.

All QuickBooks windows will close.

Making Deposits

If you have utilized the Undeposited Funds account (as you did in Chapter 3, Working with Customers), you will need to take one more step to move your payments to your bank account. This step is accomplished through the Make Deposits window. The Make Deposits window can also be used when you make a sale and do not need a sales receipt, or when you want to deposit a lump sum that will credit an income account and debit your bank account.

Reviewing the Undeposited Funds Account

In Chapter 3, Working with Customers, you learned that funds received through the Receive Payments and Enter Sales Receipts windows are deposited into the Undeposited Funds account by default. Think of it as a "holding tank" that stores all of the funds you have collected together until you are ready to make a deposit. In this section, you will learn how to empty the Undeposited Funds account.

If you have payments sitting in your Undeposited Funds account and you click the Record Deposits task icon on the Home page, you will get the Payments to Deposit window. Here you can choose which payments you wish to deposit.

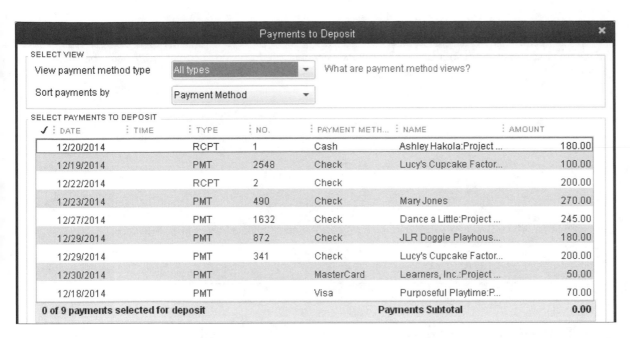

The Payments to Deposit window

TIP

You can always click OK if you are not ready to deposit the payments shown in the Payments to Deposit window yet still need to work with the Make Deposits window.

By clicking this drop-down arrow, you can select any bank account that you have set up in QuickBooks.

The Memo fields are optional, but keep in mind that you can display your memos on reports.

If you wish to keep cash back from the deposit, you can indicate that here. You will learn about petty cash in *QuickBooks Pro 2014: Level 2*.

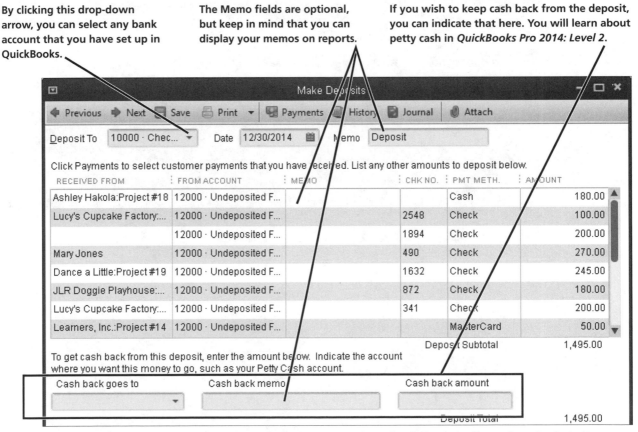

The Make Deposits window. You can click the Print button to print a detailed report of your deposits, including deposit slips if you choose to purchase and use them.

If you make deposits from your Undeposited Funds account, the following accounting will occur behind the scenes.

10000-Checking		12000-Undeposited Funds	
1,495.00			1,495.00

If you use the Make Deposits window to record sales, the accounting involved is as follows.

10000-Checking		43200-Design Income	
200.00			200.00

QUICK REFERENCE	MAKING DEPOSITS
Task	**Procedure**
Make a deposit from the Undeposited Funds account	■ Choose Banking→Make Deposits. ■ Choose the payment(s) you wish to deposit; click OK. ■ Choose the correct bank account and date for the deposit. ■ Click Save & Close or Save & New.
Make a deposit directly to a bank account	■ Choose Banking→Make Deposits; click OK if the Payments to Deposit window appears. ■ Choose the correct bank account and date for the deposit. ■ Enter all of the deposit information including the customer (if desired), account, payment method, and amount. ■ Click Save & Close or Save & New.

Use the Make Deposits Window

In this exercise, you will work with the Make Deposits window to deposit funds from the Undeposited Funds account and to make a deposit without a sales form.

1. Click the **Home** button on the Icon Bar.

2. Click the **Record Deposits** task icon in the Banking area of the Home page.

3. Click the **Select All** button; QuickBooks will place a checkmark to the left of all nine payments waiting to be deposited.

Notice that after you click the Select All button, it is grayed out. It is no longer a valid selection since all payments are already selected.

4. Click **OK** to accept the payments for deposit and move on to the Make Deposits window.

5. Click the drop-down arrow for the **Deposit To** field, and then choose **10000•Checking**; click **OK** in the Setting Default Accounts window, if necessary.

6. Tap Tab, and then type **123014** as the date.

7. Click the **Save & New** button to make the deposit to your Checking account. Leave the Make Deposits window open for the next step.

BTS BRIEF
10000•Checking DR 1,495.00; **12000•Undeposited Funds CR <1,495.00>**

Your insertion point should be in the Deposit To field of a clear Make Deposits window. If it's not, choose Banking→Make Deposits.

Make a Deposit Without Specifying a Customer

Guy and Allison worked at a Quick Sketch fundraiser where people could meet with a graphic artist for 15 minutes to describe a need they have for their organization and for $15 receive a sketch and description of a possible solution to their stated need. Average Guy Designs made $5 from each of the quick consultations. Since there were multiple customers whom Guy does not want to track individually, Allison will make a deposit to Checking, directly crediting Design Income.

8. Tap Tab to move to the Date field.

9. Follow these steps to complete the deposit:

Ⓐ Tap ⊞ until the date reads **01/03/2015**.

Ⓑ Tap Tab, and then type `Quick Sketch Event`.

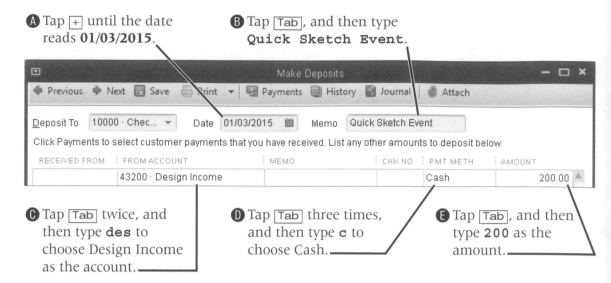

Ⓒ Tap Tab twice, and then type **des** to choose Design Income as the account.

Ⓓ Tap Tab three times, and then type **c** to choose Cash.

Ⓔ Tap Tab, and then type **200** as the amount.

Note that you don't fill in an item in this form, but you do fill in the account. Remember that an item is used to direct funds to the underlying account. You cannot leave the From Account field blank because you must specify the account that will be credited since you will be debiting a bank account with the deposit.

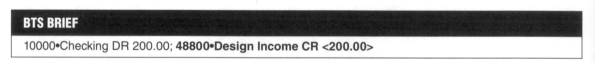

BTS BRIEF

10000•Checking DR 200.00; **48800•Design Income CR <200.00>**

10. Click **Save & Close**; your deposit will be recorded, and the window will close.

Moving Funds Between Accounts

Most people have transferred money between their bank accounts. QuickBooks has a feature that allows you to record this transfer. If you use online banking, you may even be able to set QuickBooks to perform the transfer for you when you go online (if your financial institution allows it).

Since you are transferring funds between two asset accounts, you want to debit the account that is increasing and credit the account that is decreasing. Look at the following T-accounts to visualize this transaction.

FLASHBACK TO GAAP: MONETARY UNIT

Remember that it is assumed a stable currency is going to be the unit of record.

In this illustration, you are transferring funds from the Checking account to the Savings account.

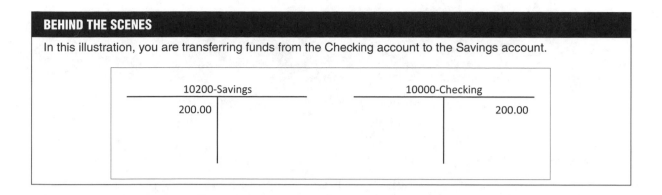

10200-Savings		10000-Checking	
200.00			200.00

QUICK REFERENCE	TRANSFERRING FUNDS BETWEEN ACCOUNTS
Task	**Procedure**
Transfer funds	■ Choose Banking→Transfer Funds.
	■ Choose the account from which you wish to draw the funds.
	■ Choose the account to which you wish to send the funds.
	■ Type the amount to be transferred and, if you wish, a memo.
	■ Click Save & Close or Save & New to record the transfer.

Move Funds Between Accounts

In this exercise, Allison will transfer funds between the Checking and Savings accounts.

1. Choose **Banking→Transfer Funds**.

2. Follow these steps to complete the funds transfer:

Ⓐ Type **010315**.   Ⓑ Click to choose **10000•Checking**.

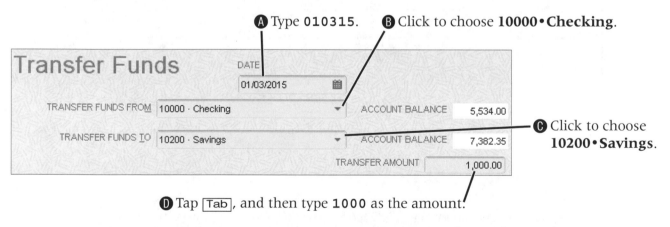

Ⓒ Click to choose **10200•Savings**.

Ⓓ Tap ⌐Tab⌐, and then type **1000** as the amount.

Notice that QuickBooks displays the account balances of the accounts involved in the transfer so you can verify sufficient funds are available.

BTS BRIEF

10200•Savings DR 1,000.00; **10000•Checking CR <1,000.00>**

3. Click **Save & Close** to record the transaction.

Managing Credit and Debit Card Transactions

Credit cards give business owners an easy way to track their expenses. QuickBooks allows you to track credit card transactions just as you track checking and savings account transactions. You can set up as many credit card accounts as you need and simply choose the account you want to work with in the Enter Credit Card Charges window.

If you use your personal credit cards occasionally for business purposes, you should *not* enter them in QuickBooks as business credit cards. Only create accounts for business credit cards.

Credit card transactions are classified as either a charge (when you make a purchase) or a credit (when you make a return). As you will use the same form for both types, you need to choose the correct type when entering transactions.

You can choose from all of your credit card accounts.

You choose to record a purchase or a refund. Purchase/Charge is selected by default when you open the window.

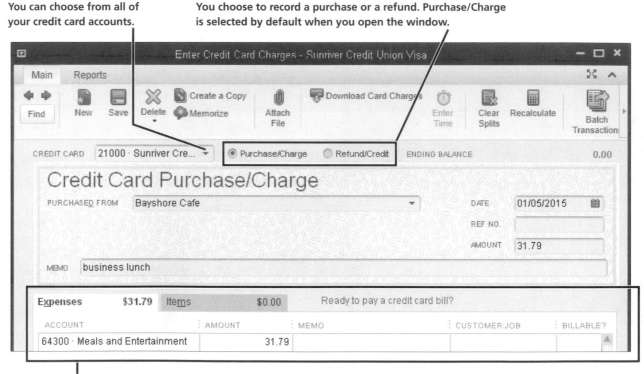

This section looks like the lower section of both the Write Checks and Enter Bills windows.

Type of Account and Normal Balance

A credit card is a liability, so its normal balance is a credit. This means you credit the account when you make a purchase (a "charge") and debit the account when you make a payment (a "credit").

The term credit is a bit confusing at this point, as you will debit your credit card account if you enter a "credit" transaction. However, if you think of it from the perspective of the merchant, it makes perfect sense!

Pay a Bill with a Credit Card

If you have entered a bill into QuickBooks, you do have the option to pay it with a credit card. Make sure that you use the Pay Bills window to accomplish the task, though, as you must remove the amount from Accounts Payable!

If you use a credit card to pay a bill that you entered through the QuickBooks Enter Bills window, you must use the Pay Bills window when you pay it—or expenses and Accounts Payable will be overstated!

Dealing with Debit Card Transactions

When you make a purchase or pay a bill with a debit card, funds are taken directly from your checking account, which is different from what occurs for credit card purchases. Use the Write Checks window to handle debit card transactions. If you use the Enter/Pay Bills windows in QuickBooks, you can continue to use them when working with debit card purchases. This means that if you have entered a bill in QuickBooks and then choose to use a debit card to pay it, you must enter that payment through the Pay Bills window. Otherwise, the expenses will be overstated, and you will leave the bill hanging out in Accounts Payable.

When you enter a debit card transaction in the Write Checks window, indicate it by entering a code such as "DB" in the No. field.

Other Types of Transactions Affecting the Checking Account

In addition to debit card transactions, you may have other ones that draw funds from the checking account as well. For instance, ATM cards and a service such as PayPal™ can withdraw funds directly from your bank account. All of these transactions will be entered using the Write Checks window; you just need to create common codes that will be used in the No. field to record each type of transaction. Common codes include DB for debit card, ATM for an ATM card transaction, and PP for a PayPal payment. You do not have to use the codes suggested here; however, you should choose one code for each type of transaction and stick with it!

A purchase credits the credit card account, as shown here.

64900-Office Supplies	64300-Meals and Entertaintment	21000-Sunriver CU Visa
57.84	31.25	89.09

A payment or refund debits the credit card account, as shown here.

64900-Office Supplies	21000-Sunriver CU Visa
10.46	10.46

When you use a credit card to pay a bill, the following occurs behind the scenes for you.

20000-Accounts Payable	21000-Sunriver CU Visa
363.27	363.27

Using a debit card to make the same bill payment as above looks like the following behind the scenes.

20000-Accounts Payable	10000-Checking
363.27	363.27

When you use a debit card to purchase office supplies, the following occurs behind the scenes for you.

64900-Office Supplies	10000-Checking
363.27	363.27

	RECORDING CREDIT AND DEBIT CARD TRANSACTIONS
Task	**Procedure**
Record a credit card transaction	■ Choose Banking→Enter Credit Card Charges. ■ Choose the account to record a purchase or refund to. ■ Enter the transaction information. ■ Click Save & Close or Save & New.
Record a debit card transaction	■ Choose Banking→Write Checks. ■ Select the bank account to which the debit card is linked. ■ Enter "DB" or the code you have chosen in the No. field. ■ Enter information into the payee, amount, and memo fields. ■ Ensure the proper expense/asset accounts are indicated on the Expense and/or Item tab. ■ Click Save & Close or Save & New.
Record a debit card transaction for a bill already entered into Accounts Payable	■ Choose Vendors→Pay Bills. ■ Select the bill you wish to pay by debit card. ■ Set the date and account to which the debit card is linked. ■ Choose to Assign check number in the Payment Method area; click Pay Selected Bills. ■ Type your code in the Assign Check Numbers window; click OK. ■ Click Done in the Payment Summary window.

DEVELOP YOUR SKILLS 5-4

Manage Credit Card Transactions

Guy needs to purchase some supplies for the office. He has also decided to purchase refreshments for clients who stop in. In this exercise, you will help Allison to enter a credit card purchase and a return, as well as pay a bill with a credit card.

1. Click the **Enter Credit Card Charges** task icon in the Banking area of the Home page.

Enter Credit Card Charges

Since you have only one credit card set up at this time, the information will fill in to the Credit Card field. If you had multiple cards, you would need to choose the appropriate one before entering other information.

2. Follow these steps to record the credit card charge:

Ⓐ Tap `Tab` three times, and then type **a**.

Ⓑ Tap `Tab`, and then type **010315**.

Ⓒ Tap `Tab` twice, and then type **89.09**.

Ⓓ Tap `Tab`, and then type the memo displayed.

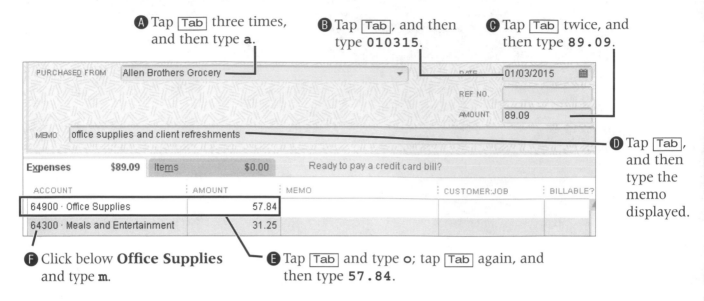

Ⓕ Click below **Office Supplies** and type **m**.

Ⓔ Tap `Tab` and type **o**; tap `Tab` again, and then type **57.84**.

The amount for the Meals and Entertainment split will automatically fill in for you.

BTS BRIEF

64900•Office Supplies DR 57.84; 64300•Meals and Entertainment DR 31.25; **21000•Sunriver Credit Union Visa CR <89.09>**

3. Click the **Save & New** button.

Record a Credit Card Return

In the next transaction, Guy returns a calculator he purchased at Allen Brothers Grocery, as he realized he didn't need it once he got back to the office.

4. Follow these steps to record the credit card refund:

Ⓐ Click to choose the **Refund/Credit** option.

Ⓑ Tap `Tab`, and then type **a**.

Ⓒ Tap `Tab`, and then use `+` to change the date to **1/6/15**.

Ⓓ Tap `Tab` twice, and then type **10.46**.

Ⓔ Tap `Tab`, and then type **office supplies return**.

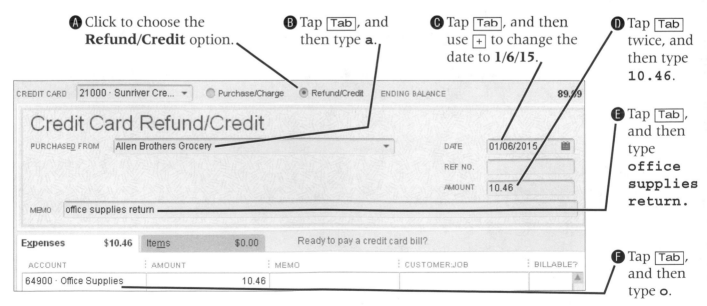

Ⓕ Tap `Tab`, and then type **o**.

5. Click the **Save & Close** button.

   QuickBooks records the transaction and closes the Enter Credit Card Charges window.

Pay a Bill with a Debit Card

You can record a bill paid by debit card in QuickBooks, although you must use the Pay Bills window in order to properly affect Accounts Payable.

6. Click the **Pay Bills** task icon in the Vendors area of the Home page.

7. Follow these steps to pay a bill with a debit card:

Ⓐ Click to place a checkmark in this box.

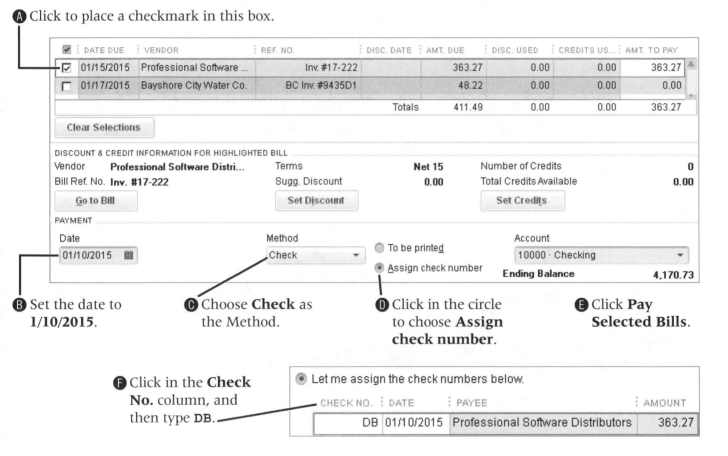

Ⓐ Click to place a checkmark in this box.

Ⓑ Set the date to **1/10/2015**.

Ⓒ Choose **Check** as the Method.

Ⓓ Click in the circle to choose **Assign check number**.

Ⓔ Click **Pay Selected Bills**.

Ⓕ Click in the **Check No.** column, and then type **DB**.

Ⓖ Click **OK**.

   When you pay a bill with a debit card, you are affecting the Checking account, so you will need to assign the transaction the "check number" that you use for all debit card transactions. In the scenario above, that would be "DB."

8. Click **Done** in the Payment Summary window.

   QuickBooks records the bill payment, debiting Accounts Payable and crediting Checking for you.

Dealing with Bounced Checks

Unfortunately, almost all business owners must deal with customers whose checks are returned for non-sufficient funds (NSF) at some time or another. Many people call these "bounced check," and this is the term also used in QuickBooks. This book uses the terms *NSF* and *bounced check*, though the latter is used more often because it is the term used in QuickBooks.

With the new Bounced Check feature, you can easily account for NSF checks received from invoiced customers.

With the 2014 version, QuickBooks makes it very easy to account for bounced checks right from the Receive Payments window. However, if you receive a bounced check that was originally received on a sales receipt or directly through a deposit, you will need to account for it using the alternate method described in the following Quick Reference tables.

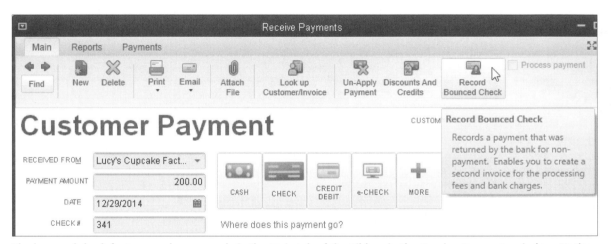

The bounced check feature can be accessed via the Main tab of the Ribbon in the Receive Payments window. Notice the ToolTip that appears when you place your mouse pointer over the Record Bounced Check button.

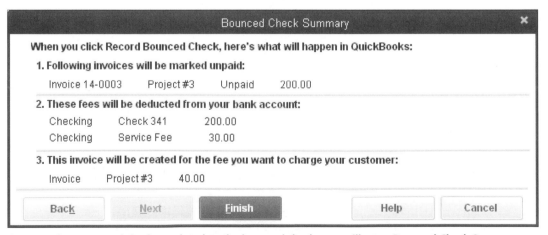

Once you have entered the fees related to the bounced check, you will see a Bounced Check Summary.

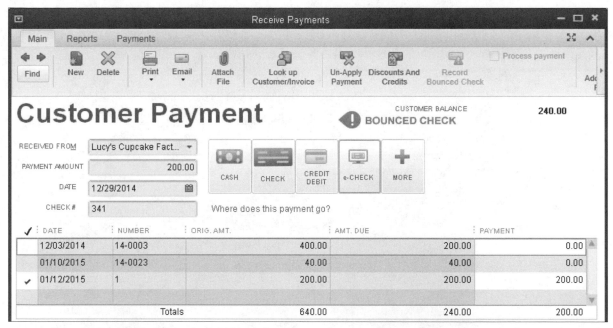

Once the bounced check has been entered for a customer payment, you will see the Bounced Check stamp displayed.

A bounced check associated with a sales receipt or a straight deposit can be dealt with by generating a statement for the customer.

The bank may charge you a lesser amount than you choose to pass on to the customer for a bounced check.

BEHIND THE SCENES

When you deal with a returned check, you will affect multiple accounts behind the scenes.

11000-Accounts Receivable		10000-Checking	
200.00			200.00
40.00			30.00

60400-Bank Service Charges		48910-Returned Check Charges	
30.00			40.00

QUICK REFERENCE	DEALING WITH BOUNCED CHECKS
Task	**Procedure**
Process a bounced check associated with an invoice	■ Open the Receive Payments window and locate the returned check. ■ Click the Record Bounced Check button. ■ Set the fees for the bounced check; click Next and then Finish.
Account for a bounced check received on a sales receipt or through the Make Deposit window	■ Create an Other Charge item for the service charge, directing it to the Other Income account. ■ Record the bank's fee in your bank account register (Bank Service Charges as account). ■ Record the check in your bank account register (customer/job as payee; Accounts Receivable as account). ■ Enter a statement charge for the customer's fee. ■ Send the customer a statement that shows the bounced check and fee.

DEVELOP YOUR SKILLS 5-5

Handle a Bounced Check

In this exercise, you will account for a check that was returned to Average Guy Designs for non-sufficient funds.

1. Click the **Receive Payments** task icon in the Customers area of the Home page.

Receive Payments

2. Click the **Previous** button two times until the payment received on check #341 from **Lucy's Cupcake Factory** is displayed.

3. Click the **Record Bounced Check** button on the Main tab of the Ribbon.

Record Bounced Check

4. Follow these steps to set the fees for the bounced check:

Ⓐ Type **30** as the **Bank Fee**.   Ⓑ Tap [Tab], and then type **011215**.

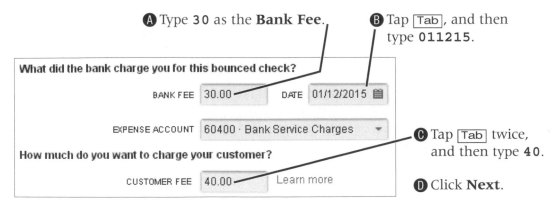

What did the bank charge you for this bounced check?

BANK FEE 30.00   DATE 01/12/2015 📅

EXPENSE ACCOUNT 60400 · Bank Service Charges ▼

How much do you want to charge your customer?

CUSTOMER FEE 40.00   Learn more

Ⓒ Tap [Tab] twice, and then type **40**.

Ⓓ Click **Next**.

A Bounced Check Summary will be displayed.

5. Click **Finish**.

The Receive Payments window will again be displayed and you will see that the check has been marked as bounced and a new invoice has been created to account for the bounced check.

BTS BRIEF

11000•Accounts Receivable DR 240.00; 60400•Bank Service Charges DR 30.00; **10000•Checking CR <230.00>; 48910•Returned Check Charges CR <40.00>**

Reconciling Accounts

It is important to make sure that your account records in QuickBooks match those of the bank. The process of matching your accounts to the bank statements you receive is called reconciliation.

Clicking here will allow you to focus on transactions associated with the statement you are reconciling.

| Reconcile - Checking | | | | | | | | | |

For period: 12/31/2014 ☑ Hide transactions after the statement's end date

Checks and Payments

✓	DATE ▲	CHK#	PAYEE	AMOUNT
✓	12/10/2014	1245	Graphic Supp...	302.50
✓	12/10/2014	1246	Ricky's Electri...	245.00
✓	12/10/2014	1247	Sandy Proper...	750.00
✓	12/29/2014	1249	Rankin Famil...	125.49
✓	12/29/2014	1250	Popelka Broa...	50.00
✓	12/30/2014	1248	Bayshore Cafe	37.49
	12/30/2014	**1252**	**Sandy Prope...**	**750.00**
✓	12/30/2014	1253	Popelka Broa...	115.17

Deposits and Other Credits

✓	DATE ▲	CHK#	MEMO	TYPE	AMOUNT
✓	12/15/2014		Deposit	DEP	1,340.00
✓	12/30/2014		Deposit	DEP	1,495.00

☑ Highlight Marked   [Mark All] [Unmark All] [Go To]   [Columns to Display...]

Beginning Balance	5,432.67	
Items you have marked cleared		
2 Deposits and Other Credits	2,835.00	
7 Checks and Payments	1,625.65	

[Modify]

Service Charge	-9.50
Interest Earned	0.00
Ending Balance	6,632.52
Cleared Balance	6,632.52
Difference	0.00

[Reconcile Now] [Leave]

QuickBooks bank account reconciliation window

QuickBooks' Reconciliation Features

You should be aware of some important reconciliation features in QuickBooks. You can save your reconciliation reports in PDF so they are ready to send via email and are viewable with the free Adobe Reader program (also known as Acrobat Reader). In QuickBooks Pro, when you reconcile a new statement, the reconciliation report replaces the prior report with the new month's information. You should save each report as a PDF file to a storage location such as your hard drive, a cloud service, or a network drive if you are using the Pro edition. In QuickBooks Premier and Enterprise editions, QuickBooks stores all reconciliation reports as PDF files for you, and you can access them through QuickBooks at any time.

Locating Discrepancies

QuickBooks also provides a feature that helps you to locate discrepancies if there is a difference in balances during the reconciliation process. You can run a Reconciliation Discrepancy Report that lists transactions affecting the reconciliation balance. The types of transactions that can affect the balance are:

- Deleted transactions
- A change to a previously cleared amount
- Transactions that were manually un-cleared in the register
- Transactions in which the date was changed to a different statement period

When Your Accounts Don't Match

It is important to take the time when performing reconciliations to ensure there are no errors. As you clear each transaction, make sure the amounts are exactly the same. It is very frustrating when you get to the end of the transactions, and they don't balance.

Once you have cleared transactions through the reconciliation process, it is important to *not* change them. Changes may alter your starting balance for the next reconciliation. If you find yourself in such a situation, you can run a Reconciliation Discrepancy report to find the problem(s).

Problem Resolution Process

If you do find yourself in the unfavorable situation of finishing your reconciliation without balancing, consider the following suggestions:

- Look for a transaction that is exactly the same amount as the difference and ensure whether or not it should be cleared.
- Determine whether you are missing a deposit or a payment by looking at the totals of each on the bank statement and the QuickBooks reconciliation window.
- Compare the number of transactions on the bank statement to the number of cleared transactions in QuickBooks.
- Verify the individual amount of each transaction on the bank statement and compare it to the amounts you have in QuickBooks.
- Determine whether it is a bank error (the bank may have recorded a transaction for the wrong amount).
- If it is a bank error, you can create an adjustment transaction in QuickBooks, notify the bank, and then reverse the adjustment transaction after the bank corrects the error.
- Run a Reconciliation Discrepancy report to see if any changes were made to previously cleared transactions. If changes were made to previously cleared transactions, undo the last reconciliation and redo it.

Reconciling Credit Cards

You can reconcile your credit cards the same way as you reconcile your bank account, although you access the command through the Chart of Accounts.

Once you have reconciled the credit card, you have the option to pay any amount due. You can choose to either write a check or enter a bill for the payment. QuickBooks takes the balance due on the credit card and fills it in to either the Enter Bills or the Write Checks window. If you don't plan to pay the entire amount owed, you can change the amount manually. You will reconcile the credit card in the "Tackle the Tasks" section at the end of the chapter.

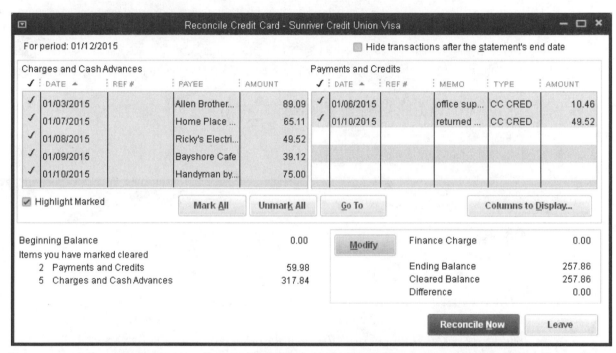

You can access the command to reconcile a credit card through the Chart of Accounts, rather than the Banking option on the menu bar. The process from there looks the same as it does when you reconcile a bank account.

After you complete the reconciliation of a credit card, you will be prompted to either write a check or enter a bill for the balance due, as displayed in the illustration.

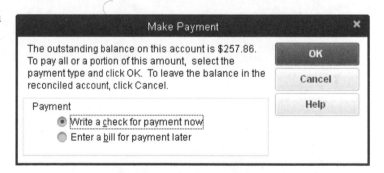

FLASHBACK TO GAAP: ASSUMPTION OF A GOING CONCERN

Remember that it is assumed that the business will be in operation indefinitely.

| RECONCILING BANK AND CREDIT CARD ACCOUNTS

Task	Procedure
Reconcile a bank account	■ Choose Banking→Reconcile.
	■ Choose the account you wish to reconcile; enter the statement date and ending balance.
	■ Enter any service or finance charges; click Continue.
	■ Compare the QuickBooks transactions to the bank statement; mark off cleared transactions.
	■ Once the difference between QuickBooks and the bank statement is zero, click Reconcile Now.
Reconcile a credit card	■ Choose Lists→Chart of Accounts; single-click the desired credit card account.
	■ Click the Activities button at the bottom of the window; choose Reconcile Credit Card.
	■ Choose the account; enter the statement date and ending balance.
	■ Enter any service or finance charges; click Continue.
	■ Compare the QuickBooks transactions to the bank statement; mark off cleared transactions.
	■ Once the difference between QuickBooks and the bank statement is zero, click Reconcile Now.

DEVELOP YOUR SKILLS 5-6

Reconcile the Checking Account

In this exercise, you will reconcile the checking account in QuickBooks. First, you will help Allison prepare to reconcile the checking account for Average Guy Designs. The bank statement for this account that you will use to complete the reconciliation is displayed here.

Before You Begin: You will be working with a bank statement. You can use the illustration shown, or you can print Develop Your Skills 5-6 from your file storage location.

```
                    Sunriver Credit Union
                         487 Merrifield Lane
                         Bayshore, CA 91547

Statement of Account Prepared For:
  Average Guy Designs
  110 Sampson Way
  Bayshore, CA 91547
                                  Account Number: 11111-44444

                                  Statement Period: Dec 1 - Dec 31, 2014
     Total                              Total
  Deposits:   $8,267.67            Payments:      $1,625.65
  Beginning                           Ending
   Balance:   $5,432.67             Balance:      $6,632.52

Transactions:
   Date       Transaction type    Payment    Deposit     Balance
  12/1/2014   Beginning Balance                          $5,432.67
  12/10/2014  Check #1245          302.50                $5,130.17
  12/10/2014  Check #1247          750.00                $4,380.17
  12/10/2014  Check #1246          245.00                $4,135.17
  12/15/2014  Deposit                        1,340.00    $5,475.17
  12/29/2014  Check #1250           50.00                $5,425.17
  12/29/2014  Check #1249          125.49                $5,299.68
  12/30/2014  Check #1248           37.49                $5,262.19
  12/30/2014  Deposit                        1,495.00    $6,757.19
  12/31/2014  Check #1253          115.17                $6,642.02
  12/31/2014  Service Charge         9.50                $6,632.52
              Ending Balance                              6,632.52
```

1. Click the **Reconcile** task icon in the Banking area of the Home page.

   QuickBooks displays the Begin Reconciliation window.

Reconcile

2. Using the illustration of the bank statement provided or the one you printed, follow these steps to prepare for reconciliation:

Ⓐ Ensure that **10000•Checking** is the account displayed.

Ⓑ Tap Tab, and then type **123114**.

Ⓒ Tap Tab, and then type **6632.52**.

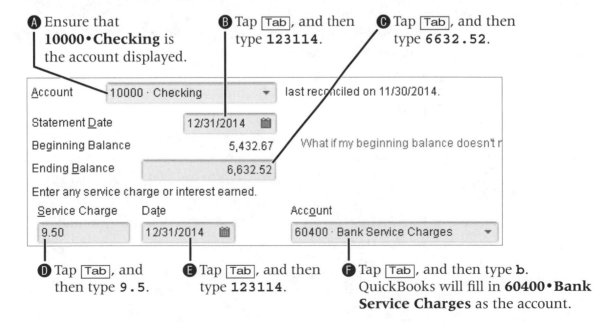

Ⓓ Tap Tab, and then type **9.5**.

Ⓔ Tap Tab, and then type **123114**.

Ⓕ Tap Tab, and then type **b**. QuickBooks will fill in **60400•Bank Service Charges** as the account.

There will be a difference in the beginning balance between this window and the bank statement because this is the first reconciliation performed since you started your QuickBooks company file.

3. Click **Continue** to move to the Reconciliation-Checking window.

   The Reconciliation-Checking window shows all transactions waiting to be cleared.

Reconcile a Checking Account

Now that you have finished the prep work, it is time to begin the actual reconciliation.

4. Click to place a checkmark to hide all transactions after the statement's end date.

5. Click in the **Checkmark** column to the left of each transaction in QuickBooks that is also on the bank checking statement displayed above step 1.

   When you are finished, your Reconciliation-Checking window should match the following illustration.

For period: 12/31/2014									☑ Hide transactions after the statement's end date

Checks and Payments

✓	DATE ▲	CHK #	PAYEE	AMOUNT
✓	12/10/2014	1245	Graphic Supp...	302.50
✓	12/10/2014	1246	Ricky's Electri...	245.00
✓	12/10/2014	1247	Sandy Proper...	750.00
✓	12/29/2014	1249	Rankin Famil...	125.49
✓	12/29/2014	1250	Popelka Broa...	50.00
✓	12/30/2014	1248	Bayshore Cafe	37.49
	12/30/2014	**1252**	**Sandy Prope...**	**750.00**
✓	12/30/2014	1253	Popelka Broa...	115.17

Deposits and Other Credits

✓	DATE ▲	CHK #	MEMO	TYPE	AMOUNT
✓	12/15/2014		Deposit	DEP	1,340.00
✓	12/30/2014		Deposit	DEP	1,495.00

6. Look at the **"Difference"** at the bottom right of the window to see if you have successfully reconciled your account.

   The goal when you perform a reconciliation is for the Difference to be 0.00. The Difference is calculated by determining the difference between the transactions on the bank statement and those that you have marked cleared in QuickBooks.

Beginning Balance	5,432.67		Modify	Service Charge	-9.50
Items you have marked cleared				Interest Earned	0.00
2 Deposits and Other Credits	2,835.00			Ending Balance	6,632.52
7 Checks and Payments	1,625.65			Cleared Balance	6,632.52
				Difference	0.00

7. Click the **Reconcile Now** button, and then click **OK** in the Information window.

   There is a pause as QuickBooks records the marked transactions as cleared.

8. Click **Close** to choose to not produce a report at this time.

   You will learn about reconciliation reports in the next section.

Dealing with Oops in Banking Transactions

It is inevitable that you will need to deal with either errors or modifications to transactions in QuickBooks. It is very important that you do this properly to ensure that everything behind the scenes is correct. You have already seen what errors dealing with customer- and vendor-transactions look like, so now we will look at possible errors when working with banking accounts.

Fixing Errors

The following table outlines an error related to the Chart of Accounts as well as an error that occurs when dealing with a debit card transaction incorrectly, the effects of the errors behind the scenes, and how to correct them.

COMMON ERRORS AND FIXES

Error	Effect Behind the Scenes	The Fix
The wrong account type was chosen when creating a new account in the Chart of Accounts	The types of accounts involved will determine what the damage will be behind the scenes (but there will be damage!)	Edit the account through the Chart of Accounts and choose the correct account type
A debit card transaction was entered in the Enter Credit Card Charges window	The wrong account is credited, and you will have an inflated amount displayed in Checking as well as the credit card account	Delete the credit card transaction and reenter it through a window that affects Checking

Correct Banking Errors

In this exercise, you will execute two tasks incorrectly and then fix them.

Do It the Wrong Way – Set the Account Type

The business has just received a Discover card that will be used for expenses. In this next example, you will set up the account incorrectly for the purpose of learning how to fix the error and do it correctly.

1. Choose **Lists→Chart of Accounts**.

2. Click the **Account** menu button, and then choose **New**.

3. Select **Expense** as the type of account, and then click **Continue**.

4. Type **62300** as the Number, tap Tab, and then type **Discover Card** as the Account Name.

5. Click **Save & Close**.

No doubt you have already realized what the error is in this example! While you will be using the card to pay for expenses, you should not set it up as an expense account. This will have huge ramifications behind the scenes, so you need to fix it pronto!

Do It the Right Way – Set the Account Type

In order to fix the error of setting up an account as the wrong type, you need to open the Edit Account window. The Chart of Accounts should still be open from the last step.

6. Right-click **62300•Discover Card** in the Chart of Accounts window, and then choose **Edit Account** from the menu.

7. Follow these steps to fix the error:

   A Click the drop-down arrow, and then choose **Credit Card**.

   B Tap ⟦Tab⟧, and then type **23000**.

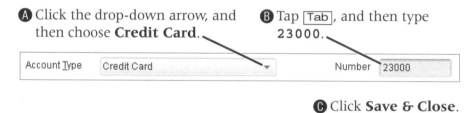

   C Click **Save & Close**.

You must change the account number when you change the account type.

8. Close the **Chart of Accounts** window.

Do It the Wrong Way – Enter a Debit Card Transaction as a Credit Card

Allison has just received a receipt from Guy for graphic art supplies. He used his debit card, but you will enter it as a credit card transaction, incorrectly, for the purpose of learning how to fix the error and do it correctly.

9. Choose **Banking→Enter Credit Card Charges**; ensure **Sunriver Credit Union Visa** and **Purchase/Charge** are selected.

10. Follow these steps to enter the transaction:

Ⓐ Click the drop-down arrow and choose **Graphic Supply Shoppe**.

Ⓑ Tap Tab , and then type **122914**.

Ⓒ Tap Tab twice, and then type **164.50**.

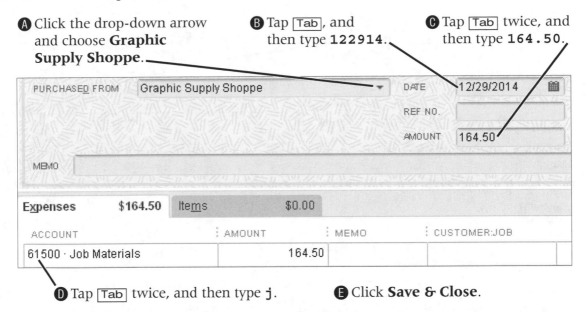

Ⓓ Tap Tab twice, and then type **j**.

Ⓔ Click **Save & Close**.

Think about this transaction. What is wrong with it? By entering the debit card transaction in the Enter Credit Card Charges window, you have increased the balance in the credit card account and have not removed the funds from your Checking account.

BTS BRIEF

61500•Job Materials DR 164.50; **21000•Sun River Credit Union Visa CR <164.50>**

Do It the Right Way – Enter a Debit Card Transaction and Credit Checking

To fix the debit card transaction that was handled improperly, you must delete it and reenter the payment using the Write Checks window.

11. Choose **Banking→Enter Credit Card Charges**.

12. Click the **Previous** button until the transaction you just entered is displayed.

You can look for a transaction by using the Previous and Next buttons, if you believe the transaction to be easy to locate. If not, use the Find or Search feature.

13. Choose **Edit→Delete Credit Card Charge**; click **OK** in the Delete Transaction window.

FROM THE KEYBOARD
Ctrl + d to delete the selected transaction

14. Close the **Enter Credit Card Charges** window.

15. Click the **Write Checks** task icon in the Customers area of the Home page.

16. Follow these steps to enter the debit card purchase correctly:

Ⓐ Tap Tab, and then type **DB**.

Ⓑ Tap Tab, and then type **122914**, if necessary.

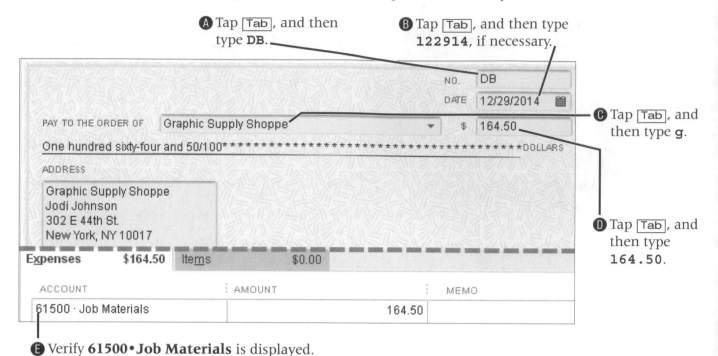

Ⓒ Tap Tab, and then type **g**.

Ⓓ Tap Tab, and then type **164.50**.

Ⓔ Verify **61500•Job Materials** is displayed.

> **BTS BRIEF**
>
> 21000•Sunriver Credit Union Visa DR 164.50; **61500•Job Materials CR <164.50>**
> 61500•Job Materials DR 164.50; **10000•Checking CR <164.50>**

17. Click **Save & Close**.

Before moving on, think about what you have just completed and make sure you understand the "why" behind it. You have ensured the balances in the Checking and credit cards accounts are now correct by recording the debit card purchase correctly.

Working with Banking and Balance Sheet Reports

In this section, you will learn about reports that can tell you stories about your banking activities in QuickBooks as well as those that display information about your balance sheet accounts (asset, liability, and equity). You will also have an opportunity to look at the snapshots available in QuickBooks. You can access snapshots relative to your payments, company, and customers.

Banking Reports

The QuickBooks banking feature comes with preset reports for you to use to get answers from your data. Banking reports deal with answers to questions such as:

- What are all of the transactions involving a specific payee?
- What checks have not cleared the bank as of the last bank statement?
- Which payments still need to be deposited?
- Where can I find a list of all transactions that affect my checking account?
- What changes in transactions may affect my next reconciliation?

Register QuickReports

Register QuickReports are run right from a register window. Once you have selected a transaction and clicked the QuickReport button, you will receive a report that shows all transactions for the payee of the selected transaction.

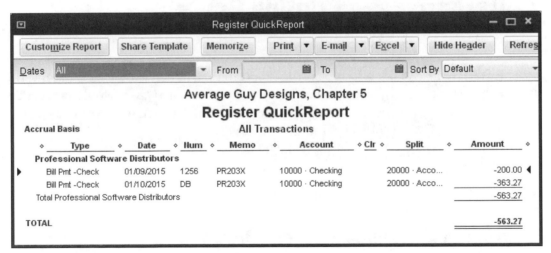

This is an example of a register QuickReport based on Average Guy Designs' transactions with Professional Software Distributors.

Reconciliation Reports

Reconciliation reports show transactions that have cleared as well as those that have yet to clear the bank. QuickBooks allows you to save reconciliation reports in a PDF format.

Average Guy Designs, Chapter 5
Reconciliation Summary
10000 · Checking, Period Ending 12/31/2014

	Dec 31, 14
Beginning Balance	5,432.67
Cleared Transactions	
Checks and Payments - 8 items	-1,635.15
Deposits and Credits - 2 items	2,835.00
Total Cleared Transactions	1,199.85
Cleared Balance	6,632.52
Uncleared Transactions	
Checks and Payments - 1 item	-750.00
Total Uncleared Transactions	-750.00
Register Balance as of 12/31/2014	5,882.52
New Transactions	
Checks and Payments - 8 items	-2,151.29
Deposits and Credits - 1 item	200.00
Total New Transactions	-1,951.29
Ending Balance	3,931.23

Take note of what a reconciliation report will display for you. In this example, you can see a Reconciliation Summary report, and you will produce a Reconciliation Detail report in the next exercise.

Alternatives to Printing Reports

Of course you can send any report to the printer. QuickBooks also gives you options for storing or working with a report:

■ **Email:** QuickBooks can convert the report to PDF, which can be viewed with the free Adobe Reader program. This allows viewing of the report exactly as it would print even to those who do not have QuickBooks. When you choose to email a form or report to a customer, the form or report will be converted automatically to PDF for you.

■ **Export:** QuickBooks can export the report to Microsoft Excel so you can use Excel's powerful spreadsheet features to work with your data. You will have an opportunity to work with QuickBooks reports in Excel in *QuickBooks Pro 2014: Level 2*.

Saving Reports and Forms as PDF

PDF copies of QuickBooks reports and forms make emailing forms and reports convenient for you. They are also a great way to create copies to save for your own records. You learned about printing a file to PDF in the How do I save as a PDF? section of Chapter 1 (page 12).

QUICK REFERENCE	PRODUCING BANKING REPORTS
Task	**Procedure**
Produce a register QuickReport	■ Open the register from which you wish to create the report. ■ Click within the transaction on which you wish to base the report. ■ Click QuickReport on the register toolbar.
Produce a reconciliation report	■ Choose Reports→Banking→Previous Reconciliation. ■ Choose the correct account and the statement ending date. ■ Choose whether you want a detail or summary report (or both); click Display.
Produce a reconciliation discrepancy report	■ Choose Reports→Banking→Reconciliation Discrepancy. ■ Choose the correct account; click OK.

Produce Banking Reports and a PDF Copy of a Report

In the last exercise, you reconciled the checking account for Average Guy Designs. In this exercise, you will help Allison to produce two banking reports and save one of them as a PDF file.

1. Choose **Reports→Banking→Previous Reconciliation**.

2. Ensure **10000•Checking** is displayed and that the circle to the left of Detail is selected.

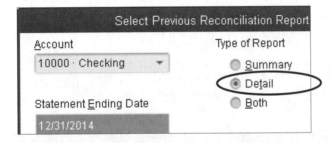

3. Click the **Display** button to produce the report.

   QuickBooks generates this report as a PDF file that can be saved, printed, or emailed.

4. Close the **Reconciliation Detail** report window.

Run a Register QuickReport
You will now create a report based on information contained within your Checking account.

5. Click the **Check Register** task icon in the Banking area of the Home page.

6. Click **OK** to choose the **10000•Checking** account.

   The Average Guy Designs Checking register will be displayed.

Check Register

7. Follow these steps to produce the register QuickReport:

Ⓐ Scroll up until the January transactions for **Professional Software Distributors** are visible; single-click anywhere within either of the transactions.

Ⓑ Click the **QuickReport** button on the toolbar.

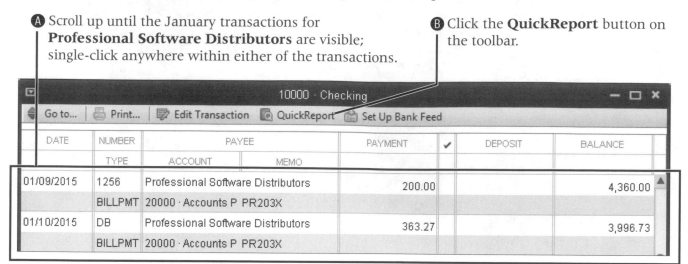

A report will be displayed that shows all of the transactions from the checking register for Professional Software Distributors. Notice the various buttons on the toolbar that you can use to print, email, export, and perform other tasks with this report. Leave this report open for the next step.

FROM THE KEYBOARD

Ctrl+q to display a QuickReport

Produce a PDF Copy of a Report

Now you will help Allison to save a PDF copy of this report. You will save it in your default file location.

8. Make sure that the QuickReport for **Professional Software Distributors** is still the active window, and then choose **File→Save as PDF** from the main QuickBooks menu bar.

A Save document as PDF window will appear.

9. Follow these steps to save a copy of the report as a PDF file:

Ⓐ Navigate to your file storage location.

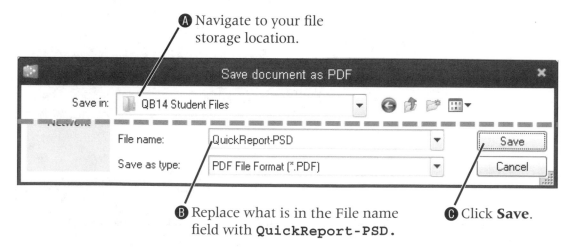

Ⓑ Replace what is in the File name field with **QuickReport-PSD**.

Ⓒ Click **Save**.

QuickBooks will process the command, saving a copy of the file to your default file location.

10. Choose **Window→Close All**.

Balance Sheet Reports

In Chapter 4, Working with Vendors, you learned how to produce one of the main company reports, Profit & Loss. In this section, you will look at another vital report, the balance sheet report.

Types of Accounts Displayed on a Balance Sheet Report

A balance sheet report displays all of your asset, liability, and equity accounts (hence the designation the "balance sheet accounts"). You can customize your report to show only the accounts you wish to display.

Average Guy Designs, Chapter 5
Balance Sheet
As of December 31, 2014

	◇ Dec 31, 14 ◇
ASSETS	
Current Assets	
Checking/Savings	
▶ 10000 · Checking	5,718.02 ◀
10200 · Savings	7,382.35
Total Checking/Savings	13,100.37
Accounts Receivable	
11000 · Accounts Receivable	2,680.00
Total Accounts Receivable	2,680.00
Total Current Assets	15,780.37
TOTAL ASSETS	15,780.37
LIABILITIES & EQUITY	
Liabilities	
Current Liabilities	
Accounts Payable	
20000 · Accounts Payable	563.27
Total Accounts Payable	563.27
Total Current Liabilities	563.27
Total Liabilities	563.27
Equity	
30000 · Opening Balance Equity	12,815.02
Net Income	2,402.08
Total Equity	15,217.10
TOTAL LIABILITIES & EQUITY	15,780.37

Average Guy Designs, Chapter 5
Balance Sheet
As of January 15, 2015

	◇ Jan 15, 15 ◇
▼ **ASSETS**	
▼ **Current Assets**	
▼ **Checking/Savings**	
▶ 10000 · Checking	3,766.73 ◀
10200 · Savings	8,382.35
Total Checking/Savings	12,149.08
▼ **Accounts Receivable**	
11000 · Accounts Receivable	2,920.00
Total Accounts Receivable	2,920.00
Total Current Assets	15,069.08
TOTAL ASSETS	15,069.08
LIABILITIES & EQUITY	
Liabilities	
Current Liabilities	
Accounts Payable	
20000 · Accounts Payable	48.22
Total Accounts Payable	48.22
Credit Cards	
21000 · Sunriver Credit Union Visa	78.63
Total Credit Cards	78.63
Total Current Liabilities	126.85
Total Liabilities	126.85
▼ **Equity**	
30000 · Opening Balance Equity	12,815.02
32000 · Owners Equity	2,402.08
Net Income	-274.87
Total Equity	14,942.23
TOTAL LIABILITIES & EQUITY	15,069.08

Note the balance sheet as of December 31, 2014 on the left compared to the one dated January 15, 2015 on the right. The Net Income has been "rolled" into Owner's Equity for you at the end of the accounting period and "starts over" at the beginning of the next one.

Visualize!

Tab: Reports
Topic: Balance sheet

Company Snapshot

The Company Snapshot window gives you a quick view of your company's bottom line in one convenient place. You can customize it to include "at-a-glance" reports that are most important to your company. The Company Snapshot can be accessed via a button on the Icon Bar or by choosing Reports→Company Snapshot from the menu bar. The Company Snapshot will show information only within a preset date range. If you don't see anything displayed, it is likely because the date for which you are performing the exercise is past the date range available through the snapshot.

 Tab: Reports
Topic: Company Snapshot

Browse for content panels to include in your Company Snapshot.

Bring back any removed panels, reset any date range changes, and remove any added panels.

These drop-down menus provide options to print, print preview, or save as an image your content panel data.

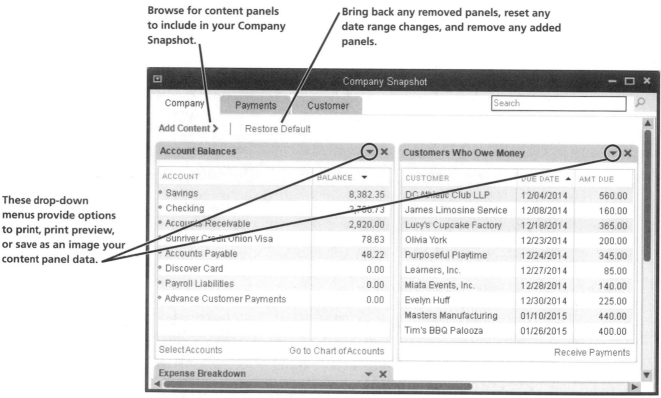

Information in the Company Snapshot is contained within content panels, each with its own Close button. You can customize the Company Snapshot to display information that is of value to you. Notice the three tabs at the top of the window that allow you to switch between the three snapshot views.

QUICK REFERENCE	WORKING WITH BALANCE SHEET REPORTS AND COMPANY SNAPSHOTS
Task	**Procedure**
Produce a balance sheet report	■ Choose Reports→Company & Financial→Balance Sheet Standard.
Produce a Company Snapshot	■ Choose Reports→Company Snapshot. ■ Customize the snapshot to meet your needs.

View a Balance Sheet Report and a Company Snapshot

In this exercise, you will create both a balance sheet report and a company snapshot for Average Guy Designs. When you create a balance sheet report, it will be based as of a certain date rather than for a period of time (as is the case for a Profit & Loss report).

1. Choose **Reports→Company & Financial→Balance Sheet Standard**.

2. Tap [Tab], type **123114**, and then tap [Tab] again.

   QuickBooks displays a balance sheet report showing the asset, liability, and equity account balances as of December 31, 2014.

3. Close the **Balance Sheet** window, choosing not to memorize the report.

Display and Customize the Company Snapshot

You will now help Allison to customize the Company Snapshot and then restore the default.

4. Choose **Reports→Company Snapshot**.

   Depending on the actual date that you perform this exercise, you may or may not have information displayed since all of the transactions we have entered up to this point are dated in December 2014/January 2015. Don't worry about the data displayed in the content panel for this exercise, but rather focus on how to manipulate it.

5. Follow these steps to remove a content panel from the snapshot:

Ⓐ Click the **Close** button to remove the Income and Expense Trend panel.

Ⓑ Click **OK** in the Remove Content window.

Notice that once you have removed the Income and Expense Trend panel, the Account Balances panel "snaps" up into the vacated space. You will now restore the default content panels to the snapshot.

6. Click the **Restore Default** link above the Account Balances panel.

7. Click **Yes** in the Restore Default window.

8. Close the **Company Snapshot** window.

9. Once you are finished learning about Banking Online with QuickBooks, choose the appropriate option for your situation:

   ■ If you will continue working, leave QuickBooks open.

   ■ If you are finished working in QuickBooks for now, choose **File→Exit**.

Working with QuickBooks Bank Feeds

There are a variety of tasks that can be carried out online with QuickBooks. With the 2014 version of QuickBooks, the online banking features have taken on a new name of "bank feeds." Bank feeds allow you to download transactions, view the transactions that have cleared your account, see your current balance, and add new transactions to QuickBooks from your financial institution. This feature allows you to save time from having to type in all your transactions, helps you to maintain better accuracy in your records, and also assists in cash flow management.

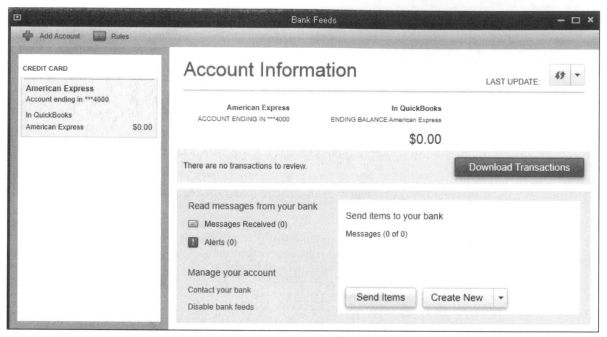

Once you have set up at least one bank feed in QuickBooks, the Bank Feeds Center will be available to you.

What you can do through bank feeds is determined by your financial institution, so you must check with it to verify what services are offered (or if any are offered at all). Also, there is no fee to use bank feeds in QuickBooks, but your financial institution may charge a fee for the service.

 Bank Feeds is a new QuickBooks feature that builds on and improves the previous online banking features.

Bank Feeds Exclusivity

In Chapter 2, Creating a Company, you learned about multi-user mode. If you do work on your company file with others, be aware that only one person at a time can be using bank feeds. The person who will be performing bank feed tasks must acquire exclusive use. If you are working in single-user mode, you do not need to acquire exclusivity as you already have it.

The Modes of Bank Feeds

You can choose how to work with your banking transactions through bank feeds as there are two different modes:

- **Express**—This mode is the new and improved QuickBooks online banking experience. In this mode, you work within the Transactions List window in order to match and add transactions, and renaming rules are created for you automatically.

- **Classic**—This mode is what was available in QuickBooks 2013 and earlier versions. In this mode, you work within account registers to match and add transactions, and you work with aliases to match names.

BANK FEEDS

View and enter downloaded transactions using:

⦿ Express Mode (new in QuickBooks 2014)

  ☑ Create rules automatically
  ☑ Always ask before creating a rule

○ Classic Mode (Register Mode)

You can choose to switch between the modes of bank feeds on the Company tab of the Checking category in the Edit Preferences window.

You do not have to choose one mode with which to work as you can switch between the two at any time. However, renaming rules from Express mode and aliases from Classic are not available in the other mode if you switch.

Bank Feeds and Reconciliation

Earlier in this chapter you learned about reconciling your QuickBooks records with the bank. When you use bank feeds you still must reconcile your accounts in the same way as you learned in this chapter. The advantage of reconciling when you use bank feeds, however, is that the majority (if not all) of your transactions have been matched already and reconciliation will be quicker. If you do have a discrepancy, then use the same problem-solving process outlined in this chapter to resolve it.

Setting Up Bank Feeds in QuickBooks

Before you can use the bank feeds feature in QuickBooks, you must complete any required applications with your financial institution(s) for your banking, credit card, or other eligible accounts. The set-up process involves four steps that QuickBooks will guide you through.

You will be able to match your bank accounts to your
QuickBooks account or create a new QuickBooks account here.

Note the four steps in the setup process.

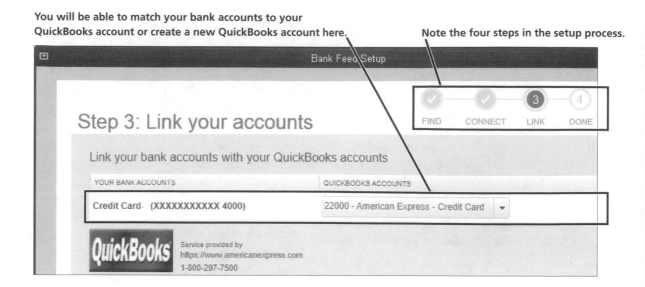

Matching and Recording Bank Feeds

Once you have set up bank feeds in QuickBooks, you will be able to download transactions from your financial institution(s), match them to transactions you have entered into QuickBooks, and properly record (remember you have to get it right behind the scenes!) new transactions that are not yet entered into QuickBooks.

Once QuickBooks is done downloading transactions in the Bank Feeds Center, you will see a link to the Transaction List and a summary of what your next step is.

QuickBooks attempts to match transactions for you by looking at check numbers, amounts, dates, and payees. You can also choose to unmatch or manually match a transaction if QuickBooks didn't get the matching right.

Recording Deposits

Many times your bank deposits comprise more than one payment, but it is recorded as one. Once you have downloaded your bank feeds, you will need to match the individual items in your register to the downloaded information. You will learn how to do this through the WebSim exercise in this section.

Recording Expenses

In the same way that you may have downloaded a deposit that doesn't match a single transaction in your QuickBooks register, you may also have a transaction that doesn't match an expense.

Record a Credit Card Transaction

Credit card transactions are treated the same as other banking transactions when working with bank feeds. You will need to create a bank feed for your QuickBooks credit card account(s) the same as you did for your bank accounts and then follow the procedures to match and record transactions once they have downloaded.

You can also choose multiple transactions and then process all of them as a batch.

You can choose what you wish to do with each transaction that you have downloaded in the Action column.

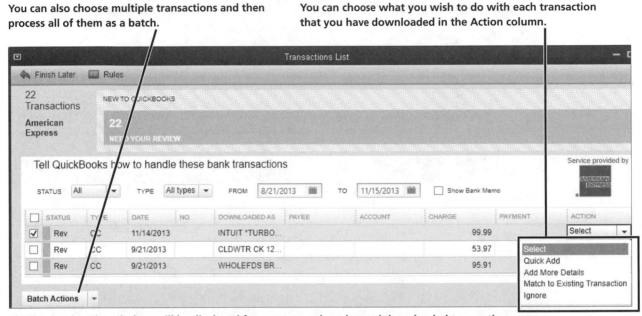

The Transaction List window will be displayed for you to match and record downloaded transactions.

Passing Notes with Your Financial Institution

If you have a direct connection with your financial institution, you can exchange messages back and forth with it. Make sure to pay attention to messages you have received, as some require you to complete a task before they can be deleted.

Electronic Invoice Payment Processing

Another feature available in QuickBooks is that you can email invoices to your customers and then receive payment from them electronically via the Internet. You will learn more about this invoicing and payment processing feature in *QuickBooks Pro 2014: Level 2*.

Making Vendor Payments with Bank Feeds

If your bank offers the service, you can make payments to your vendors through bank feeds as well. If your institution does not offer this service, you can still pay your bills through QuickBooks by using the QuickBooks Bill Pay Service that has you work with a vendor that partners with Intuit.

QuickBooks Doc Center

The Doc Center allows you to store electronic documents on your local computer, network drive, or other storage location accessible from your computer station that can be attached to your QuickBooks transactions and customer, vendor, and employee list items for no additional fee.

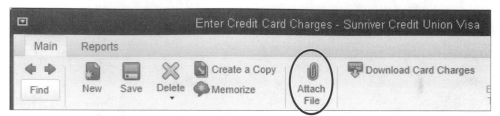

Notice the Attach buttons available in the Vendor Information area of the Vendor Center and on the toolbar of the Enter Credit Card Charges window.

QUICK REFERENCE	WORKING WITH BANK FEEDS AND THE DOC CENTER
Task	**Procedure**
Set up an account for online access	■ Contact your financial institution and find out what services they offer; complete an application, if necessary. ■ Choose Banking→Bank Feeds→Setup Bank Feed for an Account. ■ Progress through the steps in the Bank Feeds Setup interview.
Acquire exclusive use of Bank Feeds	■ Choose Banking→Bank Feeds→Acquire Exclusive Use.
Switch between bank feed modes	■ Choose Edit→Preferences. ■ Click the Checking category, and then display the Company Preferences tab. ■ In the Bank Feeds section, select the mode option; click OK.
Open the Doc Center	■ Choose Company→Documents→Doc Center.

Working with Web-based Simulations

The next exercise you will complete in this book will be a web-based simulation (WebSim) that requires you to have an Internet connection. With a WebSim, you will be working as if you were using QuickBooks; however, the exercise is actually being performed on a web page.

Work with Bank Feeds

WebSim   Work with Bank Feeds

1. Navigate to the Student Resource Center.

2. From the left navigation bar, click **Chapter 5**. In the main content window click **Develop Your Skills 5-10 Work with Bank Feeds.**

3. Follow the instructions on your screen.

Tackle the Tasks

Now is your chance to work a little more with Average Guy Designs and apply the skills that you have learned in this chapter to accomplish additional tasks. You will use the same company file you used in the Develop Your Skills exercises throughout this chapter. Enter the following tasks, referring back to the concepts in the chapter as necessary.

Create banking accounts	Use the following information to create two new accounts: 10400•Money Market; Sunriver Credit Union 22000•American Express
Make a deposit	On 1/5/15, Guy traveled to a local business and provided assistance to the owner who was trying to edit a video. He received $250 cash and chose to not enter the customer in QuickBooks. Deposit the funds from this transaction to Checking on the same day.
Transfer funds	On 1/5/15, transfer $1,000 from Checking to Money Market.
Enter credit card transactions	Enter the following Sunriver Credit Union Visa transactions: On 1/7/15, purchased a customer appreciation lunch from Home Place Pizzeria (add as a new vendor) for $65.11, using the 64300•Meals and Entertainment account. On 1/8/15, purchased a new computer mouse from Ricky's Electric City for $49.52, using 64900•Office Supplies as the account. On 1/9/15, took a new client out to lunch at Bayshore Café for $39.12, using 64300•Meals and Entertainment as the account. On 1/10/15, paid $75.00 to Handyman by the Bay for work he did to wire Allison's new workstation, using 67200•Repairs and Maintenance as the account. On 1/10/15, returned the computer mouse to Ricky's Electric City.
Reconcile a credit card	Now it is time to reconcile your Sunriver Credit Union Visa credit card. From the Student Resource Center, open the file labeled Credit Card Statement. Once you have reconciled the credit card, choose to enter a bill for payment later (QuickAdd Sunriver Credit Union as a vendor) and create a summary reconciliation report.
Produce reports	Display a summary previous reconciliation report for the Checking account. Display a balance sheet detail report as of 12/31/14.

```
                    Sunriver Credit Union
                       487 Merrifield Lane
                       Bayshore, CA 91547

Visa Statement Prepared For:
   Average Guy Designs
   110 Sampson Way
   Bayshore, CA 91547

                          Account Number: XXXX XXXX XXXX 7777

            Statement Period: December 13, 2014 - January 12, 2015
   Total                                    Total
   Charges:    $317.84                      Payments:      $59.98
   Beginning                                Ending
    Balance:    $0.00                        Balance:     $257.86

Transactions:
   Date          Description        Charge    Credit    Balance
               Beginning Balance                         $0.00
   1/3/2015    Allen Brothers Grocery   89.09            $89.09
   1/6/2015    Allen Brothers Grocery            10.46   $78.63
   1/7/2015    Home Place Pizzaria      65.11            $143.74
   1/8/2015    Ricky's Electric City    49.52            $193.26
   1/9/2015    Bayshore Café            39.12            $232.38
   1/10/2015   Handyman by the Bay      75.00            $307.38
   1/10/2015   Ricky's Electric City             49.52   $257.86
   1/12/2015   Periodic Finance Charge    0              $257.86
               Ending Balance                            $257.86
```

Concepts Review

To test your knowledge of the key concepts introduced in this chapter, complete the Concepts Review quiz on the Student Resource Center.

Reinforce Your Skills

Angela Stevens has just relocated her company, Quality-Built Construction, from California to Silverton, Oregon. You will be working with a QuickBooks Sample Company File in this exercise as it will allow you to run full payroll in a future chapter without having to purchase a payroll subscription.

Before you begin the Reinforce Your Skills exercises, complete one of these options:

- Open **RYS_Chapter05** from your file storage location.

- Restore **RYS_Chapter05 (Portable)** from your file storage location. For a reminder of how to restore a portable company file, see Develop Your Skills 3-1. Add your last name and first initial to the end of the filename.

REINFORCE YOUR SKILLS 5-1
Work with Bank Accounts and Make a Deposit

In this exercise, you will take care of the banking tasks for Quality-Built Construction. Since Angela's business checking account does not earn interest, she has decided to open a money market account. You will begin by helping her to set up this account.

1. Choose **Lists→Chart of Accounts**.

2. Click the **Account** menu button and choose **New**.

3. Choose **Bank** as the account type, and then click **Continue**.

4. Type **Company Money Market Account** as the new account name, and **1150** as the account number.

5. Click **Save & Close**, choosing **No** in the Set Up a Bank Feed window.

6. Close the **Chart of Accounts** window.

Move Funds Between Accounts

Since the money market account earns interest, Angela has decided to transfer some funds from her checking account into it.

7. Choose **Banking→Transfer Funds**.

8. Set the date to **1/2/19**.

9. Choose **Company Checking Account** as the Transfer Funds From account.

10. Choose **Company Money Market Account** as the Transfer Funds To account.

11. Type **80000** as the transfer amount.

12. Click **Save & Close** to record the transfer and close the window.

Make Deposits

Angela did a presentation for a local organization on the steps you need to take prior to building a new home. She needs to deposit the fee she earned into her checking account along with the funds that are currently in the Undeposited Funds account. You will do this in two separate steps.

13. Choose **Banking→Make Deposits**.

14. Select all of the payments in the **Payments to Deposit** window, and then click **OK**.

15. Ensure **Checking** is the Deposit To account. Click **OK** if the default account information window appears in order to acknowledge it and move to the Make Deposits window.

16. Set the deposit date as **1/03/19**, and then click **Save & New**.

17. Change the Date for the next deposit to **1/4/19**, tap Tab, and then type **Presentation** as the memo.

18. Click in the **From Account** column, and then type **consu** to fill in **Consultation Income** as the income account.

Remember, you do not have to enter a customer, but you must enter an income account!

19. Enter the payment in the form of a check: number **753** for **$800**.

Your screen should resemble the following illustration.

20. Click **Save & Close** to record the transaction and close the window.

Reconcile a Bank Account

The bank statement has just arrived. In this exercise, you will reconcile Quality-Built Construction's Company Checking Account. You may print your own statement (Reinforce Your Skills 5-2 Bank Statement) from your file storage location or refer to the illustration shown after step 2.

1. Choose **Banking→Reconcile**.

2. Use the back statement to reconcile the Checking account for Angela.

Tradesman Credit Union

Statement of Account Prepared For:	Account Number: 555-777
Quality-Built Construction	Statement Period: December 1 - 31, 2018
Angela Stevens	
316 Maple Street	
Silverton, OR 97381	

Total Deposits:	$33,500.00		Total Payments:	$120,253.43
Beginning Balance:	$186,145.28		Ending Balance:	$99,391.85

Date	Transaction type	Payment	Deposit	Balance
	Beginning Balance			$186,145.28
12/4/2018	Check #11327	27.05		$186,118.23
12/5/2018	Check #11329	35,034.00		$151,084.23
12/5/2018	Check #11328	24,098.00		$126,986.23
12/5/2018	Check #113342	11,986.00		$115,000.23
12/5/2018	Check #11341	4,521.00		$110,479.23
12/5/2018	Check #11337	3,567.09		$106,912.14
12/5/2018	Check #11332	3,400.00		$103,512.14
12/5/2018	Check #11333	2,790.03		$100,722.11
12/5/2018	Check #11338	2,380.00		$98,342.11
12/5/2018	Check #11330	2,350.00		$95,992.11
12/5/2018	Check #11331	1,250.00		$94,742.11
12/5/2018	Check #11344	936.00		$93,806.11
12/5/2018	Check #11340	400.00		$93,406.11
12/5/2018	Check #11334	227.00		$93,179.11
12/5/2018	Check #11336	185.00		$92,994.11
12/5/2018	Check #11339	180.00		$92,814.11
12/5/2018	Check #11335	100.00		$92,714.11
12/5/2018	Check #11343	12.00		$92,702.11
12/5/2018	Transfer	6,100.00		$86,602.11
12/8/2018	Check #10769	999.42		$85,602.69
12/15/2018	Check #10768	200.00		$85,402.69
12/15/2018	Deposit		33,500.00	$118,902.69
12/15/2018	Check #11345	32.05		$118,870.64
12/18/2018	Check #11351	4,800.00		$114,070.64
12/20/2018	Check #11346	2,300.00		$111,770.64
12/20/2018	Check #11347	1,635.02		$110,135.62
12/20/2018	Check #11349	1,364.55		$108,771.07
12/20/2018	Check #11350	512.22		$108,258.85
12/20/2018	Check #11348	227.00		$108,031.85
12/20/2018	Check #11352	180.00		$107,851.85
12/22/2018	Transfer	8,100.00		$99,751.85
12/23/2018	Check #11355	100.00		$99,651.85
12/26/2018	Check #11356	250.00		$99,401.85
12/31/2018	Service Charge	10.00		$99,391.85
	Ending Balance			$99,391.85

Pay attention to the following hints when you reconcile:

- *Make sure to set the reconciliation date to 12/31/2018.*

- *In the Begin Reconciliation window, make sure to enter the ending balance and the service charge.*

- *In the Reconcile-Checking window, make sure to mark only those transactions that have cleared the bank (and are on the bank statement) and that have zero differences before you click Reconcile Now.*

- *If the difference is not zero, see the Problem Resolution Process section on page 184.*

3. Choose to not create a reconciliation report now.

Manage Credit Card Transactions

In this exercise, you will help Angela to set up and use her new Visa credit card in QuickBooks.

1. If necessary, choose **Lists→Chart of Accounts**.

2. Click the **Account** menu button and choose **New** from the context menu.

3. Choose **Credit Card** as the account type, and then click **Continue**.

4. Name the new account **2070•Marion CU Visa**.

5. Click **Save & Close** to enter the new account and close the window, choosing **No** when asked if you want to set up bank feed services.

Enter a Credit Card Charge

Angela is purchasing oil filters for the business vehicles. She is not sure of the exact filter for one of the trucks, so she will purchase two and return one of them later.

6. Choose **Banking→Enter Credit Card Charges**, and ensure that the **Marion CU Visa** is selected.

7. Tap Tab three times, and then type **Auto Supply Warehouse** as the vendor. Tap Tab again, and then choose to **Quick Add** the store as a vendor.

8. Set the date to **1/2/19**, tap Tab twice, and then type **$150** as the amount.

9. Click in the **Account** column and choose **6101•Gas and Oil** as the expense account.

10. Click **Save & New** to record the transaction.

Enter a Credit Card Credit

Now you will process the return for Angela. The Enter Credit Card Charges window should still be open from the last step; if it isn't, choose Banking→Record Credit Card Charges→Enter Credit Card Charges.

11. Choose **Auto Supply Warehouse** as the vendor.

12. Set the date to **1/4/19**.

13. Choose the **Refund/Credit** option to show it is a return.

14. Type **$30** as the amount and ensure that **6101•Gas and Oil** is the account.

15. Click **Save & Close** to record the refund and close the window.

Produce Banking and Balance Sheet Reports

Angela wants to run some banking reports to get answers from hers data. In this exercise, you will help her to do just that. Angela has already performed the reconciliation, and she asks you to print the reconciliation report.

1. Choose **Reports→Banking→Previous Reconciliation**.

2. Choose to create a **Summary** report for the reconciliation you just performed (statement ending date of 12/31/2018).

3. Click **Display** to produce the report.

4. Preview how the report will print, and then close the **Reconciliation Summary** window.

Run a Deposit Detail Report

Angela would like to see all of her bank deposits for December, so she will run a report to display them.

5. Choose **Reports→Banking→Deposit Detail**.

6. Tap ⎡Tab⎤, and then type **120118**; tap ⎡Tab⎤, and then type **123118**.

7. Click the Refresh button on the report toolbar.

   You will see a report that displays the details for each deposit in December.

If you tap ⎡Tab⎤ after changing the date, QuickBooks will automatically refresh the report for you, too.

8. Choose **File→Save as PDF**.

9. Choose to save a copy of the report in your default storage location, naming it **December 2018 Deposits**.

10. Close the **Deposit Details** report window, clicking **No** when asked to memorize the report.

Display a Balance Sheet Report

11. Choose **Reports→Company & Financial→Balance Sheet Standard**.

12. Tap ⎡a⎤ to change the date range to **All**.

13. Choose **Window→Close All**.

14. Choose the appropriate option for your situation:
    - If you will continue working, leave QuickBooks open.
    - If you are finished working in QuickBooks for now, choose **File→Exit**.

Apply Your Skills

Before you begin the Apply Your Skills exercises, complete one of these options:

- *Open* **AYS_Chapter05** *from your file storage location.*
- *Restore* **AYS_Chapter05 (Portable)** *from your file storage location. For a reminder of how to restore a portable company file, see Develop Your Skills 3-1. Add your last name and first initial to the end of the filename.*

APPLY YOUR SKILLS 5-1
Manage Banking and Deposits

In this exercise, you will help Dr. James with some basic banking tasks.

1. Open the **Chart of Accounts** and create two new accounts for Wet Noses: a bank account named `Money Market` and a credit card account named `American Express`. Choose to not set up online services for either account.

2. Open the **Make Deposits** window and choose to deposit all four payments from the Undeposited Funds account into your Checking account on 6/8/14.

3. Open the **Transfer Funds** window and transfer $30,000 from Checking to Money Market on 6/10/14.

APPLY YOUR SKILLS 5-2
Enter Credit Card Transactions

In this exercise, you will enter transactions into the credit card account you just created.

1. Open the Enter Credit Card Charges window.

2. Enter the following **American Express** charges for the month.

   Quick Add any vendors not on the Vendor List and use your best judgment in selecting an expense account.

Date	Vendor	Amount	Memo
6/1/14	Thrifty Grocery	$26.73	Bottled water and soda for office
6/4/14	Glen's Handyman Service	$108.70	Office repairs
6/4/14	Malimali Hardware Store	$43.20	Supplies for office repairs
6/8/14	Labyrinth Veterinary Publications	$94.85	Reference books
6/11/14	Thrifty Grocery	$18.49	Refreshments for office
6/14/14	Bothell Pet Supply Co.	$115.43	Boarding supplies
6/14/14	Karel's Gardening Service	$60.00	Monthly garden maintenance
6/20/14	Beezer Computer Repair	$145.00	Computer repair
6/20/14	Bothell Pet Supply Co.	-$38.29	Return-Boarding supplies
6/22/14	Laura's Café	30.21	Business lunch with partner

3. Close the **Enter Credit Card Charges** window when you are finished.

Deal with a Returned Check

In this exercise, you will help Dr. James to account for check #6666 from Mary Ann Gulch for $145.65 that was returned for non-sufficient funds.

1. Choose **Customers→Receive Payments**.

2. Click the **Previous** button until the bounced check used to pay invoice **167** is displayed.

3. Click the Record Bounced Check button.

Enter the Fee Information

4. Enter a **Bank Fee** of **$25** on **6/6/2014**, using **Bank Service Charges** as the account.

5. Enter a **Customer Fee** of $45.

Reconcile a Credit Card Account

In this exercise, you will reconcile the American Express account.

1. Open the **Chart of Accounts** and begin the process to reconcile the **American Express** account using the following illustration.

American Express
6539 Beck Place
New York, NY 07852

Credit Card Statement Prepared For:
Wet Noses Veterinary Clinic
589 Retriever Drive
Bothell, WA 98011

Account Number: 3333-888888-55555

Statement Period: May 21 - June 20, 2014

Total Charges:	612.40		Total Credits:	$38.29
Beginning Balance:	$0.00		Ending Balance:	$574.11

Transactions:

Date	Description	Charge	Credit	Balance
	Beginning Balance			$0.00
5/1/2014	Thrifty Grocery	26.73		$26.73
5/4/2014	Glen's Handyman	108.70		$135.43
5/4/2014	Malimali Hardware Store	43.20		$178.63
5/8/2014	Laby Vet Pub	94.85		$273.48
5/11/2014	Thrifty Grocery	18.49		$291.97
5/14/2014	Bothell Pet Supply	115.43		$407.40
5/14/2014	Murray Gardening Service	60.00		$467.40
5/20/2014	Beezer Computer	145.00		$612.40
6/20/2014	Bothell Pet Supply		38.29	$574.11
	Periodic Finance Charge	0		$574.11
	Ending Balance			$574.11

---

2. When you have completed the reconciliation, write a check to **American Express** for the entire amount on 6/22/2014, choosing for it to be printed later. Then, display a **summary reconciliation report**.

Answer Questions with Reports

In this exercise, you will answer questions for Dr. James by running reports. You may wish to display the Report Center in List View to help you answer the questions. Ask your instructor if you should print the reports, print (save) them as PDF files, export them to Excel, or simply display them on the screen.

1. What are the details of the checks that have been written during June 2014?

2. Which transactions were cleared and which were not cleared when the American Express account was reconciled?

3. Is it possible to get a detailed list of all deposits for June 2014?

4. Are there any missing or duplicate check numbers in the Checking account?

5. What is the balance of all of the balance sheet accounts as of June 22, 2014?

6. Submit your reports based on the guidelines provided by your instructor.

7. Choose the appropriate option for your situation:

- If you will continue working, leave QuickBooks open.
- If you are finished working in QuickBooks for now, choose **File→Exit**.

Extend Your Skills

In the course of working through the following Expand Your Skills exercises, you will be utilizing various skills taught in this and previous chapter(s). Take your time and think carefully about the tasks presented to you. Turn back to the chapter content if you need assistance.

5-1 Sort Through the Stack

Before You Begin: Restore the EYS1_Chapter05 (Portable) file or open the EYS1_Chapter05 company file from your storage location.

You have been hired by Arlaine Cervantes to help her with her organization's books. She is the founder of Niños del Lago, a non-profit organization that provides impoverished Guatemalan children with an engaging educational camp experience. You have just sat down at your desk and opened a large envelope from her with a variety of documents and noticed that you have several emails from her as well. It is your job to sort through the papers and emails and make sense of what you find, entering information into QuickBooks whenever appropriate and answering any other questions in a word-processing document saved as **EYS1_Chapter05_ LastnameFirstinitial**. Remember, you are digging through papers you just dumped out of an envelope and addressing random emails from Arlaine, so it is up to you to determine the correct order in which to complete the tasks.

- Scribbled on a scrap of paper: I looked at QuickBooks and saw money in an account called "Undeposited Funds." Why isn't it in the Checking account? Can you move it for me? I deposited those funds into the Checking account on 7/11/2014!

- New credit card document on desk: From Jasper State Bank, number 7777 2222 0000 2938, $7,500 credit limit.

- Note: Opened a new Money Market bank account at Jasper State Bank on 7/10/14. Transferred $1,000 from Savings to fund the new account. Need QuickBooks account set up.

- Bank deposit slip: Check #2323 dated 7/14/2014 for a $2,500 deposit to Checking. Handwritten message on slip reads, "From Hanson Family Trust."

- Credit card receipt: Dated 7/15/2014; for office supplies; $75.11; paid to Supplies Online.

- Note: Would you please create a report that shows all of the activity in the Checking account for July 2014 and save it as a PDF file so I can email it to the accountant?

- Bank deposit slip: Dated 7/30/2014 for $750; handwritten on slip, check #1835 from Lakeside Christian School for remaining balance due.

- Credit card receipt: Dated 7/23/2014; payable to Casey's Service Station; for auto fuel; amount of $35.61. (Hint: This is for travel to a workshop site.)

- Scribbled note from Arlaine: Can you produce a report for me that shows the balances for all of the asset, liability, and equity accounts as of 7/31/2014?

5-2 Be Your Own Boss

Before You Begin: Complete Extend Your Skills 4-2 before starting this exercise.

In this exercise, you will build on the company file that you outlined and created in previous chapters. If you have created a file for your actual business, then enter your bank and credit card accounts and deposit any funds waiting in Undeposited Funds; complete any fund transfers between accounts and enter all credit and debit card transactions; enter any bounced checks; finally, use the bank statements received from your financial institution and reconcile all accounts. If you are creating a fictitious company, then create at least two banking accounts and one credit card account. Deposit all funds received in Chapter 4 into a bank account and transfer funds between your two bank accounts; account for a bounced check. You will make up the names and information for this exercise.

Create Balance Sheet and Deposit Detail reports and submit them to your instructor based on the instructions provided.

Open the company file you worked on in Extend Your Skills 4-2 and complete the tasks outlined above. When you are done, save it as a portable company file, naming it as **EYS2_Chapter05_ LastnameFirstinitial (Portable)** and submit it to your instructor based on the instructions provided.

5-3 Use the Web as a Learning Tool

Throughout this book, you will be provided with an opportunity to use the Internet as a learning tool by completing WebQuests. According to the original creators of WebQuests, as described on their website (http://WebQuest.org), a WebQuest is "an inquiry-oriented activity in which most or all of the information used by learners is drawn from the web." To complete the WebQuest projects in this book, navigate to the Student Resource Center and choose the WebQuest for the chapter on which you are working. The subject of each WebQuest will be relevant to the material found in the chapter.

WebQuest Subject: Online banking with QuickBooks

Need to Know Accounting

Even though QuickBooks does everything for you "behind the scenes," it is important that you have a basic understanding of what is happening to your books.

In this appendix, you will learn about the basic financial statements important to any business and the accounts that appear on these reports. You will also learn about the double-entry accounting system and the debits and credits that must always be equal.

Working with Financial Statements

There are two main reports that a company will produce periodically to illustrate its financial well-being.

- A **Balance Sheet** report displays all of the holdings of the company along with the debts as of a particular date.
- An **Income Statement**, otherwise known as a Profit & Loss Report, displays the income and expenses for a specified period of time.

Understanding the accounts that make up each of these reports is key to understanding your company's books.

The Accounting Equation and the Balance Sheet

The first equation you need to learn when it comes to accounting is simply termed the accounting equation:

$$Assets = Liabilities + Equity$$

This means that if you take all of your company's debt and add any investments (equity), you will have a value equal to all of the assets that your company owns.

A balance sheet is a financial statement that displays all asset, liability, and equity accounts (the balance sheet accounts). Take a look at the following illustrations to see how the accounting equation works and is represented in a balance sheet.

Average Guy Designs
Balance Sheet
As of February 28, 2015

	◇ Feb 28, 15 ◇
▼ ASSETS	
▼ Current Assets	
▼ Checking/Savings	
10000 · Checking	1,269.38
10200 · Savings	3,382.35
10400 · Money Market	1,000.00
10500 · Petty Cash	247.76
Total Checking/Savings	5,899.49
▼ Accounts Receivable	
11000 · Accounts Receivable	250.00
Total Accounts Receivable	250.00
▼ Other Current Assets	
12100 · Inventory Asset	1,379.00
13200 · Prepaid Rent	3,500.00
13300 · Prepaid Insurance	875.00
Total Other Current Assets	5,754.00
Total Current Assets	11,903.49
▼ Fixed Assets	
15000 · Furniture and Equipment	2,639.00
16000 · Vehicles	4,500.00
Total Fixed Assets	7,139.00
TOTAL ASSETS	**19,042.49**

▼ LIABILITIES & EQUITY	
▼ Liabilities	
▼ Current Liabilities	
▼ Other Current Liabilities	
24000 · Payroll Liabilities	24.60
25000 · Customer Deposits	300.00
Total Other Current Liabilities	324.60
Total Current Liabilities	324.60
▼ Long Term Liabilities	
26000 · Loan - Vehicles (Vespa - 1)	4,050.00
28300 · Loan -Office Furniture	2,639.00
Total Long Term Liabilities	6,689.00
Total Liabilities	7,013.60
▼ Equity	
30000 · Opening Balance Equity	12,815.02
32000 · Owners Equity	2,402.08
Net Income	-3,188.21
Total Equity	12,028.89
TOTAL LIABILITIES & EQUITY	**19,042.49**

Notice that the amount for Total Liabilities & Equity is $19,042.49.

Notice that the amount for Total Assets is also $19,042.49.

The upper section (displayed here on the left) represents the left side of the accounting equation and displays all assets. The lower section (displayed here on the right) represents the right side of the accounting equation and displays all liability and equity accounts.

The Income Statement

The accounts that you find on the Income Statement (or Profit & Loss report) are income and expense. In the following illustration you can view an Income Statement and the accounts that appear on it.

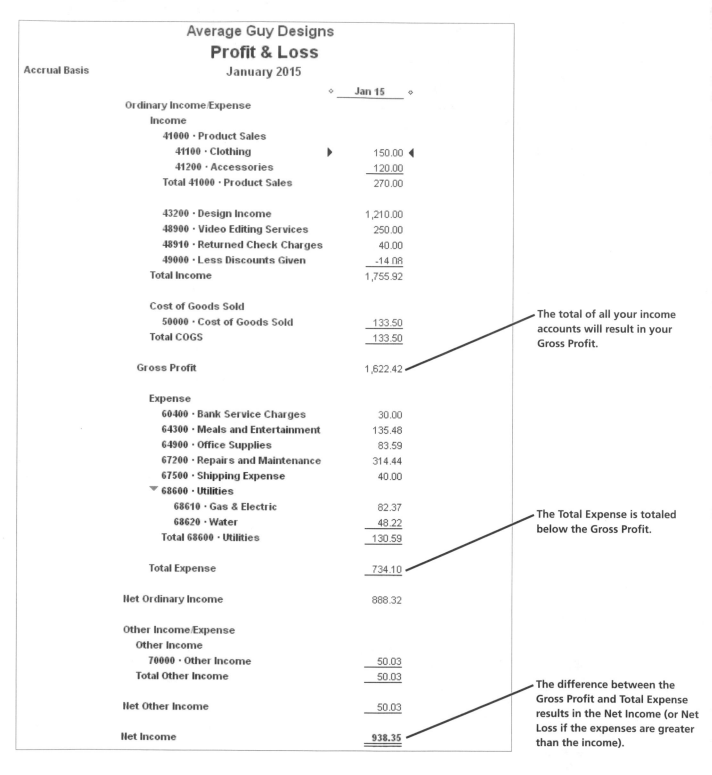

Average Guy Designs
Profit & Loss
January 2015

Accrual Basis

	Jan 15
Ordinary Income/Expense	
Income	
41000 · Product Sales	
41100 · Clothing	150.00
41200 · Accessories	120.00
Total 41000 · Product Sales	270.00
43200 · Design Income	1,210.00
48900 · Video Editing Services	250.00
48910 · Returned Check Charges	40.00
49000 · Less Discounts Given	-14.08
Total Income	1,755.92
Cost of Goods Sold	
50000 · Cost of Goods Sold	133.50
Total COGS	133.50
Gross Profit	1,622.42
Expense	
60400 · Bank Service Charges	30.00
64300 · Meals and Entertainment	135.48
64900 · Office Supplies	83.59
67200 · Repairs and Maintenance	314.44
67500 · Shipping Expense	40.00
68600 · Utilities	
68610 · Gas & Electric	82.37
68620 · Water	48.22
Total 68600 · Utilities	130.59
Total Expense	734.10
Net Ordinary Income	888.32
Other Income/Expense	
Other Income	
70000 · Other Income	50.03
Total Other Income	50.03
Net Other Income	50.03
Net Income	938.35

The total of all your income accounts will result in your Gross Profit.

The Total Expense is totaled below the Gross Profit.

The difference between the Gross Profit and Total Expense results in the Net Income (or Net Loss if the expenses are greater than the income).

Debits and Credits: The Double-Entry Accounting System

There is another equation in accounting that is paramount for us to keep in mind: Debits must always equal credits! Most people who do not work in the accounting field are confused about debits and credits, though.

Accounts are often displayed in a "T" format in accounting (which you can see in all of the Behind the Scenes sections of this book). The T accounts allow you to place the name of the account on the top, account debits on the left side, and account credits on the right side. This means that the left side (debits) must always equal the right side (credits) when entering accounting transactions (hence the term "double-entry").

Account Name	
Debit Side	Credit Side

A simple way to view an account is to use the T format.

In order to understand debits and credits a bit better, we will now look at the types of accounts and their normal balances.

Types of Accounts and Normal Balances

We have looked at the two main financial statements and the types of accounts included in each. The balance sheet is composed of asset, liability, and equity accounts. The income statement is composed of income and expense accounts. Before we look deeper into each account type, it is important to understand normal balances.

Take a look at Chapter 2, Creating a Company, to view all of the account sub-types that you can create in QuickBooks.

About Normal Balances

Each type of account must have a normal balance of either a debit or a credit. The normal balance is the side that will increase the amount of the account. Assets and expenses both have debit normal balances and will increase when debited and decrease when credited. Liabilities, equity, and income all have credit normal balances and will increase when credited and decrease when debited.

The concept of normal balances makes sense if you think of the balance sheet. Assets with a debit normal balance must equal the sum of the liabilities and equity, which both have a credit normal balance. Think of this as the marriage of the accounting equation and the fact that debits must equal credits!

The following table describes the primary account types and their normal balances.

Account Type	Description
Assets	An asset is anything that a company owns or monies that are owed to the company. Examples of assets are checking accounts, accounts receivable, and autos. Assets have a debit normal balance.
Liabilities	A liability is something that a company owes such as an auto loan or a credit card balance. Liabilities have a credit normal balance.
Equity	Equity accounts are both investments into the company (Owner's Equity or Stockholder's Equity) and the net income or loss from the operation of a business (Retained Earnings). Equity accounts have a credit normal balance.
Income	Income accounts reflect the sales and fees earned during an accounting period. Income accounts have a credit normal balance.
Expenses	Expense accounts record the expenditures that a company accrues while conducting business. Expense accounts have a debit normal balance.

The Trial Balance Report

At the end of an accounting cycle a trial balance is prepared that shows all accounts affected during the cycle. The balance of each account is entered in the appropriate column based on its normal balance. The net income or net loss is the difference between income and expenses. If the income is greater than the expenses, an excess credit balance will result and will increase the equity account (a net income). If the expenses are greater than the income, an excess debit balance will result and will decrease the equity account (a net loss).

```
                      Average Guy Designs
                        Trial Balance
                     As of February 28, 2015

                                            Feb 28, 15
                                    ◇   Debit   ◇   Credit   ◇
   10000 · Checking                  ▶ 1,269.38 ◀
   10200 · Savings                     3,382.35
   10400 · Money Market                1,000.00
   10500 · Petty Cash                    247.76
   11000 · Accounts Receivable             0.00
   12000 · Undeposited Funds              0.00
   12100 · Inventory Asset             1,379.00
   13200 · Prepaid Rent                3,500.00
   13300 · Prepaid Insurance            875.00
   15000 · Furniture and Equipment    2,639.00
   16000 · Vehicles                   4,500.00
   20000 · Accounts Payable              0.00
   21000 · Sunriver Credit Union Visa    0.00
   24000 · Payroll Liabilities                        24.60
   25000 · Customer Deposits                          300.00
   25500 · Sales Tax Payable             0.00
   26000 · Loan - Vehicles (Vespa - 1)             4,050.00
   28300 · Loan -Office Furniture                   2,639.00
   30000 · Opening Balance Equity                  12,815.02
   32000 · Owners Equity                              85.35
   41100 · Clothing                                  150.00
   41200 · Accessories                               120.00
   43200 · Design Income                           3,200.00
   48800 · Print Layout Income                       200.00
   48900 · Video Editing Services                    690.00
   48910 · Returned Check Charges                     40.00
   49000 · Less Discounts Given          16.70
   50000 · Cost of Goods Sold           133.50
   60300 · Bad Debt Expense             345.00
   60400 · Bank Service Charges          30.00
   61700 · Computer and Internet Expenses 563.27
   63300 · Insurance Expense            175.00
   64300 · Meals and Entertainment      169.23
   64900 · Office Supplies               83.59
   66100 · Company-Paid Benefits        203.50
   66200 · Company-Paid Taxes           188.20
   66300 · Gross Wages                2,460.00
   67100 · Rent Expense                 700.00
   67200 · Repairs and Maintenance      314.44
   67500 · Shipping Expense              58.49
   68610 · Gas & Electric                82.37
   68620 · Water                         48.22
   70000 · Other Income                                50.03
   TOTAL                              24,364.00    24,364.00
```

The debits and credits in a Trial Balance must be equal.

Finding Additional Accounting Resources

Want to learn more about what happens to your company's books behind the scenes in QuickBooks? Visit the student resource center to explore a variety of online learning resources or purchase a copy of *Accounting Basics: An Introduction for Non-Accounting Majors*, which is also published by Labyrinth Learning.

Glossary

accountant's copy A special copy of your QuickBooks file that can be created if your accountant needs to make adjustments to your QuickBooks file, but you do not want to lose access to it while it is being adjusted

accounting cycle A series of steps to help a business keep its accounting records properly during the fiscal period

accrual basis In the accrual basis of accounting, income is recorded when the sale is made and expenses recorded when accrued; often used by firms or businesses with large inventories

activities Affect what is happening behind the scenes; can be easily input into forms such as invoices or bills

administrator QuickBooks user who controls the access of all users of a QuickBooks file; administrator also controls all company preferences in the Edit Preferences window

assets Anything owned by a company or that is owed to a company; items such as a checking account, a building, a prepaid insurance account, or accounts receivable

audit trail Allows you to track every entry, modification, or deletion to transactions in your file; accessed through the Accounting category in the Report Center or the Report option on the menu bar

Average Cost A method of inventory tracking where the value of the inventory is determined by dividing the total value of the inventory by the total number of inventory items

backup The process of creating a condensed copy of your QuickBooks file to ensure you don't lose your data or to allow yourself or another person the ability to view your company file on another computer

bad debt Funds owed to you that are not collectable and need to be written off

balance sheet accounts The asset, liability, and equity accounts, such as bank, credit card, current liabilities (sales tax payable and payroll liabilities), accounts receivable, accounts payable, and retained earnings

Balance Sheet by Class Report Balance sheet report on which each class appears as a separate column; should be used only by expert users

balance sheet report A report that displays all assets, liabilities, and equity as of a specific date

batch invoicing Feature that lets a user create invoices that are basically the same for multiple customers at one time

batch timesheets Feature that allows you to create timesheets for multiple employees who work the same hours on the same jobs and using the same payroll item(s)

behind the scenes The accounting that QuickBooks performs for you when you enter transactions

bounced check A check returned by the bank due to non-sufficient funds in the account; also called a "NSF" check

browser A software application used to locate and display web pages, such as Netscape Navigator and Microsoft Internet Explorer

Budget In QuickBooks, create a budget for your company either from scratch or based on actual values from a previous period

cash basis In the cash basis of accounting, income is recorded when cash is received and expenses recorded when cash is paid; commonly used by small businesses and professionals

Cash Flow Forecast A report that gives you a glimpse of what you can expect a company's cash flow to look like in the near future based on current data in the company file

centers QuickBooks has four centers: Customer, Employee, Report, and Vendor; centers allow you to view the Customers & Jobs, Employee, and Vendor lists, access QuickBooks reports, and view snapshots of information (of an individual customer, vendor, or employee)

classes Classes are used to rate; not tied to any particular customer, vendor, or item; used to track only one particular aspect of your business, such as location or individual programs

closing the books During this process at the end of your fiscal year, QuickBooks transfers the net income or net loss to Retained Earnings, restricts access to transactions prior to the closing date (unless you know the password), and allows you to clean up your company data; you are not required to "close the books" in QuickBooks

company file The QuickBooks file you use when working with your company's day-to-day operations

company setup Takes you through the steps necessary to set up a new company in QuickBooks

Company Snapshot A window that offers a quick view of your company's bottom line in one convenient place

Contributed reports Feature that allows you to look for a report submitted by another user so you don't have to "reinvent the wheel"; you can also share your custom reports with this feature

Customers & Jobs List A list in QuickBooks that stores all information related to your customers and the jobs associated with them

Customer & Vendor Profile Lists Lists QuickBooks provides to track customer and vendor information

Depreciation Provides a business with a way to match income to expenses; a fixed asset is used to produce income over a period of time, and depreciation allows you to record the appropriate expense for the same period; many small businesses record depreciation transactions just once a year, but they can be entered monthly or quarterly if the business produces financial statements for those periods

Doc Center Feature that allows you to store your source documents electronically, attaching them to the transactions or list entries to which they belong

draw An owner's withdrawal of funds from the company

edition Intuit creates a multitude of editions of QuickBooks to choose from: QuickBooks Online, QuickBooks Pro, QuickBooks Premier, and QuickBooks Enterprise

electronic payments   Some companies receive payments from customers electronically; they can be handled by using a new payment type called Electronic Payment

Employees List   A list in QuickBooks that helps you to keep track of your employee data; can be used as a source of information to run payroll in QuickBooks; accessed through the Employee Center

equity accounts   Reflect the owner's investment in the company and have a credit normal balance; in a Sole Proprietorship, equity is what the owner has invested in the company and in a corporation, the equity is what the shareholders have invested in the company

estimates   Feature that allows a user to create a proposal for a customer or job

Express Start   In this method of company creation, QuickBooks asks you for your basic company information, and it will be up to you to set up certain items such as payroll and inventory later

field   A box into which data is entered

file storage location   Location where you store files for this course (USB flash drive, the My Documents folder, or a network drive at a school or company)

filtering   Filtering allows you to include only the essential data in your report; choose to filter out many types of data such as accounts, dollar amounts, and types of customers; allows you to closely examine and report on a specific group of data

finance charge   A charge assessed to an overdue customer balance

Fixed Asset   An asset you don't plan to use up or turn into cash within the next year; businesses use fixed assets in a productive capacity to promote the main operations of the company; are depreciable, which means that you don't expense the assets when you purchase them, but rather over the useful life of the asset

fixed asset account   Type of account that tracks the activities associated with a fixed asset

fonts   QuickBooks displays its preset reports in a default font; you can make many changes to the characteristics of the font in your report, such as the font name, style, color, and size

forecast   A feature that allows you to make predictions about the future; they can be created based on actual figures from the last year or from scratch

Formatting   Formatting deals with the appearance of the report; it has nothing to do with the data contained within it

Generally Accepted Accounting Principles (GAAP)   Rules used to prepare, present, and report financial statements for a wide variety of entities

graphs   Graphs in QuickBooks allow you to display your information in a more illustrative way

header and footer   Default headers and footers appear on all preset QuickBooks reports; change the information included along with how it is formatted on the Header and Footer tabs of the Additional Customization window

Income Statement   Financial report that can be found in the Company & Financial category of the Report Finder window; P&L reports reflect all transactions that have affected income and expense accounts within a specified time period; also called a Profit & Loss Report

Internet   A collection of computers all over the world that send, receive, and store information; access is gained through an Internet Service Provider (ISP); the web is just a portion of the Internet

investment   Occurs when an owner deposits funds into the company

job costing   Allows a users to determine the profitability of each job for a customer

just in time   Allows you to see summary information when entering a transaction for a customer or vendor

Layout Designer   The Layout Designer window provides rulers to line up objects, and toolbar buttons to help manipulate your template objects

Lead Center   Feature that allows you to track information about potential customers

link   Also called hyperlink; provides navigation through a website; displayed on the QuickBooks Home page to provide navigation throughout the QuickBooks program

list (database)   Allows you to store information about customers, vendors, employees, and other data important to your business

live community   A place where a user can collaborate with other QuickBooks users to get advice or to provide insights

logo   QuickBooks allows you to personalize your templates by including your company logo

Long Term Liabilities account   A QuickBooks account that tracks a liability (loan) you do not plan to pay off within the next year

online backup   QuickBooks offers an online backup option for a monthly fee that is determined based on the amount of room you wish to have available for your backup work

on the fly   When you type a new entry into a field that draws from a list, QuickBooks gives you the opportunity to add the record to the list "on the fly" as you create the transaction

Opening Balance Equity account   An equity account created by QuickBooks when you start your first balance sheet account; it allows you to have an accurate balance sheet from the start

other current assets   An account that tracks the transactions related to an asset that you plan to either use up or convert to cash within one year

outside payroll service   A service that runs payroll for a company outside of QuickBooks; the company inputs the information into QuickBooks without using the payroll features

Payroll Liabilities   The account in which you hold payroll taxes and other deductions until you are required to pay them

payroll options   Intuit provides a variety of options to run your payroll; to view and compare these options, visit the Student Resource Center

PDF file   PDF stands for "portable document format;" it is a type of file that preserves formatting, data, and graphics; saves in a portable file

permanent account   An account for which the ending balance for one fiscal period is the opening balance for the next

petty cash   Cash kept by businesses for small expenditures; in QuickBooks, Petty Cash is set up as a bank account in the Chart of Accounts

portable company file   A type of QuickBooks file that contains all company data in a compressed format; it must be restored to be utilized; it is much smaller in size than a company or backup file

preferences The way you interact with QuickBooks is controlled by the preferences you select; the Preferences window has 19 categories; company preferences are controlled by the administrator and determine how the entire company interacts with QuickBooks; personal preferences are controlled by individual users and dictate interactions between QuickBooks and only that one user

Price Level List Allows a user to set and charge different price levels for different customers or jobs

profit and loss (P&L) report A financial report that can be found in the Company & Financial category of the Report Finder window; P&L reports reflect all transactions that have affected income and expense accounts within a specified time period; also called an Income Statement

progress invoicing Allows you to invoice from an estimate in stages rather than for the entire estimate amount

purchase order A form utilized by many companies to enter items into inventory; it does not affect anything "behind the scenes"

Quick Reference tables Tables that summarize the tasks you have just learned. Use them as guidelines when you begin work on your own QuickBooks company file.

QuickReport A report that shows all the transactions recorded in QuickBooks for a particular list record, which can be run from the various list windows

QuickZoom A QuickBooks report and graph feature that allows you to zoom through underlying sub-reports until you reach the form where the data were originally entered; this can be extremely useful if you have questions about where a figure in a report or graph comes from

reconciliation The process of matching your QuickBooks accounts to the bank and credit card statements you receive. It is important to make sure that your account records in QuickBooks match those of the bank or credit card company

report A way to display your company information in various ways such as printed, onscreen, or as a PDF file

resize To change the height or width of an image, window, or object

restoring The process of decompressing a QuickBooks backup or portable company file; when you restore a file in the same location with the same name as another file, it will replace that file

sales orders Allows you to manage customer orders of both products and services; available in the Premier and Enterprise editions

search feature Allows a user to perform searches based on text entered throughout a company file and menu commands

Starter Chart of Accounts During the setup process, QuickBooks asks you to choose the business type that your company most closely resembles; QuickBooks uses your choice to create a Chart of Accounts close to what you need (it will take you less time to edit it to fit your unique business than to start from scratch); you cannot change the business type option later

Statement of Cash Flows Report that shows how viable a company is in the short term; demonstrates whether a company will be able to pay its bills, payroll, and other expenses; also indicates the financial health of the company

Statement of Owner's Equity Report that shows the capital at the beginning of the fiscal period, any additional investments, as well as draws, the net income or loss, and the ending amount

subaccounts Help you keep precise records; to track expenses more closely, you may want to have separate accounts for your office phone, office fax, cellular phone, etc.; subaccounts are a great way to track these separate expenses while keeping the number of expense accounts down

template A specific form format (with no data) on which you can base all of your future forms; QuickBooks provides several templates, but you can also create custom templates

temporary account Accounts are zeroed out at the end of each fiscal period, with the amounts from them moving into an equity account as either a net income (if income was greater than expenses) or a net loss (if expenses exceeded income for the period); also called a nominal account

Time Tracking Allows you to create weekly timesheets so you can break down the hours by customer/job or to record single activities for a customer/job

Trial Balance Report that adds up the debits and credits at the end of an accounting period so mistakes can be traced if debits don't equal credits

unearned income Funds received from a customer as a deposit or for a gift certificate; these funds should be held in a liability account until they are "earned"

units of measure Feature that allows you to convert units of measure; useful for companies that purchase and sell in different units of measure or need to indicate units on purchase or sales forms; available in the Premier and higher versions of QuickBooks

users You can set up an unlimited number of users for your QuickBooks company and assign a password for each person; users can only change their own personal preferences (the administrator controls the access each user has to the QuickBooks file)

Vendor Anyone (except employees) to whom you pay money; could be the electric company, the organization to which you pay taxes, a merchandise supplier, or subcontractors you pay to do work for your customers

Vendor List A list in QuickBooks that stores all information related to your vendors

version Intuit creates a new version of QuickBooks each year (such as QuickBooks 2011, 2012, or 2013) and each new version provides additional features that are new for that year

website Refers to a collection of related web pages and their supporting files and folders.

year-to-date amounts If you begin to use the QuickBooks payroll feature for existing employees who have received at least one paycheck from you (and it is not the first day of January), you must enter year-to-date amounts for them to ensure that QuickBooks calculates taxes with thresholds properly and you will be able to print accurate W-2s at the end of the year

Index

Notes

Notes

Notes

Notes

Notes

Notes

Notes

Notes

Notes

Notes